CALIFORNIA STUDIES IN FOOD AND CULTURE

Darra Goldstein, Editor

More Than Just Food

The publisher gratefully acknowledges the generous support of the Anne G. Lipow Endowment Fund for Social Justice and Human Rights of the University of California Press Foundation, which was established by Stephen M. Silberstein.

More Than Just Food

FOOD JUSTICE AND
COMMUNITY CHANGE

Garrett M. Broad

UNIVERSITY OF CALIFORNIA PRESS

University of California Press, one of the most distinguished university presses in the United States, enriches lives around the world by advancing scholarship in the humanities, social sciences, and natural sciences. Its activities are supported by the UC Press Foundation and by philanthropic contributions from individuals and institutions. For more information, visit www.ucpress.edu.

University of California Press
Oakland, California

Library of Congress Cataloging-in-Publication Data

Broad, Garrett M., 1986- author.
    More than just food : food justice and community change / Garrett M. Broad.
        pages   cm.— (California studies in food and culture ; [60])
    Includes bibliographical references and index.
    ISBN 978-0-520-28744-0 (cloth : alk. paper)
    ISBN 978-0-520-28745-7 (pbk. : alk. paper)
    ISBN 978-0-520-96256-9 (ebook)
    1. Food supply—Social aspects—United States.   2. Food industry and trade—Social aspects—United States.   3. Minorities—Nutrition—Social aspects—United States.   4. Social justice—United States.   I. Title. II. Series: California studies in food and culture ; 60.
    HD9005.B688   2016
    338.1′973—dc23   2015032472

24   23   22   21   20   19   18   17   16
10   9   8   7   6   5   4   3   2   1

For my teachers

CONTENTS

LIST OF ILLUSTRATIONS

ACKNOWLEDGMENTS

This project would not have been possible without the guidance, support, and insights of countless individuals and institutions—so many, in fact, that naming each and every one would require a book unto itself. In broad strokes, I am indebted to at least three main groups: collaborators and participants from the activist and practitioner community, colleagues and mentors from the academic community, and trusted friends and family from my personal life.

I am grateful to have had the chance to work with so many amazing people involved in food justice organizing, urban agriculture, and community development in the city of Los Angeles, across the United States, and around the world. The names, voices, and faces of these organizations and individuals form the foundation of this book. I thank them all for their time, dedication, and willingness to share their candid perspectives with me. Members of Community Services Unlimited (CSU) played an especially important role in this respect. Neelam Sharma, Heather Fenney Alexander, Dyane Pascall, and Lawrence DeFreitas—along with the rest of the CSU staff, board, and their community collaborators and organizational partners—were all extremely gracious in allowing me to work with and learn from them.

I have tremendous appreciation for the faculty, staff, administration, and students at the University of Southern California's Annenberg School for Communication and Journalism, where I received my PhD and wrote an earlier version of this work as part of my doctoral dissertation. Sandra Ball-Rokeach, who served as my faculty advisor, continues to be an admirable mentor and deserves an enormous amount of credit for helping to shape my scholarly approach. Sarah Banet-Weiser, Andrew Lakoff, Peter Clarke, and Larry Gross served on my graduate committees, offering invaluable feedback that helped turn disparate ideas into a cohesive project. I also learned a great deal from my graduate school colleagues—including past and present members of the Metamorphosis Project, members of my doctoral cohort, and the many others who I worked alongside in the basement offices. Special thanks, as well, go to Paul Lichterman, whose year-long ethnographic methods seminar in the Department of Sociology formed the initial basis for this research.

I was lucky to receive generous support from the University of Pennsylvania's Annenberg School for Communication as the George Gerbner Postdoctoral Fellow. The time, space, and intellectual community this position offered were vital to the completion of this book. I am particularly thankful to Michael Delli-Carpini and Carolyn Marvin for their institutional support. John Jackson, Sharrona Pearl, and Victor Pickard all provided useful commentary on my research, as did Andrew Calabrese during his visit to Philadelphia. I benefited from many conversations and interactions with faculty, staff, and students from across the Penn community. My experience at the University of Pennsylvania also helped me land a spectacular job as an Assistant Professor at Fordham University in the Department of Communication and Media Studies. Thanks to Jacqueline Reich and all of my new colleagues at Fordham for being so welcoming, encouraging, and hospitable.

I am thrilled that this work is being published by the University of California Press. My editor, Kate Marshall, proved to be a great champion for this project. Thanks are also due to Stacy Eisenstark, Zuha Khan, Dore Brown, and Genevieve Thurston for their editorial assistance, to Darra Goldstein for including this work in the California Studies in Food and Culture series, and to the entire editorial and marketing teams at UC Press. Lewis Friedland, Leda Cooks, and two anonymous reviewers provided essential feedback on draft submissions. I am grateful, as well, to Sahra Sulaiman, Heng Leng, and Nicole Samay for allowing us to include their photos and artwork in this publication.

From my earliest age, my family helped establish a core value system that has always served me well. I am forever grateful to my parents, Mindy Fineberg Broad and Spencer Broad, as well as to my brother, Matthew Broad, for being wonderful role models. I am proud to carry on a tradition of learning and teaching established by my grandfather, Lester Broad. Countless other family members and friends, some of them living and some no longer with us, have served as important inspirations. Last, but certainly not least, I am thankful to the newest member of my family—my wife, Janelle Stetz—for always reminding me how essential it is to have fun.

Despite the help of all of these influential people—and I could go on to list more—I should note that any errors or omissions in this work are entirely my responsibility.

Introduction

We've always been involved in food, because food is a very basic
necessity, and it's the stuff that revolutions are made of.

DAVID HILLIARD, *former Chief of Staff, Black Panther Party*

A few weeks into filming the second season of his ABC reality television
show, *Jamie Oliver's Food Revolution,* celebrity chef Jamie Oliver had his permit to film in the Los Angeles Unified School District (LAUSD) fully
revoked. After having been granted initial permission to film culinary classes
at West Adams Preparatory High School in Central Los Angeles, Oliver had
been hoping to set up shop a few miles away, at South Los Angeles's Manual
Arts High School. The LAUSD, however, had second thoughts. "If you look
at the last series [Oliver] did in Huntington, West Virginia, it was full of
conflict and drama, and we're not interested in that," Robert Alaniz, a media
relations official with the LAUSD, was quoted as saying.

According to the LAUSD, conversations with West Virginia's Cabell
County School District suggested that Oliver's work in Huntington—where
he attempted to transform the local school food environment into a healthier
one—may have been great for *his* career, but it had actually cost *them* dearly
in money, bad press, and ongoing legal wrangling. Officials also questioned
the motives behind the selection of Los Angeles as a site for a reality
TV nutritional intervention. Childhood obesity rates in the city had actually
begun to decline in recent years, they argued, and recent changes in the
LAUSD's cafeteria menus went above and beyond the healthy meal standards
required by the federal government. They wondered if Oliver, rather than

aiming to offer actionable solutions to help the LAUSD improve its operations, was simply looking for an excuse to spend a few months in sunny Southern California. Oliver, for his part, told a different tale, suggesting that his filming permit was terminated because he could not promise that his show would make the LAUSD look good. "They fail to see me as a positive," he explained, "and they fail to see the TV as an incredible way to spread the word, to inspire people, to inform parents, to see other teachers doing pioneering things."[1]

When the first episodes of *Food Revolution*'s second season aired in April of 2011, the LAUSD was depicted on primetime television as an obstruction-ist villain. Oliver was accused of misrepresenting LAUSD's food service operations in order to garner more attention for his reality show. "Jamie, come in and work with us," Alaniz said at a press conference after the season premier, "but leave your cameras behind." Without LAUSD's cooperation, Oliver had done his best to piece together the installment of *Food Revolution*. He set up a community kitchen in the affluent neighborhood of Westwood and partnered with celebrity health advocate Jamie Lee Curtis to judge a youth cooking competition. Eventually, Oliver was able to film an interview with the new LAUSD superintendent, John Deasy, in which the district agreed to ban the sugar-laden chocolate and strawberry flavored milks that had long been sold at the city's schools. Still, Oliver could not replicate the ratings success that he had achieved with season one of *Food Revolution* in West Virginia. After the first two episodes aired to little fanfare, the program was shelved during the high-profile May "sweeps" period, and the final four episodes were broadcast in the television graveyard of June.[2]

As a researcher and activist living in Los Angeles at the time—focusing my attention on issues related to food, health, and social justice in the city—I found it difficult to take sides in this made-for-TV debate. In one corner was the LAUSD, an enormous bureaucracy of food service, yet one that undoubt-edly hoped to do well by the more than 650,000 children who were fed in its cafeterias daily. However, even as the institution showed a sincere commit-ment to improving the quality of its food offerings, it remained inextricably linked to networks of food production and distribution that too often made highly processed, unhealthy, environmentally unsustainable, and unappetiz-ing meals the centerpiece of school lunches. And while recent changes to LAUSD menus may have played some role in reducing LA's childhood obes-ity rates, these statistics could easily deceive, since elevated rates of diet-related disease were still heavily concentrated among children in low-income neigh-borhoods and communities of color across the district.[3]

In the other corner was Jamie Oliver, a celebrity chef whose interest in spotlighting the importance of childhood nutrition seemed to be born of good intentions as well. However, his repeated claim of launching a "food revolution" through the sheer force of his personality appeared self-aggrandizing, and his barnstorming approach proved more suitable for reality television than effective advocacy. Not to be overlooked, either, was the fact that Oliver made few attempts while in Los Angeles to build connections with residents and activists from historically marginalized neighborhoods—people who could speak to the broader challenges faced by low-income community members and who could offer remedies for local food system change based on lived experience. Indeed, the fact that his much-ballyhooed community kitchen opened in one of the wealthiest areas of the city belied his understanding of the local economic and nutritional landscapes.[4]

As the conflict between the LAUSD and Jamie Oliver grabbed headlines, the media conversation continued to focus on trying to decide which side seemed best equipped to teach children to "choose the right foods" to eat, on the one hand, and which side stood in the way of community health, on the other. What was missing from the debate, however, was any substantive analysis of the broader food system, its ongoing structural failures, and potential avenues for systemic change. Conspicuously absent from the conversation, as well, were the voices and perspectives of local residents and young people themselves. As time passed and media attention waned, I regretted that we had missed another opportunity to tell a different kind of story about the enduring links between food, health, and youth development. I wanted to have a conversation that would speak of changing not only individual behaviors but also collective systems, one that would look to low-income communities and communities of color as partners in change rather than problems to be solved, and that would include the call for making healthier food choices as part of a broader agenda for *food justice*.

This book tries to tell that story.

MORE THAN JUST FOOD

The chapters to follow describe and analyze the actions of community-based food justice organizations—grassroots, people-of-color-led groups that are working to promote health, equity, and sustainability through urban food activism. This project is based on a combination of ethnographic research methods, interviews, critical analyses, and participatory inquiries; its primary aim is to highlight the capacity of community action to serve as a power base for a twenty-first century food justice movement. At the same time, however, the research cautions against overly romanticized visions of autonomous, community-based change, emphasizing instead the complicated and often contradictory nature of nonprofit food justice organizing in the contemporary moment. Shifting the dominant cultural narratives and institutional networks of the food system toward greater justice is no easy task, of course, but it is my contention that in-depth scholarship on the topic can serve as a useful tool for evaluation, strategizing, and future visioning. With that in mind, this book also offers a set of concrete recommendations—related to the food justice movement's organizing, media storytelling, and policy advocacy practices, as well as its relationship to funding agencies, movement allies, and adversaries—that could help increase the impact and staying power of its agenda for people-powered community change.

It is no coincidence that the research for this book was conducted at a moment of significant social, economic, and political strain. The Great Recession that began in 2008 led to massive unemployment and income losses among everyday people in the United States, while the so-called recovery saw inequality widen to nearly unprecedented levels. As one notable indicator among many, enrollment in the federal Supplemental Nutrition Assistance Program (SNAP, formerly known as the Food Stamps program) reached record highs during this period. That system provided support for over 46 million individuals to purchase food in 2014, approximately 20 million more than had received benefits before the economic downturn. Lower-income families and communities of color were particularly hard-hit by these developments, exacerbating already existing disparities in the domains of health, wealth, and educational opportunity.[5]

Simultaneously, while this project was taking shape, issues related to food, agriculture, and nutrition were receiving a nearly unprecedented level of public and media attention. In documentary films and on network television, in bestselling books, and in the halls of the White House, a discursive explosion related to food issues was underway. The topics of discussion varied widely—some called attention to "food deserts" and epidemics of diet-related disease, others implored viewers to discover the joys of eating like a "foodie," and still others sounded an alarm about the environmental destructiveness of industrialized agricultural practices.[6] I found myself immersed in learning about the problems of the modern *food system,* a term used to describe the interlocking dynamics of food production, distribution, and consumption that stretch from seed and sea to plate and body. And, like many others, I followed the oft-repeated suggestion to *get involved* in some of the "alternative food" initiatives that were being offered up as food system solutions. I began to think more critically about my food choices, support local farmers by purchasing at neighborhood produce markets, volunteer with grassroots urban agriculture organizations, and help to found a community garden in my own multicultural Los Angeles neighborhood.

I was also excited to have the chance to blend my alternative food activism with my scholarly research. Indeed, as an early career academic, I was working to stake my claim as an *engaged scholar,* one who hoped to use research as a way to better understand and advance social change that would promote long-term social justice. *Social change,* as I have come to understand the term, refers to any significant alteration to an enduring social structure of society as well as to the underlying cultural value systems that legitimate those social structures. *Social justice* is a related but distinct concept, a normative concern that calls for an equitable distribution of fundamental resources, a universal respect for the dignity of all peoples, and the promotion of political and social rights that ensure all minority groups can equally pursue their life's interests and voice their visions for change. Advocates for social justice recognize that social, economic, and political inequity rarely occur naturally— rather, these dynamics emerge over time through historical processes of discrimination and favor. From this perspective, then, justice is realized not only through the active promotion of equity, but also by consciously addressing and deconstructing the discrimination that created the inequity in the first place.[7]

My research helped me to fundamentally understand the ways in which the contemporary food system operates as a vast and globally networked entity, one faced with a set of intersecting environmental, economic, and public health crises. That is to say, at the same time as the system offers a bountiful and nourishing harvest to many privileged citizens of the globe, it also serves as a site of significant social injustice in both the developed and developing worlds. For reasons that will be detailed in later chapters of this book, the dominant norms of the industrialized food system are ultimately environmentally destructive; exploitative of farmers, workers, and animals; and inequitable, such that low-income and ethnic minority communities in particular lack access to high-quality affordable foods and face disparities related to food security and chronic disease. In response, diverse sets of social change initiatives have emerged with an aim to transform both the institutional structures and cultural values of our food system.

Cognizant of the unjust impacts of the ongoing economic crisis and enthralled by the possibilities of food system transformation, I set out to investigate the social justice potential of alternative food activism. It was through this scholar-activist perspective that the idea for this book emerged. Through my grassroots participation, I found that much of what I encountered did not match what I saw in the influential food-focused media productions that were garnering mainstream attention. In popular media, the nutritional, environmental, and social problems of the food system were often portrayed as having utterly simple, conflict-free solutions, generally involving nothing more than individual consumer choices and a little bit of "growing your own." If we could simply get the general public to understand the importance of healthy eating, pop culture advocates suggested, perhaps by having young boys and girls taste a tomato grown in their own school garden or by opening a community farmers' market, we would all be well on our way toward health and sustainability.

Unfortunately, missing from the design, deployment, and management of many of the alternative food initiatives I observed was any recognition that inequity in the food system was centrally linked to histories of racial and economic discrimination. As a number of scholars and activists had begun to point out, such programs often lacked substantive participation from those community members who actually faced the challenges of food injustice themselves. Largely as a result, alternative food initiatives tended to benefit mostly white, economically secure, and already healthy consumers. Low-income communities of color, by contrast, were too often treated as subjects to be taught the "right way to eat," while issues of systemic injustice in the labor force and other barriers to community health were downplayed or ignored. Without a direct social justice consciousness, the evidence suggested, achieving health and sustainability through such programs would prove elusive.[8]

At the grassroots level, by contrast, I began to take stock of a strikingly different narrative. There, I began to hear the term *food justice* used as a way to describe a different type of approach for improving the health of the eating public, of marginalized communities, and of the food system as a whole. The advocates for food justice that I came in contact with argued that the problems of the food system were not simple or conflict-free at all but were actually connected to other systemic social, economic, and racial injustices. Food-related initiatives, they suggested, could be used as a tool to develop a set of community-based solutions that might help transform the very political and economic systems that had historically oppressed low-income and ethnic minority communities across the United States and around the world. While community-based food justice advocates employed some of the same strategies that were featured in popular media portrayals—building gardens, providing nutrition education, and improving access to healthy food through alternative food networks—they did so in the purpose of a much larger cause. They situated food as a vehicle for a more expansive, people-of-color-led social justice project toward which they were fundamentally committed.

Researchers Robert Gottlieb and Anupama Joshi defined food justice as "ensuring that the benefits and risks of where, what, and how food is grown and produced, transported and distributed, and accessed and eaten are shared fairly" (6). Scholars Alison Hope Alkon and Julian Agyeman added that such efforts must remain "firmly rooted in the low-income communities and communities of color that suffer from inequalities embedded in the food system" (7).[9] Food justice, I came to learn, had emerged as a counter-force in the United States, not only to the problems of the industrial food system but also to those alternative food networks that tended *not* to place social justice in a position of primacy.

However, as I looked into the scholarship and actions of food justice work, I began to levy a parallel complaint: the solutions proffered in activist and academic settings were often overly simplified and did not match what I was seeing on the ground. Too often, I felt, case studies of community-based and people-of-color-led food justice initiatives leaned toward a general romanticizing of community-focused activity. Notably, such accounts did little to situate the efforts of those nonprofit food justice organizations that were leading the charge within realistic political, economic, and cultural networks. Instead, they tended to imply that these community-based food justice efforts operated in an entirely autonomous fashion, somehow independent of external cultural influences, structural supports, and quite often, the logic of capitalism. In other discussions of food justice, a number of critical scholars seemed to write off the social change capacity of community-based food justice organizing completely. These critics suggested that the educational and community economic development focus of food justice efforts was not so different from that of white-led alternative food initiatives, both tending to reify a neoliberal philosophy of market-driven self-improvement, a strategy that unintentionally absolves the government of its responsibility to ensure good food for all. Why spend so much time focusing on community-based activism, such accounts tended to argue, when the real levers for substantive social transformation are pulled through changes in food and agricultural policies?[10]

Through the course of my own work, I saw real value in the food justice approach, witnessing community-based groups make legitimate strides toward building community capacity, promoting youth development, and improving the ecological health of their neighborhoods from the ground up. At the same time, I recognized the strategy's limitations and contradictions. I observed that the community-based organizations that were advocating for food justice were hardly operating alone, as they partnered with hosts of public and private individuals and groups to advance their goals. Many of these partners were from *outside* of the local communities in which food justice groups organized, and many of them had become engaged in food-related work only after they were encouraged to do so by the types of popular media productions that food justice activists hoped, in part, to counter. I noticed, as well, that food justice groups were depending upon funding and support from major governmental organizations, wealthy foundations, and even major corporations. These institutions consistently pushed food justice activists to incorporate diverse sets of practices and logics into their operations, dynamics that would make them more accountable and "fundable" in the landscape of nonprofit organizing.[11]

Through it all, however, I also saw food justice groups work hard to keep their community-based, people-of-color-led mission of social transformation at the heart of their efforts. They insisted that their food justice vision was nothing short of a radical call to action, and they pushed back against encroachments from groups and forces that would attempt to co-opt or moderate their message. In a cultural environment in which food system issues had skyrocketed in popularity, they looked for opportunities to catalyze community development while also tapping into networks that would help them tell their food justice story to broader audiences.

I set out to develop a project that would paint a more nuanced and holistic portrait of these developments. The ultimate purpose of *More Than Just Food* is to use ethnographic insights to tell a story of both the potential and limits of community-based food justice organizing in the twenty-first century urban United States. Employing an analytical approach referred to as the *communication ecology perspective,* my work is particularly attentive to the networks and narratives that characterize the actions and philosophies of food justice practitioners today. Drawing from several years of engaged scholarly research, I aim to address an intersecting set of empirical and critical questions. To what extent can sustainable social change be realized through a community-based approach to food justice? What makes food a worthwhile vehicle for these efforts, and what makes the local community an operative site of action? Embedded as these community-based nonprofit initiatives are—within circuitous networks of power, knowledge, and expertise—does community-based food justice organizing have a chance of fulfilling the lofty social and environmental justice goals it has set out to address? And in the face of neoliberal cultural forces and media-savvy outsiders that are so adept at the marginalization and co-optation of social justice initiatives, can small-scale food justice groups successfully communicate their visions of social transformation to a broader public?

I argue that community-based food justice does indeed offer a valuable model for the promotion of social and racial justice in the contemporary age. The salience of food as a universal social and cultural necessity, combined with the documented ability of local organizing to serve as an avenue for capacity-building within historically marginalized communities, offers a foundation upon which an agenda for sustainable community change can be built. With that said, I do not offer simple and clear-cut solutions to the problem of community-based food injustice but rather recognize that this strategy of community action remains fraught with tension and ambivalence, while the political possibilities of the approach are necessarily constrained. That is to say, if community-based activists hope to parlay local action into a sustained food justice movement, certain criteria—related to ongoing community participation, a committed vision for systemic change, a plan for programmatic sustainability, and an ability to exert influence beyond the local—must be met.

Through the course of my research on community-based food justice organizing, many of the activists with whom I collaborated pointed to the Brazilian educator and philosopher Paulo Freire as an inspiration for their work. In his seminal book, *Pedagogy of the Oppressed,* Freire emphasized the importance of *praxis* in the organizing process, a concept he defined as "reflection and action upon the world in order to transform it" (51). For Freire and his adherents, this reinforcing combination of dialogue and application is essential for the liberation of historically marginalized communities.[12] In *More Than Just Food,* I argue that food justice activism can be understood as a *hybrid praxis,* an ever-evolving mix of philosophy and action that takes shape through an ongoing process of co-construction, collaboration, and conflict in food justice work. Understanding these complex dynamics, I suggest, will be necessary to increase the scale and scope of the food justice movement in the years to come.

THE ROAD AHEAD

More Than Just Food offers an ethnographic exploration of community-based food justice activism in urban America, using the network of Community Services Unlimited Inc. (CSU) as a centering artifact of study. CSU was initially created as the nonprofit arm of the Southern California chapter of the Black Panther Party and today stands as a leading food justice nonprofit organization in its own community of South Los Angeles, with connections to other food justice groups from across the United States and around the world. "We fulfill our mission of serving the people, body and soul, by focusing on building a sustainable community here in South LA," Neelam Sharma, CSU's executive director, explained in an interview. "Using food as an access point to engage community in that process, we raise critical awareness of the issues that impact us the most in our neighborhood and, more importantly, build responses."

However, this book is more than a single case study of a specific South LA-based food justice organization. By combining the deep dive of ethnographic research with networked concepts and multiple strategies for critical and theoretical inquiry, I use CSU as an analytical entry point, one that allows for an interrogation and assessment of the broader field of action in which community-based food justice organizing is situated today. Guided by the extended case method of ethnography, each of the chapters highlights a different set of food justice networks and narratives, employing a nonlinear, multilevel, and multimethod approach that crosses time and space. The pages to follow use participant observation to describe CSU's local organizing strategies, analyze interviews to understand the motivations of youth food justice advocates from across the nation, draw from historiography to explain the political economic foundations of nonprofit food activism, and apply critical media analysis to the branding materials of new entrants into the food justice landscape.

Taken together, this research approach is grounded in the foundations of what I refer to as the *communication ecology perspective*. Chapter 1 of this book outlines the key theoretical and methodological foundations that shape this scholarly orientation, points that are also expanded upon in the methodological appendix. The chapter provides a rationale for focusing on the local community as a site of both social change organizing and academic scholarship in an age of digital media and neoliberal politics. From there, I offer a set of working principles for sustainable community change that can be used to evaluate the utility, efficacy, and shortcomings of various community-based food justice initiatives, including those of CSU and other groups highlighted in the chapters that follow.

Chapter 2 turns the reader's attention directly toward the food system, establishing food as a vital social, economic, and environmental infrastructure of modern society, one that is faced with a host of intersecting crises on both local and global scales. Cognizant that the readership will likely have varying degrees of expertise with respect to these topics, I provide an overview of the central risks to human and environmental health that have emerged in recent decades as a result of the changing dynamics of food production, distribution, and consumption. I then describe the rise of the varied "alternative food movements" that have taken shape in response to these interlocking challenges in the food system. The chapter describes how members of community-based food justice organizations have joined a growing chorus of alternative food advocates who identify the local community as a valuable space for food system change.

Chapter 3 is an ethnographic exploration of CSU, a small nonprofit organization focused on food justice in South Los Angeles. It highlights the voices, actions, and knowledge practices of CSU staff, partners, and youth and community collaborators as they collectively endeavor to improve the health of their local neighborhoods. I track how the organization aimed to build a level of critical consciousness and a set of community-based alternative institutions that it hoped would, in its own words, "build a sustainable food system from the ground up in South Central LA, while training local youth, creating real jobs and building the local economy."[13]

Chapter 4 highlights the work of Rooted in Community, a national network of youth food justice organizations with member groups that come from across the United States. CSU served as host for a recent summit of the network that brought together over one hundred youth and dozens of organizational staff into a common space of sharing and strategizing. Linking these geographically dispersed community groups into common cause, I insist, represents a vital opportunity for a broader food justice movement to coalesce. In order for this to be possible, however, network members must remain reflexive in their attempts to find the right mix between community-focused action and broader movement-building, and they must also balance the priorities of youth-led organizing with parallel interests in policy advocacy and digital media storytelling.

Chapter 5 takes a step back in networked time, employing a genealogical approach in order to understand the historical foundations of CSU's community-based practices. The chapter begins with a discussion of the Black Panther Party and its system of community programs in the 1970s and then tracks how CSU emerged from that history to develop into a "fundable" food justice group in the twenty-first century. Investigating the numerous tensions and successes along the way, the story mirrors the challenges faced by many community-based groups whose social justice missions at times conflict with their nonprofit status. The chapter asks—how does a group go from being founded as part of the Black Panther Party to depending on grant funding from a governmental establishment like the United States Department of Agriculture?

Chapter 6 compares and contrasts the work of CSU with several other groups that have become engaged in efforts to tackle food injustice in the South Los Angeles community—specifically the Teaching Gardens Program of the American Heart Association and the viral video-launched Ron Finley Project. I use a comparison of their respective organizational networks, "theories of change," and digital media strategies to uncover the increasingly competitive nonprofit environment in which contemporary food justice organizing takes place. This environment, I suggest, is in many ways more supportive of groups that are already well capitalized, have access to powerful media channels and communication networks, and are neither "of the community" nor particularly devoted to issues of social justice at all.

The conclusion of the book discusses the implications of my research for scholarship on food justice and community-based activism in general. It also offer thoughts on the utility that the work might have for practitioners and engaged scholars participating in everyday struggles for social justice, in the food system and elsewhere. Collectively, the chapters to follow in many ways reflect the guiding mission of the food justice groups whose work forms the foundation of this account. In the face of daunting challenges across the global food system and within historically marginalized communities, the book aims to demonstrate the ways in which food offers a powerful and engaging avenue for change. However, if researchers and activists are truly committed to a sustained movement for social justice, they must incorporate more than just food at the center of that process. "Food is a way in which you can get folks to think critically about their environment," Lawrence DeFreitas, a staff member with CSU explained. "A community that understands how the environment impacts them has the ability to think critically to take action."

ON ENGAGED SCHOLARSHIP

Before bringing this introduction to a close, a few additional comments regarding my scholarly position and engaged strategy of research are in order. *More Than Just Food* is informed by a theoretical and practical commitment to methods of engaged scholarship. With the use of the term *engaged scholarship,* I refer to academic work that actively engages with research participants through community-based and participatory methods.[14] The aim of engaged scholarship, as I practice the approach, is to produce scholarly knowledge while simultaneously conducting research that may help research participants advance, facilitate, and reflect upon their own social change efforts. This engaged approach differs from some of the traditional standards in American academia, which has often called for a sharp break between researcher and research subjects. Those who follow this engaged methodology, however, believe that a collaborative research practice is ethically sound and can serve as a foundation for the production of scholarly insights that would be difficult to garner through a more neutral observational approach.[15] My own positionality as a white, middle-class male who never lived in the South Los Angeles area, where much of my research for this book takes place, nor ever faced any significant instances of food injustice in my own daily life, actually served to solidify my attachment to an engaged approach. It is my contention that only through a dialogic collaboration with community-based food justice activists could I ever have conducted research on this topic that was simultaneously respectful to those involved and insightful for the scholarly and practitioner communities.

During the development of this project, I spent years living and working in Los Angeles, engaged as both researcher and activist on food justice and urban agricultural issues. My involvement with CSU reaches back to 2009, when I first attended an informational and fundraising event hosted by the group in South Los Angeles. From that time, I intermittently served as a volunteer for various projects and attended a number of their events. More than a year later, after receiving approval from the University of Southern California's Office for the Protection of Research Subjects, I developed a more formal research relationship with the organization, and they agreed to allow me in to focus on their work as a case study for my ethnographic research. As an engaged scholar and social justice ally, I served in a variety of capacities with CSU during multiple years of fieldwork. I worked as a volunteer in their urban farms and in gardening workshops, sat on the organizing committee for several of their sponsored programs, assisted in writing specific portions of grant applications, and contributed to door-to-door outreach efforts, among other activities. Through that time, I was also engaged in a number of other urban agriculture, nutrition education, and food policy initiatives around the city of Los Angeles. It is important to note that, during my research and writing process, I was never on the payroll of CSU or any other food justice organization, and I was always transparent about the fact that I was there to serve a dual role as a researcher and a contributor to the group. Ultimately, honest transparency with my research collaborators allowed me to develop a level of critical distance that proved to be fundamental in maintaining the integrity of my scholarly project.

I recognize that my active and ongoing engagement with research participants may be objectionable to some readers with a grounding in a traditional model of objective ethnographic investigation. While I understand those critiques, I also think it is important that we consider just how increasingly untenable—and in many ways undesirable—that historically ideal approach is for scholarly practice today. Here, I draw from the thoughts of the ethnographer John L. Jackson, who in 2013 described how scholars "no longer simply *arrive* at our field-sites anymore, at least not like before. Those field-sites already come knocking at our doors or flitting across our computer screens long before we get out of bed—and in ways that actually look and feel much different from the cross-cultural state of affairs just ten or fifteen years ago" (48, emphasis in original). Today, researchers arrive at ethnographic projects to find research "subjects" already actively doing research on their own work, not to mention on the background of the potential academic research partner, as well as actively telling their own stories through a variety of communication and digital media formats. What develops, then, is an increasingly multisited ethnographic field site, a set of networked and iterative landscapes of scholarly and activist inquiry.[16]

The first chapter of this book provides more detail regarding the methodological and theoretical foundations that shaped my investigation into community-based food justice. The chapters that follow provide a mix of description, analysis, and evaluation across intersecting domains of food movement activism. Taken together, my work endeavors to document and assess the networks and narratives that have emerged as the engine for contemporary grassroots organizing for food justice. It offers insights, recommendations, and words of caution for scholars and practitioners with an interest in advancing health, equity, and sustainability in the face of enduring injustice in the food system and beyond.

Networks, Narratives, and Community Action

From the #Occupy movement to the Arab Spring, from the #BlackLivesMatter protests to the Spanish Indignados, the last several years have seen a host of high-profile mass demonstrations take shape in cities and towns across the United States and around the world. "By sharing sorrow and hope in the free public space of the Internet, by connecting to each other, and by envisioning projects from multiple sources of being," social theorist Manuel Castells described, "individuals formed networks, regardless of their personal views or organizational attachments. They came together" (2).[1] Scholars and activists have pointed to several common qualities across these twenty-first century mobilizations: they have been leaderless and horizontal in nature; they have been spontaneously linked by networked technologies and social media platforms like Twitter; and they have leveraged digital tools to occupy public space in the name of populist revolution, be it the overthrow of neoliberal global financial systems, the upending of oppressive governments, or the deconstruction of racist regimes of policing.[2]

This book, however, is not about these spontaneous mass demonstrations. Not because I deem them unimportant or because I consider their concerns and organizing practices to be disconnected from those of the food justice movement. Quite the contrary, food justice activism actually intersects in substantive ways with these mass protest movements—their actions are similarly rooted in anger toward corporate and government failure, digital technologies play a central role in shaping their respective coordination strategies, and the transformation of public space is fundamental to their missions. Still, *More Than Just Food* does not focus on spontaneous mass mobilization because years of observation and participation in food justice organizing has shown me that this is simply not where the energy of the movement has been centered.[3] Instead, the practitioners I have encountered have maintained a focus on the slow and steady of work of promoting food justice through the development of programs at the level of the local *community*—building farms and gardens, developing youth education and job training initiatives, and creating social enterprises that bring good food into neighborhoods (most often their own) that have lacked healthy and affordable options for decades.

Community Services Unlimited (CSU), based in South Los Angeles, offers as an operative example of this community-focused approach. The food injustice faced by the local residents with whom the organization collaborates is the product of decades and centuries of systemic discrimination and disinvestment on local, national, and international scales. Today, through a host of networked partnerships and shared funding sources, as well as through common narratives and shared visions of food system transformation, CSU considers its work to be part of a larger movement for food justice. It is linked to a number of other operations engaged in this field of activism—including the Social Justice Learning Institute in nearby Inglewood, California; Growing Power in Milwaukee, Wisconsin; the Detroit Black Community Food Security Network in Michigan; and even partners in Oaxaca, Mexico, and as far as Johannesburg, South Africa. As I will explore in greater detail in chapter 2, these initiatives have emerged not only in response to the failures of the contemporary food system but also in response to an inadequate alternative food movement, one that has done an insufficient job of incorporating the needs and knowledge of residents and leaders from low-income neighborhoods and communities of color into its agenda. Importantly, these food justice groups have all been bound by a common assumption that, even though many of the challenges they face are shaped by global economic and political forces, community-based food projects offer a unique and viable entry point to build an effective form of resistance. The food justice activists highlighted in this book, therefore, have not turned toward mass protest mobilization as a primary prong of their agenda but rather cultivated a strategy of building local nonprofit organizations to bolster community-based capacity and effect sustainable change.

How is it—in an age of globalized injustice and digital tools for mass communication—that community-based strategies of organizing such as this have continued to persist? With a review of relevant theory and practice related to the dynamics of neoliberalism, networked social movements, and community organizing, this chapter works to contextualize this very question. With this review in place, I then introduce a set of working principles for sustainable change in the domain of community-based food justice. These evidence-based criteria are intended to provide a framework for evaluating both the efficacy and limitations of food-related initiatives in the modern age. The chapter continues with a discussion of the *communication ecology perspective,* which has guided my research process, as I argue that ethnographic attention to the networked action and narrative practices of community-based organizations allows for an in-depth understanding of their change-making capacity. The chapters that follow then apply this research approach and use these evaluative criteria to investigate the power, possibility, and constraints of food justice organizing today, documenting the hybridity of community-based food justice work in the globalized, digital age.

COMMUNITY ACTION, NEOLIBERALISM, AND THE NONPROFIT INDUSTRIAL COMPLEX

The twenty-first century is understood as a novel historical conjuncture, one rife with both crisis and opportunity. The international community undoubtedly faces a set of intersecting, boundary-crossing, and existential risks related to health, the environment, and the economy.[4] Concurrently, global society and the tools of digital technology have been highlighted as central to tackling these crises, as they provide the necessary networking power to promote social change and empower social movements on national and international scales.[5]

While many scholars and practitioners interested in the dynamics of social change have understandably focused their attention on macro-level social movements and protests in recent years, others have actually called for an increased focus on the local community as a site where the challenges and risks of global society are experienced and addressed.[6] In providing a rationale for his focus on the way a neighborhood affects the health of its population, for instance, the distinguished social scientist Robert Sampson has argued that "macrolevel processes are lived locally and experienced on the ground in everyday life" (62).[7] Similarly, scholars such as Sandra Ball-Rokeach and Lewis Friedland have suggested that, within the context of twenty-first century global society, the local community remains a privileged site for analyzing real-world communicative activity and the machinations of democratic life and civic engagement. Along with a host of colleagues, these and other researchers have urged scholars to take a multilevel and ecological approach to the study of social change, recognizing that macro-level forces— like major media systems, government policy, and global economics—both shape and are reshaped by community-level factors, including community-based organizations, local media storytellers, and individuals, in their networks of interpersonal connections.[8]

Throughout Western democracies in the last several decades, the scholarly interest in community action has been energized by the proliferation of community-based nonprofit organizations committed to improving the health and well-being of residents at the local level. In the United States, of course, the tradition of localized voluntary and civic associations has deep roots. Chronicled by the likes of the French dignitary Alexis de Tocqueville in the early part of the nineteenth century, Americans have long looked to the Jeffersonian principles of self-governance and the model of New England town hall meetings as examples of community self-sufficiency and its merits. This commitment has persisted over time, and while the early twentieth century was characterized by massive, albeit unevenly distributed, national investments through New Deal social programs, decision-makers in the late twentieth century and early twenty-first century have increasingly placed faith in a combination of market forces and decentralized social policy in order to engender prosperity, with community-based actors playing a major role in this process.

Social theorist Michel Foucault referred to this decentralizing strategy as "governance at a distance," a primary political philosophy at the heart of what he termed *neoliberal governmentality*. Today, most of us take for granted the notion that a government will be interested in—and actively devote resources to—promoting the health and well-being of its population. Yet, as Foucault explained, it was not until the nineteenth century that these "biopolitical" concerns emerged as central to the art of government. Around this time, nations began to draw upon vast amounts of newly available biostatistical data—birth rates, causes of mortality, environmental impacts, and the like—and started to use this information to monitor, regulate, and influence the health behavior of various social groups.[9] Yet in the era of the post-welfare state, during the late twentieth and early twenty-first centuries, national governments in Western democracies rolled back their emphasis on centralization and direct biopolitical intervention, favoring instead a neoliberal strategy that delegated administrative power to lower levels of local and community-based action. As theorist Nikolas Rose explained, in this contemporary context, potential solutions to biopolitical risks are indeed championed by major political institutions and macro-level nongovernmental organizations, but the solutions they proffer are most often administered through indirect means. In other words, biopolitical interventions intended to advance health, equity, or sustainability are rarely carried out primarily by any central state institution but are rather designed and managed by organizations and individuals that operate at the level of the geographic or cultural community.[10]

The next chapter of this book will explore in significant depth the ascendance of this type of biopolitical community-based programming in the domain of food justice. But to provide a preliminary example of how this has taken shape, consider the fact that, in recent years, federal officials in the US government have become concerned that low-income Americans do not eat enough fruits and vegetables to be healthy. As one potential solution to this problem, the federal department of Health and Human Services (HHS) has looked for ways to improve access to fresh produce in low-income communities. Rather than creating and deploying a centralized and uniform national food access plan, however, the HHS has funded coalitions of organizations and researchers that create food access programs that are specific to their own local contexts.[11] In 2011, for instance, CSU was awarded nearly $200,000 in grant funds from HHS to bolster its produce distribution social enterprise in South Los Angeles. "Expanding this program will further increase access to high quality, affordable produce, support local farmers, and improve local corner markets," the project description read.[12] Since funded organizations are required to evaluate the impacts of their interventions through a variety of research strategies, in the years to come, HHS will be able to analyze the results from its numerous investments with several key questions in mind: Which local programs were most successful at encouraging low-income residents to eat more healthy foods? Which programs proved to be the most cost-effective? How should these findings influence the future funding, research, and policymaking priorities of both the government and businesses? This is neoliberal governmentality in action.

In the United States and elsewhere, the last half-century has seen the governmental philosophy of neoliberalism come to fruition through the deployment of policies and programs that promote its ideals in government, business, and civil society. Importantly, my use of the theoretical term *neoliberalism* here should not to be confused with the colloquial term *liberal,* which is commonly employed in American political parlance to refer to social progressives or simply the Democratic Party. Instead, *neoliberalism* is used to describe an influential political and economic philosophy of the modern age that encourages the marketization of social life, a movement toward widespread privatization, and a cultural commitment to decentralized and individualized self-sufficiency. In the eyes of scholar Wendy Brown, neoliberal rationality involves *"extending and disseminating market values to all institutions and social action,* even as the market itself remains a distinctive player" (7, emphasis in original).[13] Policymaking in this context is characterized by an assumption that individuals are always calculating, rational actors—members of the species *homo economicus*—whose entrepreneurial abilities and decision-making capacities make them wholly responsible for their station in life.

Those who espouse a neoliberal philosophy argue that their laissez-faire form of government is the ultimate expression of freedom and liberty, as it grants faith in individuals and on-the-ground nongovernmental institutions to make the most prudent decisions that will ultimately optimize well-being among the broader population. Such a claim is harshly rebuffed by critics of neoliberalism, including scholar David Harvey, who has argued that "the freedoms it embodies reflect the interests of private property owners, businesses, multinational corporations, and financial capital" (7).[14] Authors who write in this critical vein have little optimism that the values of neoliberalism have any value at all, and they suggest that there is little possibility for social justice and social change unless neoliberal capitalism itself is destroyed.[15]

While sympathetic to the thrust of these critical arguments, in my estimation, theorists such as Brown and Harvey at times lean toward an overdetermined and suffocating interpretation of neoliberalism. That is to say, they exhibit a tendency to overemphasize the totalizing influence of neoliberalism's market-based logic on individuals and communities, while overzealously dismissing the capacity for social justice activism to endure from within this landscape. It is for this reason that, throughout this book, I consciously refer to the broader political and economic era in which we reside not simply as *neoliberalism* but as the *age of neoliberalism,* a minor rephrasing that I believe maintains space for alternative forms of resistance and a level of optimism regarding potential social justice advocacy.[16] In this context, the neoliberal values described above certainly play a central role in shaping our social and economic lives and, quite often, in marginalizing struggles for social justice. Still, neoliberalism remains subsumed within a broader context that actually motivates oppositional modes of philosophy and practice. For those with a stake in social justice, then, it means that although activist efforts will be inherently constructed in constant conversation with neoliberalism, they need not be fully determined by neoliberal ideology.

As evidence of how this landscape takes shape, recent decades have seen policy and cultural shifts that incentivize not only the individual initiative and self-regulation most often associated with neoliberal logic but also efforts that advance community-based economic development, localized service provision, and community organizing.[17] What urban theorist Jennifer Wolch termed a "shadow state" of voluntary service organizations and community-based nonprofit groups has burgeoned. These efforts are funded largely by public money from the government, in combination with the endowments of major foundations, donor support, and, increasingly, revenue production derived from nonprofit social enterprises.[18] As Nikolas Rose has explained, in this context, "society is to be regenerated, and social justice to be maximized, through the building of responsible communities, prepared to invest in themselves. And in the name of community, a whole variety of groups and forces make their demands, wage their campaigns, stand up for their rights and enact their resistances" (136).[19]

The community offers a unique space of analysis and action where the tensions between neoliberal logics and oppositional activism are on full display. Indeed, any attempt to read the American political left-right spectrum directly onto contemporary conceptions of the community's political capacity will undoubtedly leave analysts wanting. In his classic work *Keywords*, cultural theorist Raymond Williams argued that, "unlike all other terms of social organization (*state, nation, society,* etc.) [the term *community*] seems never to be used unfavourably, and never to be given any positive opposing or distinguishing term" (76, emphasis in original).[20] Especially in times of economic austerity, many political conservatives have lauded strategies that cut out massive bureaucratic service delivery systems in favor of place-based shadow state initiatives that empower local communities to take their fate into their own hands.[21] Many political progressives—inspired by examples that include the Civil Rights movement, the philosophies of Brazilian educator Paulo Freire, and the community organizing strategies of Saul Alinsky— appreciate the participatory and people-powered opportunities that community-based approaches to social change bring to the fore.[22] While critical of the individualized service-provision strategy that has historically been favored by many major funding agencies, progressives are heartened to see that, in the words of community organizing scholar Meredith Minkler, *"community empowerment, community participation,* and *community part-nerships* are . . . among a litany of terms used with increasing frequency by health agencies, philanthropic organizations, and policymakers" (7, emphasis in original).[23]

This is not to say that the community-based strategy for community health promotion has been viewed favorably by everyone. Especially in today's political climate, some conservative activists have a knee-jerk opposi-tional reaction to pretty much any government-funded social program, even those administered at the local community level. This becomes especially true if said programs are seen to promote socially liberal norms, as many community-based initiatives do.

Among many radical, left-wing critics, by contrast, the movement of the state away from national-level social welfare initiatives, combined with the professionalization of the nonprofit sector at the level of the local commu-nity, signals a major victory for neoliberalism, at the expense of social justice activism. In the arguments of Andrea Smith and other members of the col-laborative Incite! Women of Color Against Violence, for instance, the rise of the shadow state has led to the emergence of a "nonprofit industrial complex," a development that has made social change activists increasingly dependent upon white, male-dominated, conservative foundations and other funding agencies for support. This nonprofit industrial complex has further consoli-dated power and money into the exploitative hands of corporate actors, with social movements encouraged to model themselves after capitalist structures rather than challenge them. As an outcome, social justice advocacy is consist-ently monitored and controlled, as activist energies are redirected into depo-liticized career-based organizing as opposed to transformative and values-driven mass movements.[24] In my research, I have found that debates regarding this incisive critique are ever-present among community-based food justice activists. A key aim of this book is to document these very tensions within community activism as well as to empirically assess whether and how they might be overcome in the quest for food justice.

SEEKING SUSTAINABLE COMMUNITY CHANGE IN THE SHADOW OF THE SHADOW STATE

My work, of course, builds upon that of many others who have endeavored to use their scholarship to inform the development of effective social justice activism in the age of neoliberalism. Sociologist Nina Eliasoph's exploration of youth-focused "Empowerment Projects," for instance, provides an example of how ethnographic research can offer concrete evidence of the failures that have beset many volunteer-oriented shadow state nonprofits in this context. By profiling community-based nonprofit organizations that interminably fret about funding and consciously avoid potentially uncomfortable conversations about social and racial inequity, she demonstrated how, "Rather than learning how to care about the 'bigger picture,' as some organizers hope they will, youth volunteers learn to ignore politics" (233). Still, Eliasoph offered some hope that such community-based initiatives could offer powerful avenues for civic engagement. By nourishing and building community expertise, confronting conflict, and committing to long-term partnerships, she argued, more effective community engagements are possible.[25]

Similarly, social theorist Ruth Wilson Gilmore—another member of the Incite! collaborative, mentioned above—has suggested that, while grassroots organizing in an era of the nonprofit industrial complex is hardly without its limitations, it does represent a valuable arena for change. "If contemporary grassroots activists are looking for a pure form of doing things, they should stop," she wrote (50). Building upon the thoughts of Jennifer Wolch, Gilmore argued that the prospect of community-level social justice remains when it is advanced by a subset of resistant nonprofit groups—those who persevere "*in the shadow of* the shadow state" (emphasis added). In order to make any substantive impact, she explained, these groups must always remain committed to a more expansive vision of change in their work:

> The grassroots groups that have formally joined the third sector are in the shadow of the shadow state.... They have detailed political programs and deep social and economic critiques. Their leadership is well educated in the ways of the world, whatever their level of formal schooling, and they try to pay some staff to promote and proliferate the organization's analysis and activity even if most participants in the group are unpaid volunteers. The government is often the object of their advocacy and their antagonisms—whether because the antistate state is the source of trouble or the locus for remedy. But the real focus of their energies is ordinary people whom they wish fervently to organize against their own abandonment (47).[26]

In his ethnography of immigrant rights organizing in the United States, scholar-activist Sasha Costanza-Chock further explored the tensions inherent to social justice advocacy, particularly when led by nonprofits that depend on outside funding. He highlighted the importance of both sustainability *and* autonomy as central to success for those working "in the shadow of the shadow state": "A diversified stream of resources is important not so much to avoid explicit control by funders (although that does occasionally present a problem) but to escape the long-term process of social movement profession-alization that tends to shift movements away from value-driven base building and toward issue-driven, top-down models of social change" (200). Costanza-Chock went on to emphasize the power of what he termed *transmedia organizing* as fundamental to this task, urging social justice advocates to take seriously "the creation of a narrative of social transformation across multiple media platforms, involving the movement's base in participatory media mak-ing, and linking attention directly to concrete opportunities for action" (50).[27]

Taken together, this scholarly review underscores several key points that are at the heart of the conceptual approach of this book. The first is that, in the age of neoliberalism, community-based social-change organizing repre-sents a dynamic site to explore the relationships between local activism and broader movements for social justice—in the food system and beyond. Furthermore, these critical perspectives demonstrate that, often on account of funders' lack of social justice consciousness and organizers' inability to tackle the discriminatory antecedents of inequality, many locally focused projects of the nonprofit industrial complex fail to offer any real transforma-tive agenda for change. These insights also point to the ways in which grass-roots organizations that *are* actually trying to advance radical visions of social justice—operating, therefore, "in the shadow of the shadow state"—still remain deeply embedded in networked relationships that connect them to partners and allies from varied ideological and institutional backgrounds, including members of the very entities that activists hope to undermine or transform. Yet even with these fundamental challenges in mind, many schol-ars and practitioners still see the community as a site with legitimate social justice potential. As the urban policy researchers James DeFilippis, Robert Fisher, and Eric Shragge have suggested, it seems as if the "limited capacity of community remains, as does its centrality. Accordingly, the debate over the place of community in social change should continue to locate both the pos-sibilities and limits of practice at is core" (166).[28]

The grassroots food justice organization whose network is investigated as a centering artifact in this book—CSU—attempts to navigate through the very shadows described above. Other community-based initiatives profiled in this work and connected by CSU's networked action—including the

Rooted in Community network, the American Heart Association's Teaching Gardens program, and the Ron Finley Project—also find themselves engaged with the tensions, limitations, and possibilities of community action in the nonprofit industrial complex. The chapters to follow aim to understand how the complicated and hybrid agendas of community-based food justice action are enacted and evolve over time and to articulate what these local efforts mean for the prospects of a wider-ranging movement for food justice.

Rather than simply describing the nature of these activities, however, I have an interest in providing a level of assessment that can inform food justice activism, organizing, and funding strategies moving forward. What I propose below is a set of working principles for implementing sustainable change in the arena of community-based food justice. I have devised these principles by building upon the insights of the scholars and practitioners cited in this book, my own experiences in food justice research, and my conversations with community-based activists. It should be noted that these principles are conceptualized as ideal types, and they therefore intentionally set a very high bar. It is my contention that ambitious guideposts such as these can play a role as a means of both evaluating existing food justice efforts and reflecting upon the future development of the food justice movement. With that as a preface, I suggest that, in order for the work of community-based food justice organizing to be parlayed into sustainable and enduring community change, the following elements must be present in the praxis of those organizations involved. Successful food justice organizing must

- be driven by local storytelling about food and justice—conversations that emerge from lived experience and historical realities, are rooted in place, and are grounded in community-based collaboration.
- be characterized by a theory of change that situates local food system struggles within broader legacies and visions of social justice activism.
- cultivate networked partnerships that provide programmatic and fiscal sustainability.
- exhibit a willingness and capacity to develop community-focused action into large-scale cultural and political transformation.

As I return continually to these criteria in subsequent chapters, it becomes evident that none of the organizations profiled in this book fully meet them—indeed, I am not sure there is a single food justice organization operating in the United States today that does. This assertion should not be taken as a slight against the work of food justice organizers—rather, it is based on an understanding that, while the work of specific community organizations forms the essential foundation for community development and capacity-building, the localized efforts of these groups must always be linked through networked action to diverse allies in order to increase the scale of and sustain social change.[29] In other words, no single group can do it alone, but each can contribute to the broader movement through unique means and at varied points in their respective organizational developments. This conclusion is also why I believe engaged scholarship has a productive role to play in the development of effective activism. This book, therefore, intends to use description and analysis to both theorize and strategize about how locally focused action can contribute to the long-term process of food justice movement-building.

THE COMMUNICATION ECOLOGY PERSPECTIVE

Now that my working principles have been established, this chapter continues by briefly outlining the methodological approach used to collect evidence for the ethnographic research that follows. I encourage those with interest in reading more on this topic to consult the appendix as well. Notably, although this book's exploration of community-level social change draws from an interdisciplinary set of theoretical and methodological frameworks, my training as a scholar in the field of communication studies remains a driving force of my academic research. Communication, of course, is a highly diverse arena of scholarship in its own right. My own intellectual upbringing in the field has encouraged me to focus upon two fundamental and intersecting areas of inquiry—investigations of *networks* and *narratives*. Grounded in a *communication ecology perspective,* this book bridges the study of networks and narratives to document and evaluate social change efforts that aim to advance community-based food justice.

As I offered in my definition of social change in the introduction, understanding such processes requires attention to structural concerns, on one hand, and to value systems that are at the root of enduring cultural and institutional dynamics, on the other. Historically, research on social change and social movements has tended to concentrate on either one or the other piece of this puzzle—many scholars focus on structurally oriented questions of "how" social movements mobilize resources while others focus on culturally oriented questions of "why" social change efforts take shape.[30] Finding some measure of synthesis between these often discrete approaches has been on the research agenda for some time, and one potentially promising approach to move toward this integration has come from scholars who place *networks* at the center of their research perspectives.

As Manuel Castells argued in his renowned *Information Age* trilogy, thanks to the influence of digital communication technologies, we now live in a "network society," in which a "prevailing, networking logic transforms all domains of social and economic life" (368).[31] A focus on networks in research on social change has paralleled the broader influence of networked concepts in the academic, governmental, and activist worlds.[32] As the network theorist Mario Diani has outlined, in traditional social movement research, networks—of interpersonal and interorganizational interaction—have generally been seen simply as *facilitators* of recruitment and participation for individuals and groups involved in organized social change efforts. When viewed from a network orientation, however, networks are not treated only as preconditions and resources for action but rather as the *primary analytical tool* through which social change activities can be documented and assessed. A networked approach is fundamentally relational, in that it investigates connections between and among organizations, individuals, collectives, and social structures to understand the phenomena under study.[33]

While network analysis is generally associated with a set of formal, heavily mathematical tools, Diani has argued that it is "best conceived as a broader approach to social processes. . . . To this purpose, triangulation strategies, combining qualitative and quantitative evidence, are most useful" (174).[34] On a practical level, however, the field has been dominated by quantitative, graphical research that charts networks of social change actors over time. Scholars have employed much less in the way of qualitative inquiry, and as a result, they have tended to emphasize questions related to structure at the expense of questions related to culture. Critics such as Raul Lejano, Mrill Ingram, and Helen Ingram, for instance, have argued that the network literature "gives rise to a powerful, positivist mode of analysis that emphasizes pattern and structure and, less so, meaning and identity" (29). By contrast, they encouraged an analytical approach that would reclaim questions of culture through an investigation of the *narratives* that link networked social change participants into common cause.[35]

Narrative analysts, of course, are no strangers to research efforts on social change, either.[36] Ultimately, those who are committed to exploring the narrative elements of social change efforts all agree that *storytelling*, in its various forms, provides an avenue through which we can understand social action and knowledge practices. To paraphrase the late George Gerbner—a leading thinker on this topic—stories serve a powerful function in their ability to reveal how things work, describe what things are, and tell us what to do about them.[37] Human beings are conceptualized as navigating their social worlds in narrative terms, while media systems, organizations, and institutions work in concert with interpersonal communication to shape a host of societal narratives that can prove influential in shaping social norms and motivating action.

In *More Than Just Food*, I employ a communication ecology perspective as a guide for my ethnographic research process. This approach integrates considerations of networks and narratives in order to understand both the "how" and "why" of social change organizing. The idea for the communication ecology perspective emerged from the theorizing and empirical research of the Metamorphosis Project, a research team under the leadership of sociologist and communication theorist Sandra Ball-Rokeach that has focused for decades on a variety of questions related to urban community life and communication dynamics in Los Angeles and beyond.[38] The development of the communication ecology perspective was informed by a diverse set of research threads, including the Chicago School of sociology, ecological models of public health promotion, and multilevel frameworks from communication and media studies. At its foundation, the term *communication* signals attention to networked relationships in which meaning is produced through ongoing interactions between individuals, organizations, media systems, and any other purveyors of information. The term *ecology* is representative of the dynamic, multilevel, evolving nature of these interactive elements, as well as the ways in which contextual and physical environments shape the nature of those networked relationships over time. The communication ecology perspective urges scholars to consider communication networks as a primary analytical tool for understanding social relationships. From there, scholars can qualitatively investigate the narratives that inhabit those networks as a means to explore the production of meaning and the construction of knowledge over time.

A primary method of employing this perspective comes through the conceptualization and analysis of what my colleagues and I have termed *goal-oriented communication ecologies*, which are defined as the multiple networks of communication resources constructed by an actor in pursuit of specific goals and in the context of that actor's communication environment. Both individuals and groups can be seen to have many different communication ecologies, as they will construct overlapping clusters of communication resource relations in an effort to achieve particular goals or acquire knowledge on specific topics. A person might construct one communication ecology that is oriented toward promoting her personal health, for instance, as her knowledge will be shaped through discursive interactions with networked sets of medical professionals, media sources, friends, and family members, among others. This same person might have an entirely different communication ecology that is oriented toward achieving work-related goals, with a whole other set of intersecting or distinct networks and narratives. Importantly, these communication ecologies are always constructed from within broader networks of communicative interaction, and they are fundamentally shaped by a variety of external environmental, spatial, and sociocultural forces that can serve to either limit or facilitate an actor's pursuit of a particular goal.[39]

In this book, in order to explore the "how" and "why" of food justice practice, I apply the communication ecology concept to the level of the community-based organization. I define an *organizational communication ecology* as the network of communication resource relations constructed by an organization in pursuit of a goal and in the context of its organizational environment. Through the structure and meaning that comes forth in these multiple networked organizational communication ecologies, a group can be understood to derive its organizational identity, find solidarity with other social change actors, connect with the community in which it operates, tell its story to broader publics, and achieve any number of other ideological and pragmatic goals. I use these networked structures themselves as a way to trace the flow of narrative, knowledge, culture, and identity as these elements are constructed in the evolving philosophy and action of food justice groups over time. With the insights gained through an investigation of these organizational communication ecologies, I am able to evaluate the extent to which my working principles for sustainable community change, outlined above, are achieved by those engaged in food justice organizing.

. . .

"What is the most important thing to us is that we make change in our community," Neelam Sharma, CSU's executive director, succinctly explained in an interview. This chapter has provided some theoretical context to help explain why, in an age of global risk and digital communication networks, the strategy of nonprofit community organizing toward social justice has persisted. It also introduced a set of working principles to evaluate the sustainable effectiveness of community-based change. From there, it outlined the tenets of the communication ecology perspective, a theoretical and methodological approach that guides this book's critical and empirical inquiry.

In tracing the successes and challenges of social justice nonprofits that operate "in the shadow of the shadow state," *More Than Just Food* interrogates the hybrid praxis that takes shape in the evolving action of grassroots food movement organizations. In what ways does food serve as a productive force to advance social justice at the level of the local community? How might effective community action push forth an even more expansive agenda for change? What factors restrain the food justice movement from growing, and what can be done to strengthen its force in the years to come?

The chapters to follow feature a networked exploration of South LA's CSU—a conceptual diagram of which can be found at the end of this chapter—as well as connected case studies of linked organizations in the food justice landscape. I analyze how the networked structures and narrative practices of these intersecting nonprofit groups construct distinctive organizing approaches. Guided by my working principles for sustainable community change, I provide insight into the capacity and limitations of diverse forms of community-based food justice activism in the age of neoliberalism. With this in mind, the next chapter turns its attention to the structures of the modern industrial food system itself.

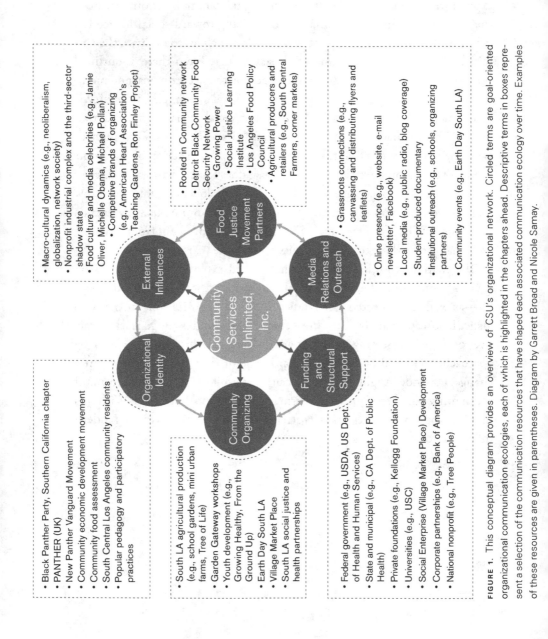

FIGURE 1. This conceptual diagram provides an overview of CSU's organizational network. Circled terms are goal-oriented organizational communication ecologies, each of which is highlighted in the chapters ahead. Descriptive terms in boxes represent a selection of the communication resources that have shaped each associated communication ecology over time. Examples of these resources are given in parentheses. Diagram by Garrett Broad and Nicole Samay.

- Black Panther Party, Southern California chapter
- PANTHER (UK)
- New Panther Vanguard Movement
- Community economic development movement
- Community food assessment
- South Central Los Angeles community residents
- Popular pedagogy and participatory practices

- South LA agricultural production (e.g., school gardens, mini urban farms, Tree of Life)
- Garden Gateway workshops
- Youth development (e.g., Growing Healthy, From the Ground Up)
- Earth Day South LA
- Village Market Place
- South LA social justice and health partnerships

- Federal government (e.g., USDA, US Dept. of Health and Human Services)
- State and municipal (e.g., CA Dept. of Public Health)
- Private foundations (e.g., Kellogg Foundation)
- Universities (e.g., USC)
- Social Enterprise (Village Market Place) Development
- Corporate partnerships (e.g., Bank of America)
- National nonprofit (e.g., Tree People)

- Macro-cultural dynamics (e.g., neoliberalism, globalization, network society)
- Nonprofit industrial complex and the third-sector shadow state
- Food culture and media celebrities (e.g., Jamie Oliver, Michelle Obama, Michael Pollan)
- Competitive brands of organizing (e.g., American Heart Association's Teaching Gardens, Ron Finley Project)

- Rooted in Community network
- Detroit Black Community Food Security Network
- Growing Power
- Social Justice Learning Institute
- Los Angeles Food Policy Council
- Agricultural producers and retailers (e.g., South Central Farmers, corner markets)

- Grassroots connections (e.g., canvassing and distributing flyers and leaflets)
- Online presence (e.g., website, e-mail newsletter, Facebook)
- Local media (e.g., public radio, blog coverage)
- Student-produced documentary
- Institutional outreach (e.g., schools, organizing partners)
- Community events (e.g., Earth Day South LA)

Community Services Unlimited, Inc.

- External Influences
- Food Justice Movement Partners
- Organizational Identity
- Media Relations and Outreach
- Community Organizing
- Funding and Structural Support

Food Systems, Food Movements, Food Justice

Combining an interactive mapping platform with data from the national census and a geographic directory of grocery stores from across the country, the United States Department of Agriculture (USDA) was proud to introduce its new online Food Desert Locator in May of 2011. Agriculture Secretary Tom Vilsack explained in the official press release that the new tool would "help policy makers, community planners, researchers, and other professionals identify communities where public-private intervention can help make fresh, healthy, and affordable food more readily available to residents."[1] The Food Desert Locator was emblematic of a broader push, picking up significant momentum over the course of the previous decade or more, to put healthy food access concerns onto the agenda of American citizens, activists, policymakers, and private businesses alike.

The term *food desert* was explicitly mentioned by the US Congress in the Food, Conservation and Energy Act of 2008—known colloquially as the 2008 Farm Bill—when federal lawmakers allocated $500,000 to investigate existing problems and potential solutions related to places "with limited access to affordable and nutritious food, particularly such an area of predominantly lower-income neighborhoods and communities."[2] Shortly thereafter, First Lady Michelle Obama publicly stated that 23.5 million Americans, including 6.5 million children, resided within these food deserts. Her national Let's Move initiative included combatting these community-based problems as central to her goal of ending childhood obesity.[3] A few years later, the Obama administration's Healthy Food Financing Initiative—a $400 million, multiyear program operated jointly by the Departments of Treasury, Agriculture, and Health and Human Services—was rolled out with a stated aim of spurring food-related economic development in food deserts across urban and rural America. The administration argued that these financing programs, which were kicked off in 2010 and expanded in subsequent federal budgets, would help "revitalize neighborhoods and communities by employing place-based approaches—strategies that target the prosperity, equity, sustainability and livability of places."[4] Several years into the second decade of the twenty-first century, a consensus seemed to have emerged that inequality in the American food system was a reality, and food deserts were identified as both a cause and manifestation of this problem.

It was around this time that I offered my volunteer research services to colleagues at Community Services Unlimited (CSU). They were in the process of drafting a multiyear grant application to the Community Economic Development Program of the United States Department of Health and Human Services, and they asked for my assistance in outlining the relevant scholarly literature on food deserts and community health outcomes in South Los Angeles. For the proposed project, funds would be used to spur the growth of CSU's social enterprise—the Village Market Place (VMP)—as the grant would allow for new hiring, youth job-skill training, and an expansion in the distribution and marketing of the program. "Scaling up the VMP would allow for the continued development of a vibrant local food economy in a community that has traditionally experienced economic and nutritional inequality," the proposal, which was ultimately funded, asserted.[5]

CSU was in the process of growing its community-based social enterprise at a time when observers from diverse political perspectives agreed that the global food system was entering an era of significant strain. Climate change, intensifying droughts, the loss of fertile lands, and a host of market disruptions were spiking food prices and exacerbating food insecurity across the developing world.[6] In the United States, unhealthy eating habits were being blamed as a primary driver of the nation's battles with obesity and other metabolic disorders, maladies that were particularly acute within low-income communities and communities of color. Articulating what had become a commonplace refrain, the Robert Wood Johnson Foundation described the situation as "one of the most challenging health crises the country has ever faced," insisting that medical costs and productivity losses were "hampering America's ability to compete in the global economy" (3).[7]

Even in the face of these global and national food system challenges, however, I found that many advocates for food system reform continued to propose a set of locally focused, community-based initiatives that combined governmental support with private entrepreneurship and the hard work of local residents and activists as viable solutions to advance health, equity, and sustainability across urban America. This chapter aims to explore why and how community-based approaches have become central to food activism, broadly speaking, and to food justice organizing, specifically. While hardly an exhaustive compendium on food system issues, it serves as a primer of sorts on the dynamics of the contemporary food system and of movements for food system change. My intention here is to help the reader situate the ethnographic research on community-based food justice that forms the heart of this book within relevant social, political, and economic contexts. To achieve this goal, the pages to follow highlight the networked structures and cultural narratives that characterize the past, present, and potential futures of the food system. The chapter provides a brief sketch of agricultural history, offers an overview of the central risks that have emerged as a result of food system industrialization, and describes the various alternative food initiatives that have taken aim at this industrialized status quo.

I argue that global and local food systems today are characterized by a paradox of coexisting abundance and injustice. As a means to remedy this structural inequity, locally focused program development has emerged as a driving force for twenty-first century food activism in the United States.[8] As I discussed in chapter 1, in the age of neoliberalism, decentralized strategies of community-based capacity-building—often spearheaded by shadow state nonprofit organizations—bring with them a set of inherent advantages and constraints. Alternative food activism offers a prime example.

Indeed, recent years have seen countless community-based food and agriculture initiatives take shape, all with overlapping aims to improve the economic, ecological, or nutritional health of the food system. While these programs have undoubtedly benefitted a number of food system stakeholders, their results have proved uneven. Notably, many alternative food initiatives have consistently overlooked the systemic racialized and economic components of food-related inequality, and as a result, they have failed to promote justice for all. In response to these intersecting concerns, a people-of-color-led movement for community-based food justice has emerged in urban America. Yet, as sympathetic critics of food justice organizing insist, that movement also faces significant challenges in its quest to advance sustainable community change.

Food has long been central to the development of human civilization. It has served as a dynamic force for the emergence of cultural identity and societal stability and encouraged economic exchange and regional cooperation while stoking significant conflict and spurring long-term exploitation. Operating at local, regional, national, and global scales, the contemporary food system consists of complex networks of, to name just a few key players, individuals, organizations, transnational corporations, governments, and a host of other public and private institutions. It includes the states, corporations, and financial institutions that invest money and resources into food and agricultural development; farmers and laborers who grow crops; animals who are utilized in food production; processors who refine and package food; distributors and retailers who sell food; consumers who cook and eat food; and those involved with the infrastructures that deal with food waste. Over time, shifts toward a more industrialized food system have been encouraged by a widespread desire for the improvement of agricultural processes, the growth of capital markets, the rise of corporate food industries, advances in transportation and communication infrastructure, global consumer demand, and an ever-evolving set of other social and technological dynamics. Today, the multi-trillion dollar global food system represents one of the largest—and most important—industries in the world.[9]

From the start, there has been one basic question at the heart of these processes: can we produce enough food to support and nourish a growing population, or will we go hungry? At its core, the contemporary food system has been shown to offer great promise in the enduring quest to feed the world. Yet, on account of several intersecting economic, social, and environmental challenges, the system has fallen short of fulfilling this task, while the industrialization of food itself has created an entirely new set of risks with which society must grapple.

Of course, for the vast majority of humanity's existence—some 190,000 years—the basis of the food system encompassed groups of humans who spent their time foraging, hunting, doing basic cooking, and traveling. The transition to farming and herding—which likely began between 10,000 and 12,000 years ago—represented perhaps the most fundamental shift in the organization of social life throughout all of human history. At some point in this range, groups of humans decided to abandon gathering and hunting as their primary modes of acquiring food and shift to agriculture. Over the course of the next few thousand years, agricultural practices began to develop across a number of continents, with a rapid and large-scale adoption of plant and animal domestication occurring during the span of years approximately 10,000 to 7,000 years before the present time.[10]

Preindustrial agriculture was largely defined by slash-and-burn farming methods, a low-technology style of subsistence farming in which natural vegetation is cut down and burned away and crops are grown in its place until the area is deemed fallow, at which point farmers move to new areas. These subsistence practices call for the agro-ecological integration of multiple elements of the landscape—including cropland, forests, waterways, and seas—into a holistic process. Still practiced in similar forms by countless residents of the developing world today, slash-and-burn farming methods, along with other styles of small-scale subsistence agriculture, have hardly been easy rows to hoe, so to speak. The methods place food production at the whim of unpredictable weather patterns, crop and animal diseases, soil fertility and productivity constraints, and external strife and war. Collectively, these dangers have always threatened the ability of subsistence farmers to produce enough food to nourish local and rural communities, while the increasingly urban and global populations of the modern age unequivocally call for more intensive and reliable agricultural strategies.[11]

Food production practices developed in different ways across different regions of the globe, as innovations in plant and animal breeding, irrigation, organic fertilization, and food preservation came as a result of agro-ecological management that was specific to varied locales. Still, the fundamentals of agricultural practice remained mostly stable over the course of many centuries. It was starting in earnest around the fifteenth century that the development of cities, colonial expansion, increased trade, and technological advances in both agriculture and transportation began to shift this state of affairs. In the centuries to follow, exploitative European imperialism, which depended on slave-based agricultural labor as a foundational element of its economic base, pushed agriculture toward a new model of capitalist agro-industrialism.[12]

As the Industrial Revolution took hold in the eighteenth and nineteenth centuries, proponents of "scientific agriculture" in Europe sought to maximize agricultural production while using less land and fewer farmworkers. Through empirical experimentation and technological innovation, they worked to improve the efficiency of tools, provide better irrigation, and select and breed crops and animals that would yield more productivity. However, as Europe and its colonial agro-industrial outposts began to specialize crop development and increase yields on wide swaths of land—abandoning a tradition of farming systems that had integrated all elements of the natural landscape—problems of soil fertility became paramount.[13]

It was at this time that advances in chemistry came into the purview of food production and an emerging capitalist agribusiness. Agriculture became a specific subfield for scientists and economists in Europe, in the developing powerhouse of the United States, and around the world. Increasingly intensive agricultural practices were seen as imperative for the advancement of nineteenth century technological progress, a way to finally eliminate the long-standing dangers of hunger for growing population centers while raising the standards of living for all. The introduction of nitrogen-enriched inorganic fertilizers, petroleum-based pesticides, and plants bred to optimally coexist in a landscape with these new chemical innovations laid the foundation for what is now often referred to as "conventional" or "traditional" agriculture. When considering the arc of agricultural history, however, it is clear that these adjectives are hardly appropriate labels, given that such a radical transformation had taken place.[14]

The push toward intensification would only grow more central to agricultural practices in the coming years. In the twentieth century, state-led development projects established during the Cold War touted further modernization of agriculture as the key to saving the bustling world from widespread hunger. Building on the ideology of intensive cultivation that had developed in the West in earlier centuries, this Green Revolution in agriculture was characterized by the industrialization of farm inputs and the massive application of petrochemical fertilizers and other chemical processes. Post-World War II, chemical corporations that had previously developed biocides as potential biological warfare agents were able to shift their productive capacity from waging war against foreign enemies to waging war against weeds and pests. In the immediate post-war years, these corporations and their partners in government successfully advanced a narrative that such natural nuisances, if not dealt with, would stand in the way of agricultural abundance, consumer freedom, and the long-term elimination of global hunger.[15]

In many ways, industrial agriculture in this post-war period provided a basis for the development and growth of modern global civilization as we now know it. The introduction of nitrogen fertilizers, pesticides, and insecticides boosted global food production to unprecedented levels. Concurrently, global population growth accelerated from approximately 1 billion in 1800, to 3 billion in 1960, to 6 billion in 1999, to over 7 billion at the time of this writing (and the number is always rising). The increasingly intensive food production of the last several centuries proved to be a response to, as well as a trigger for, the ever-growing trends in global population with which we have become accustomed.[16]

What, then, became of the great promises of the Green Revolution in industrial agriculture? In wealthy nations like the United States, the Green Revolution's most clear accomplishment was in the domain of consumer purchasing opportunities. The heretofore unfathomable scale and relative consistency of industrial agriculture allowed for the development of modern-day supermarkets and produce markets, as strawberries became available in the wintertime and tomatoes began to look identical from grocer to grocer. Combined with scientific advances in transportation and chemical-based food preservation, industrialization also made possible the growth of massive industries in the production and sale of processed, fast, and convenient foods. Make no mistake—the scope and reliability of food availability across the developed world today is an inarguably remarkable break from the millenniums-long history of human society. Additionally, on account of Green Revolution technology and economies of scale, the food delivered to largely urban consumer populations has come to be sourced from shrinking rural communities in which fewer and fewer people are actually engaged in farming occupations, allowing more of the populace to pursue other nonagricultural lifestyles and professions.

When it came to the developing world—those global regions in which poverty was increasingly concentrated in the twentieth and twenty-first centuries—for a time, mechanization, industrialization, and chemicalization demonstrated some success in tackling the great, enduring challenges of hunger and malnutrition. In sheer numbers, the world began to reliably produce a volume of crops that could provide populations worldwide with sufficient caloric intake. Following the Green Revolution, several decades in the latter part of the 1900s witnessed decreases in the overall percentage of global citizens who experienced hunger. However, with global populations still rising, the Green Revolution hardly eliminated hunger, a fact that remains clear to the present day. Indeed, the Food and Agriculture Organization of the United Nations has estimated that, during the years from 2010 to 2014, somewhere between 925 million and 805 million people did not have enough food to eat, with 98 percent of those people residing in developing nations.

Many more suffer from micronutrient vitamin and mineral deficiencies due to lack of diversity in their diets.[17]

What is at the root of this paradox of agricultural abundance and stability, on one hand, and hunger and inequity, on the other? In the wake of the Green Revolution, widespread poverty, inadequate food distribution, geopolitical power imbalances, and a market-driven global agricultural system that emphasized the production of a limited set of commodity crops ensured that the promise of feeding the world would remain unfulfilled. As scholar-activists Eric Holt-Gimenez and Raj Patel have described, "The overlapping histories of development, the Green Revolution, Northern subsidies, structural adjustment and free trade agreements constitute an agrarian saga of global proportions and helps to explain why poverty and overproduction—not scarcity and overpopulation—are the main causes of hunger in the world" (25).[18] This paradox demonstrates that the key question of whether or not humanity could someday produce enough food to feed an ever-growing global population does not sufficiently engage with the challenges that characterize the food system in the age of neoliberalism. Instead, as society has been forced to grapple with the realities of inequitable allocations of risk, questions of justice have been brought to the fore.

RISK AND INJUSTICE IN THE INDUSTRIAL FOOD SYSTEM

The networked actors of the food system today are required to engage with a historically novel set of economic, environmental, and public health risks. Indeed, crises in the contemporary food system are in many ways typical of what scholars Ulrich Beck, Anthony Giddens, and others have termed "world risk society." "The threats and uncertainties in question," Beck wrote, "in contrast to earlier eras, are not the result of the errors of modernization but of its *successes*" (7, emphasis in original).[19] The newfound, self-generated risks that have emerged bring with them local and global implications, and they involve complex systems in their long-term management. Still, just as these risks have emerged, so too have a set of heterogeneous social-movement formations that, through varying means and on the basis of diverse sets of philosophies, have attempted to allay the risks that industrialization in the food system has engendered.

It is useful to think of contemporary risk in the food system as coalescing around three intersecting conceptual areas. First, there are economic and occupational concerns—these issues are fundamentally grounded in the widespread corporate consolidation that has come to characterize the food system, and such dynamics have implications for how power is exercised and exploitation is enacted across the globe. Second, there are environmental and nonhuman animal concerns—notably, the practices of large-scale and chemically intensive industrial agriculture have proven detrimental to the well-being of natural resources and the health of nonhuman life. Third, there are dietary and public health concerns—a host of chronic diet-related diseases and food safety and access issues have joined hunger and malnutrition as central nutritive challenges that characterize the contemporary age.

From an economic perspective, buffered by market-based governmental policies and subsidies that support monopolistic growth, large-scale capitalist agribusiness has enforced widespread consolidation in the global food industry over the last several decades. A few major multinationals aggressively control the majority of global food production, processing, and distribution. In nearly every sector—including soybean processing (85 percent global control by top four firms), beef slaughter (82 percent global control by top four firms), wet corn milling (87 percent global control by top four firms), broiler chicken slaughter (53 percent global control by top four firms), and food retail (64 percent US market control by top twenty firms)—competition has decreased while market power has become more concentrated. An "hourglass" picture of agricultural development has taken shape, such that, in the words of scholar Terry Marsden, "thousands of farmers feed millions of consumers through an increasingly corporately controlled system that involves webs of interconnected input suppliers, food processors and retailers" (138).[20] Names such as Monsanto, Dupont, Archer Daniels Midland, Cargill, ConAgra, Tyson, and Wal-Mart dominate decision-making from seed to table.[21] Bolstered by powerful public relations apparatuses and often unquestioned by major media systems, these dominant actors tell the story that the food system is a market just like any other, one that provides the greatest benefits when private interests are free to pursue economic gain.

Flexing this technological, economic, and ideological muscle, the United States has dominated North America and much of the global food system with a market-oriented model of agricultural production and distribution.[22] Consolidated corporate industries exercise significant power in shaping and marginalizing the practices of small US farmers, while the exploitation of low-wage and migrant farmworkers has become a normative reality across much of the American system of labor.[23] Many small- and medium-sized farming operations across the globe, meanwhile, have found themselves in serious debt to corporate interests and are often put out of business. A rash of farmer suicides in India and collective resistance from farmers in nations as disperse as South Korea, Guatemala, and the Philippines points to the ways in which global corporate agribusiness has not had the best interest of local farmers in mind.[24]

A host of environmental risks have emerged in concert with these economic shifts. Ecological principles related to the long-term health of the land and concerns for biodiversity and public health have been fundamentally marginalized by a market-based ideology that idealizes a commitment to economic efficiency and technological innovation above all else.[25] Globalized industrial food production relies on heavy inputs of petrochemical fertilizers, pesticides, and a monocultural growing process, as single commodity crops—mostly wheat, soy, and corn—are grown over large areas of land to feed into global markets. Modern agriculture has developed processes in which the same piece of land can be used more frequently, increasing the specialization of productive crops in order to improve yields and ease the processes of mechanization. As former US Secretary of Agriculture Earl Butz infamously described during his tenure in the 1970s, the mantra of this strategy is to "get big or get out."[26]

Proponents of a second Green Revolution, characterized by the introduction of genetically modified (GM) foods and touted by multinational agricultural conglomerates, have promised that biotechnology could reduce agricultural chemical use and further increase yields. Essentially, the story told by agribusiness corporations and their allies in government and philanthropy has been that genetic modification will finally solve the interminable task of "feeding the world" through environmentally sound methods.[27] Some of the most vocal critics of this approach warn that the production and consumption of these "frankenfoods" will lead to outright environmental devastation and the emergence of unknown cancers and other health risks. The reality is that both of these perspectives remain based on incomplete bodies of evidence. Decades after GM products entered the food supply, there remains little credible data to demonstrate that the worst direct health outcomes detractors asserted would inevitably emerge have actually taken shape. Yet GM proponents consistently hype the limited successes of targeted agricultural interventions while overlooking the very real social and environmental risks that remain embedded in their strategy. In reality, GM agriculture has done little to actually increase agricultural yields, and its proliferation has reduced seed biodiversity while increasing monoculture. Meanwhile, a growing body of evidence demonstrates that, when supported through investment and competent management, diversified organic farming practices can be just as successful in boosting yields as chemically intensive or GM strategies—while also supporting local economies and promoting sustainable livelihoods. Within this landscape of debate about the merits of GM foods, perhaps the clearest conclusion is that its widespread introduction has continued to consolidate power into the hands of fewer and fewer major agribusiness interests.[28]

While the long-term benefits or drawbacks of GM products with respect to the environment remain unknown, we do know that industrialization in general has had serious negative ramifications for the long-term viability of soil fertility, pest management, ecological diversity, pollution control, and broader environmental sustainability. Emissions of greenhouse gases from industrialized agriculture, combined with drastic land use changes, have emerged as central drivers of climate change. The current practices in food production are ultimately causing fresh water, available land, and valuable energy inputs to rapidly disappear at the same time as the global population rises and demand increases. In addition, nutrient leaks from herbicides and fertilizers have been associated with the deterioration of fisheries, the development of "dead zones" in bodies of water like the Gulf of Mexico, and widespread soil erosion. As global demand for animal-derived products has skyrocketed, industrial farm animal production (IFAP)—commonly known as factory farming—has proven particularly environmentally devastating. IFAP has been identified as a leading emitter of the greenhouse gas emissions that contribute to climate change, while massive amounts of waste and agricultural runoff stand as a leading cause of air pollution, water pollution, and soil degradation. Additionally, concerns related to animal cruelty within IFAP are of course worthy of consideration in their own right.[29]

All of these various environmental concerns remain intricately linked to occupational and environmental justice risks. Low-income and migrant farmworkers have commonly been exposed to a variety of harmful and disease-causing chemicals, while those employed in industrialized animal production have been forced to operate at hazardous and exhausting speeds. In the United States and around the world, these laborers generally have little access to legal recourse to remedy the exploitation they face at the hands of major corporate players.[30]

Food consumers face their own set of challenges. In the United States, for instance, 14.3 percent of households (17.5 million) were "food insecure" at some time during 2013, meaning that their access to adequate food was limited at some point by a lack of money or other resources.[31] Although increasingly under attack by so-called budget reformers, an emergency food safety net remains tenuously in place, preventing the type of widespread hunger that still exists in the developing world from becoming a part of the fabric of American life. As I mentioned in the introduction, over 46 million low-income Americans received food-purchasing support through the federal Supplemental Nutrition Assistance Program (SNAP, formerly known as the Food Stamp Program) in 2014. As another indicator, in the 2012–2013 school year, 21.5 million children received free or reduced-price lunches as part of the National School Lunch Program.[32]

Ultimately, the story that tends to grab the most attention in public health and popular media circles is not necessarily the lack of overall foods available to Americans but rather the types of foods that have come to dominate the shelves of grocery and convenience stores across the nation. Minimally processed whole foods, such as fruits and vegetables, are generally agreed to be health promoting, but they make less money for the corporations involved in their production, distribution, and sales.[33] By contrast, ultra-processed foods, such as breads, meat products, sugary snacks, and frozen dinners—which have as their foundation oils, fats, flours, starches, and sugars and are then combined with complex additives to make them more palatable and habit forming—are, as medical nutrition researcher Carlos Monteiro has described, "typically branded, distributed internationally and globally, heavily advertised and marketed, and very profitable" (730). While aspects of the science behind their contentions remain contested, researchers and public health officials have attributed a significant portion of the rise in chronic diseases like hypertension, coronary heart disease, diabetes, and obesity to diet, linking the risk of contracting these diseases to the increased consumption of these poor-quality processed foods.[34]

In the face of growing criticism, the story told by dominant powers in food production and processing is that they are simply feeding consumer demand. There is plenty of evidence to suggest, however, that they have actually worked strategically to create a demand that must be fed.[35] In the name of offering "cheap food" to the consuming public, government has directly and indirectly subsidized the production of commodity grains—namely wheat, corn, and soy—that form the foundation of processed foods and animal products. Meanwhile, massive industries in food science and marketing have sprung up in order to encourage greater consumption. As food scholar

Marion Nestle has described, the combination of food advertising, convenience, larger portions, and the gustatory components of habit-forming processed foods, in conjunction with "systematic, pervasive and unrelenting" lobbying efforts, have ensured that more and more of these foods are purchased and eaten (26).[36] Furthermore, federal assistance initiatives like SNAP and the National School Lunch Program have proved to be dumping grounds where the worst of the worst low-quality processed foods are able to find captive consumer markets, while the consolidated food retail sector has provided another perfect outlet for ultra-processed food exchanges to take place.[37] This American-made model is now spreading across the developing world, where a so-called nutrition transition has wedded increased industrialization with greater consumption of ultra-processed foods and the subsequent appearance of chronic and degenerative diet-related diseases.[38] As sociologist Michael Carolan has explained, while this system may create foods that are objectively "cheap" at the check-out line, when we take into account the great economic, environmental, and public health costs that they eventually bring about, the food system can hardly be seen to produce an abundance of food that is truly "affordable."[39]

This is not to say that processed foods do not bring some valuable levels of pleasure and convenience to eaters or that, in moderation, they can likely be part of a healthy diet. It must also be reiterated that, for many privileged global citizens today, the reliability of food availability and the diversity in eating options is undoubtedly greater than at any other time in the course of human history. What this admission brings to light, however, is the striking inequity that remains embedded in the food system, both between the developed and developing world and within developed nations themselves. In the United States, as an operative example, diet-related diseases affect residents of all social classes and ethnic backgrounds. Yet, as has already been established, low-income communities and communities of color are far more likely to live inside food deserts in which fast-food restaurants and unhealthy, cheap, ultra-processed options are far easier to find than fresh and affordable minimally processed whole foods. Residents who are surrounded by these poor food environments have been consistently found to have less health-promoting diets and higher rates of chronic disease and to suffer from a host of other health disparities.[40]

It is important to emphasize, however, that the local food environment *alone* does not provide a direct link between food consumption and health outcomes, as is sometimes interpreted. More plausible than a one-to-one ratio, it seems, is that poor food environments in the United States and elsewhere contribute to a process of what has been termed *deprivation amplification*. That is, problems related to food access amplify the economic, environmental, and social disadvantages already faced by low-income communities and communities of color.[41] A host of intersecting concerns—related to poverty, the built environment, environmental injustice, education, racial bias in the criminal justice system, and a lack of economic opportunity, among other factors—intersect with food issues to influence health and well-being.[42] The chronic disease rates that have been connected to food deserts, then, are unlikely to be solved by simply adding a few more grocery stores or limiting the presence of fast food restaurants in such neighborhoods.[43] Instead, if food access initiatives hope to achieve their health promotion aims, they must be included as part of a more systemic movement for sustainable social change.

ALTERNATIVE FOOD MOVEMENTS
AND THE TURN TO COMMUNITY

The dynamics of capital-driven, industrialized food production exponentially compound the landscape of risk faced by the already marginalized and exploited citizens of the developed and developing worlds alike. In the face of these unjust practices, recent decades have seen a host of local and global actors emerge as a productive counterforce. Activists have worked hard to inject new narratives into the food system conversation, while simultaneously constructing new networks that aim to advance food system sustainability and sustenance. In the United States and elsewhere, these new social movement activities have often been referred to as the "alternative food movement." [44] Yet, as the prominent journalist Michael Pollan has pointed out, it is probably more accurate to describe the emergence of plural "food *movements,*" since these efforts are "unified as yet by little more than the recognition that industrial food production is in need of reform because its social/environmental/public health/animal welfare/gastronomic costs are too high."[45] There is great diversity, in fact, with respect to the philosophical foundations, motivations, focus areas, goals, and strategies employed by the number of individuals and organizations who could be considered as engaged in these "alternative food movements."

Try as one might, this diversity makes it extremely challenging to determine where, exactly, the dominant structures of the food system end and the food movements begin. As Eric Holt-Giménez has described, a variety of initiatives for food system reform and improvement have actually been introduced by members of the "corporate food regime" itself. There is a clear recognition among many neoliberal power brokers—including major agrifood corporations, financial institutions, and the US government, as well as global humanitarian and social service institutions like the United Nation's Food and Agriculture Organization and the Bill and Melinda Gates Foundation—that sustainably feeding growing global populations is a vital challenge of the twenty-first century. Still, these groups tend to fall short of being true alternatives to current practices. Instead, the story they tell—one that is amplified through powerful media and institutional channels—is that some combination of technological solutions, trade liberalization, food aid, and individualized consumer initiatives will best provide sustainable goods and services for all. Any transformation of dominant social structures or cultural values— that is, any shift that emphasizes how inequity in the food system has been shaped by legacies of exploitation and systemic injustice—is deemed unnecessary, if considered at all. As I will continue to explore throughout this book, alternative food movements remain in many ways linked to the structures and cultures of the corporate food regime. However, their efforts follow a distinctly different narrative—the global industrial food system, food movement activists argue, is fundamentally flawed, unsustainable, and in need of a drastic overhaul.[46]

As perhaps the most prominent food movement organization in the developing world, La Vía Campesina (The Peasant Way) serves as an illustrative example of how this global opposition has coalesced. A coalition of grassroots farmers' organizations, La Vía Campesina was founded in 1993 and has developed into a leading voice for peasant farmers in global agricultural debates. Connected by collective organizing and the power of digital communication technologies, their work aims to advance what they call *food sovereignty*. Similar in ideology to the food justice approach, food sovereignty advocates tend to be centered in the Global South and are overtly radical in their critique of neoliberalism and its influences. Members of La Vía Campesina promote a sustainable and culturally oriented agriculture that "ensures that the rights to use and manage lands, territories, water, seeds, livestock and biodiversity are in the hands of those who produce food and not of the corporate sector."[47] Far from being a singular and cohesive entity, though, the organization itself is actually made up of approximately 150 local and national organizations, representing 200 million farmers in 70 countries across all continents. Each member group must therefore develop strategies that respond to its own specific set of conditions, opportunities, and constraints.[48]

Like La Vía Campesina, much of the food movement energy in the Global South has emerged from grassroots radicalism—activists advocate for the dismantling of corporate agrifood's monopoly power, call for redistributive land reform, and seek a revival of agroecologically managed peasant agriculture. In the Global North, food movements have tended to be driven by political progressives, who work in pursuit of their own culturally derived visions of sustainability, equity, and justice. As geographer Rachel Slocum has described, the target of progressive activists in the United States has been "the conventional food system that privileges corporate agriculture, commodity subsidies, trans-continental shipping and foods high in fats, salt and sugars" (522).[49]

Recent decades have witnessed the creation of countless initiatives that respond to the varied economic, environmental, and nutrition-related risks of industrialized food in the United States. While some progressive food movement activists have concentrated their attention on advocating for alternative food policy on national and international scales, a larger number have focused on the entrepreneurial development of alternative food projects and programs. Many of these projects explicitly advance the interests of local farmers, as farmers' markets, community-supported agriculture arrangements, and "buy local" campaigns have become commonplace across much of the nation. Other projects remain attuned primarily to environmental concerns, as advocates champion agro-ecological production initiatives, work to improve soil fertility and plant biodiversity, promote organic foods, and provide alternatives to factory farming. A host of school and other locally focused projects that are committed to using nutrition education, gardening, and farm-to-table initiatives to tackle the challenges of chronic diet-related disease and obesity have been implemented. Gastronomically minded "foodies," represented by numerous local groups and national entities like Slow Food USA, have worked to highlight the pleasures of eating gourmet and culturally diverse cuisines. Other efforts remain grounded in a vision of greater justice in the food system, focused on advancing the rights and labor conditions of local and global farmworkers, building cooperative ownership in food retail, investing in healthy food projects in underserved communities, and promoting youth and economic development in historically marginalized neighborhoods of color. Many of these projects, of course, combine various elements of these intersecting agendas into their work, and they have increasingly come together with actors in local government, business, and civil society to participate in collaborative bodies such as Food Policy Councils.[50]

Meanwhile, several prominent figures have garnered media attention to bring the story of alternative food to broader audiences. First Lady Michelle Obama catapulted nutrition issues onto the national stage with the launch of her Let's Move initiative in 2010. Dedicated to "solving the problem of obesity in a generation," Let's Move endeavored to provide information to parents and facilitate public-private partnerships to foster healthy food environments in homes, schools, and communities.[51] Around the same time, British celebrity chef Jamie Oliver launched *Jamie Oliver's Food Revolution* on the ABC television network, hoping to "create a strong, sustainable movement to educate every child about food, inspire families to cook again and empower people everywhere to fight obesity."[52] *New York Times* columnist Mark Bittman, food studies scholar Marion Nestle, and Chez Panisse restaurant founder Alice Waters are among a number of prominent public intellectuals who are regularly granted high-profile media spaces in order to critique the food industry and offer suggestions for change. Several successful food system documentaries—including *Super Size Me* (2004), *King Corn* (2007), and *Forks Over Knives* (2011)—have also received widespread distribution and acclaim. Perhaps the most influential work in this genre has been *Food, Inc.* (2009), Robert Kenner's Academy Award-nominated film, which prominently featured the perspectives of Michael Pollan, author of *The Omnivore's Dilemma,* and *Fast Food Nation's* Eric Schlosser. The film took aim at the marginalizing power of corporate agriculture, highlighted the plight of low-income urban food consumers and rural farmers, peered inside confined animal feeding operations, and pointed to processed foods as villains in America's battle against chronic disease. Still, the film ended on an optimistic note, urging viewers to "vote to change" the food system "three times a day" (at every meal) and insisting that "you can change the world with every bite."

Taken together, this media storytelling has often been lauded as a game-changing wake-up call for the American public and the food industry alike. The call to "vote with your fork" has undoubtedly become a familiar refrain within progressive food circles.[53] For a variety of philosophically distinct proponents for food system change—from Michelle Obama on the reformist side to food co-op retail markets on the more radical side—individual consumption has been consistently lauded as a valuable entry point for activism and empowerment. This rhetorical and policy strategy, however, has not gone without criticism.

Indeed, on the political right, governmental and public support for particular food purchasing decisions has often been derided as a "nanny state" approach, one that encroaches upon individual liberty and pushes the nation toward irrational elitism.[54] On the other side of the political spectrum, critics from the left have been consistently disappointed that food reform initiatives do not go far enough. Changing individual consumer habits, they argue, may be valuable for one's personal health and peace of mind, but can it really serve to reshape our broken food system? And, given the preponderance of alternative food movement spokespersons who come from upper-income backgrounds—sometimes with close professional ties to the corporate food regime itself—do their consumer-oriented solutions really reflect the voices, needs, and desires of those Americans who daily experience food injustice?[55]

It is my contention that an important element is often missing from all sides of this "vote with your fork" debate. Notably, the conversation tends to hover around the limits and potential of *individual* action in transforming the food system, but in doing so, it overlooks the parallel role played by the *community* in these popular initiatives. In chapter 1 of this book, I explained how the logic of neoliberal governmentality has encouraged the ascendance of a shadow state of third-sector organizations, those nonprofit groups that promote health and wellness at the community level in the United States. Above all else, the action of the American alternative food movement has been characterized by the rise of nonprofit organizations with this type of community-based orientation. Indeed, these efforts have not only urged individuals to use consumer power as a force for health and sustainability but also consistently emphasized the importance of cultivating family, community-based, and institutional environments that support these "good food" decisions.

The term *community food security,* for instance, has been coined to encapsulate this perspective. It is a concept defined by food scholars Michael Hamm and Anne Bellows as "a situation in which all community residents obtain a safe, culturally acceptable, nutritionally adequate diet through a sustainable food system that maximizes community self-reliance and social justice."[56] From the late 1980s up through the present, a new funding infrastructure has emerged as a means of advancing these community food security aims. While some community food projects have been designed as wholly or partially self-sustaining through entrepreneurial revenue-generation, most depend upon significant support from public, private, and foundation-based grants and donations. Advocacy from a coalition of alternative food movement practitioners, for instance, led to the inclusion of the USDA Community Food Projects Competitive Grants Program in the 1996 federal Farm Bill. Offering multiyear grants of up to $250,000 to organizations, the initiative has provided millions of dollars for community-based food and agriculture projects, and it has also shaped the direction of community food activism through its training and technical assistance programs.[57] The W. K. Kellogg Foundation—with its $7.3 billion endowment—has emerged as another key funder, with "food and community" established as a signature focus area in its broader pursuit of family and child health promotion. By providing funds to strengthen community and school-based food systems and fostering collaboration across networks of community-based food movement practitioners, the foundation works to promote "a nation where all children, families and communities have equitable access to good food."[58] As the movement's profile has grown, community food security initiatives have also relied upon the funding and technical support of countless local and municipal government authorities, donations, and pro bono assistance from private philanthropists and volunteers and partnerships with businesses and food companies as part of corporate social responsibility campaigns.

As diverse as the alternative food movement networks of the early twenty-first century have come to be, they have found widespread appeal in a narrative that champions the value of community-led approaches blended with some entrepreneurial initiative and smart individual decision-making on the path to food system transformation. Given what we know about the challenges of the contemporary food system, however, it begs the question—does this community-based approach do enough to combat the structural power of the corporate food system? Or does its reformist scope and vision ultimately reinforce the tendencies of an exploitative, unsustainable, and unjust status quo?

COMMUNITY-BASED FOOD JUSTICE

As alternative food movements have picked up steam in the United States, a number of sympathetic critics have called into question the capacity of community food security projects to make any real dent in the dominant practices of the food system. The food justice movement has emerged largely in response to this, rooted in two intersecting critiques of progressive food activism—the first critique cultural, the second structural. From the cultural perspective, progressive initiatives have been criticized for what scholars David Goodman, Melanie DuPuis, and Michael Goodman have deemed an "unreflexive localism." That is to say, in scholarship and practice, the value and capacity of local action has been romanticized as offering a utopian vision for food system change, one free of thorny social justice concerns or imbalances of power.[59]

In truth, progressive food movement projects have been shown to disproportionately benefit and serve the interests of those who are already economically advantaged and, most often, white communities. In whose neighborhoods, for instance, are new farmers' markets or community gardens being constructed, and based upon whose knowledge and experiences are nutrition education programs being devised? The argument follows that alternative food movements are permeated by a normative whiteness and an ethos of "color blindness." Projects are too often initiated and controlled by well-meaning but uninformed privileged whites, and their programs consistently ignore racial and cultural difference with respect to inequities in the food system—an ignorance that prohibits such initiatives from achieving transformative and sustainable goals. In this reading, alternative food initiatives have not done enough to make sure that residents and activists in low-income communities, particularly people of color and residents with other marginalized cultural identities, are in control of the conceptualization and management of these projects from the start.[60]

The structural critique takes on the political and economic foundations of alternative food movements. Notably, the commitment to notions of local entrepreneurial economic development and individualized consumer choice that remains at the heart of many progressive projects is criticized as limiting at best and regressive at worst. Reflecting what Julie Guthman has called a "fairly delimited conception of the politics of the possible" (277), such practices have been seen to reify market-based solutions and bolster a neoliberal ideal that absolves government and policymakers of responsibility. From this perspective, these initiatives create uneven and spurious solutions at the community level while downplaying the need for transformative structural change across the entire food system.[61]

The food justice response, therefore, has taken shape as a counter not only to the injustice of the industrial food system but also to the structural and cultural deficiencies embedded in the alternative food movement itself. At a basic level, movements for food justice expand on "environmental justice" activism that initially developed as reaction to the limits of environmentalism in the 1980s. Traditional environmentalists were accused of being disconnected from the environmental hazards that everyday people—and particularly people of color—faced in those spaces where residents "live, work, and play."[62] In the twenty-first century, food justice efforts have built upon this concept to include concerns over places where residents "live, work, play, *and eat.*"[63]

Universalized concerns over racial equity, economic opportunity, and community-based self-determination are at the root of the food justice approach, and the concept has been applied to a variety of causes across the domains of food production, distribution, and consumption. In *More Than Just Food,* I focus on a central community-based strain of this broader food justice perspective. In urban America, food justice has proved particularly resonant as a framework for guiding alternative food movement practices that are established in historically marginalized, low-income communities of color. While a variety of community-based alternative food projects have operated in these neighborhoods for some time—school gardens, urban farms, community-supported agriculture projects, and nutrition education programs among them—food justice has expanded the narratives and networks of these initiatives. What I refer to as "community-based food justice" groups have blended alternative food movement organizing with critical perspectives from the environmental justice movement and a historical understanding of struggles against economic and racial exploitation.

Since at least the early twenty-first century, new people-of-color-led community-based food justice groups have formed, some as extensions of already existing community-based nonprofit organizations, others created specifically to tackle food injustice in their local areas. CSU is one such group— deeply connected to its community of practice, it is also linked through formal partnerships, shared funding sources, and a host of informal personal and organizational exchanges with other community-based food justice groups from across the United States and around the world. Together, these groups are bound by a mission to use food as a vehicle to advance broader projects related to social justice, economic empowerment, and urban sustainability, using local food organizing to combat legacies of discrimination and inequity within their own communities. Each group brings with it a set of contemporary and historical particularities, shaped by the personal and cultural backgrounds of its membership, constituency, and geography.[64]

For instance, since delving into food justice organizing, CSU has built connections with groups like the Detroit Black Community Food Security Network, an organization that has focused since 2006 on building "community self-reliance" and works to "change our consciousness about food" through urban agriculture projects, local policy development, and cooperative buying.[65] Another networked peer of CSU, the Milwaukee-based Growing Power, has emerged as a leader in creating jobs through promoting local food systems, guided by a mission to "transform communities by supporting people from diverse backgrounds and the environments in which they live through the development of Community Food Systems." Other networked connections have been forged by CSU in the Los Angeles area with groups like Inglewood's Social Justice Learning Institute, an organization that uses critical food system education and agricultural projects as a way of furthering its mission of "improving the education, health, and well-being of youth and communities of color by empowering them to enact social change through research, training, and community mobilization."[66] In recent years, direct opportunities for discussion and collaboration between these and other groups has helped the food justice movement grow and evolve. Participation in a variety of conferences and events—including the W. K. Kellogg Foundation's Food and Community Gathering, Growing Power's Growing Food and Justice Initiative, and the Rooted in Community network's annual summit (which is detailed in chapter 4)—has allowed for local, national, and transnational consciousness-raising and strategizing on food justice concerns to be sustained over time.

While community-based food justice organizations are still a minority in the broader landscape of American alternative food movements, their numbers have risen exponentially in recent years, while the possibilities of these people-of-color-led food system initiatives have been championed by a host of scholars and practitioners. To some, food justice has signaled that a new type of movement has the ability to transcend the histories of white supremacy that have characterized the oppressive dominant food system and permeated the alternative food movement itself. As Malik Yakini, a founder of the Detroit Black Community Food Security Network, articulated, the status quo of white-led programming "suggests that their worldview should universally be accepted, that their standards of behavior are best and that their theories of change should define how social movements proceed." He added, "we should defend the right to define what is best for our communities based on our understanding of the historical factors that have created our circumstances and on our own lived experience."[67]

Others emphasize the potentially powerful capacity of these efforts to move activism beyond the logics of neoliberal capitalism en route to food system transformation. Focusing on the work of Mesoamerican and Latin@ farmer groups in the United States, anthropologist Teresa M. Mares has argued that both food justice and the related food sovereignty movement "transcend geophysical boundaries to challenge the political and market-based structures that are responsible for food injustices" (35).[68] In a piece they wrote together, Mares and fellow anthropologist Devon G. Peña offered the case of the South Central Farmers of Los Angeles, a group of mostly Latin@ immigrants whose urban farm was destroyed after a lengthy property rights battle with a developer. Despite this injustice, the South Central Farmers persisted and were able to maintain an eighty-acre farm in a nearby county. Championing the resistant and revolutionary potential of people-of-color-led food activism, the researchers argued that the practice and scholarship of alternative food movements should do more to "focus on the possibility that autonomous food cultivation practices enable the families and communities working in these landscapes to create and sustain decommodified relationships to food" (205).[69]

For some sympathetic critics of alternative food movements, however, food justice has not demonstrated itself to be particularly transformative at all. From the perspective of these critics, although the movement's emphasis on racial inequity and class consciousness has certainly provided a valuable response to the heretofore dominant whiteness of alternative food practices, food justice is still limited by many of the same neoliberal tendencies as its more mainstream counterparts. Critical geographer Julie Guthman, for one, has argued that food justice remains constrained by its being embedded in market-driven systems, by its reliance on community-based educational and entrepreneurial strategies, and by its often-isolated focus on the plight of urban consumers at the expense of other injustices in the food system. "Precisely because social movement possibilities are so constrained by neoliberal logics of the market," Guthman argued, "many dedicated activists barely see other ways forward besides educating people to the qualities of food and bringing good food to low-income people in acts of charity or through nonprofit subsidies in the name of health and empowerment" (154).[70] Alison Hope Alkon levied a similar critique in her ethnographic analysis of the West Oakland Farmers Market, a green economic project whose African American participants consistently pointed to the example of the Black Panther Party as an inspiration for their community-based initiatives. Since the Black Panther Party was, in Alkon's interpretation, "radically opposed to capitalism," it was an inherent contradiction to map what was a historically socialist agenda onto a new market-driven initiative. The social justice potential of farmers markets, Alkon argued, is severely constrained, since "the broader context of neoliberalization pushes activists toward adopting green economic strategies, even as they profess visions of justice and sustainability that are strongly rooted in anticapitalist histories and traditions" (146).[71]

The chapters to follow engage with the tensions that are brought to the fore in these debates. In one sense, I remain indebted to the scholars and activists who have articulated the ways in which knowledge and power is deeply embedded—and too often overlooked—within historically marginalized communities of color, those who could and should help lead the charge toward sustainable community change. With that said, I am also skeptical of rhetoric that situates community-based food justice efforts as fully "autonomous" or "decommodified" movements for food system transformation. As Guthman and Alkon's critiques intimate, in the time that the concept of food justice has increased in salience, so too has the movement's interaction with market-based logics, governmental structures, and philanthropic initiatives—a topic that is explored in depth in subsequent sections of this book. The Detroit Black Community Food Security Network's acquisition of a $750,000 multiyear grant from the Kellogg Foundation—funds that will be used, in part, to create a retail co-op—and the organization's involvement in the City of Detroit's Food Policy Council serve as operative examples of this.[72] Additionally, although it was glossed over in Mares and Peña's account of the South Central Farm, mentioned above, the South Central Farmers received substantial assistance from a variety of external allies—including pro bono legal support, the media advocacy of actress Darryl Hannah, an irrigation system installed by a local Toyota dealer, and the sixty acres of land that was gifted to the farmers by an anonymous donor, which is today being used to support the farm's nonprofit social enterprise business.[73] Similarly, as chapter 5 of this book details, the Black Panther Party, while anticapitalist in its initial ideological foundation, over time built relationships with a host of Black entrepreneurs and wealthy white capitalists. Such partnerships call into question Alkon's claim that the organization was "radically opposed to capitalism" throughout its history.[74] Therefore, in this networked context, terms like "autonomous" and "decommodified" hardly seem to characterize the complex dynamics at play.

By no means do I make such points to denigrate or foreclose the potential of community-based, people-of-color-led food justice activism. Quite the contrary, while I take seriously those critics who believe food justice's relationship to neoliberalism constrains its social change capacity, I also push back against the tendency to dismiss the potential of those food justice activists who operate "in the shadow of the shadow state" to creatively navigate, and at times overcome these very barriers.[75] Indeed, in the pages of *More Than Just Food,* I advocate for an open-minded perspective that neither romanticizes nor overlooks the capacity of community-based social justice activism. My aim in this work is to understand how food justice actually operates, what potential for social change it represents, and in what ways it is limited in its capacity to promote food system transformation. Ultimately, the story of community-based food justice activism that this book tells is not one of decommodifed autonomy nor of outright neoliberal co-option but rather of ongoing and evolving structural and cultural hybridity. The working principles for sustainable community change, outlined in chapter 1, provide a framework for assessing the extent to which the ideals of community-based food justice can be achieved from within this complicated environment.

. . .

The aim of this chapter was to situate the contemporary movement for community-based food justice in urban America within its proper social, economic, and historical contexts. Tracing the food system from its early agricultural foundations up through the age of industrialization and into the era of biotechnology, I highlighted the networked structures and cultural narratives that have served to define food production, distribution, and consumption through these epochs. Research demonstrates that today's food system is characterized by an enduring paradox—for some citizens of the world, it is an infrastructure that promotes abundance and nourishment, while for others, it operates as a force of injustice and unsustainability. In the face of this paradox, activists engaged in alternative food movements—working throughout both the developed and developing worlds—have entered public life. Together, they insist that the modern industrialized food system has not lived up to its promise. Yet they do not speak in a unified voice. Motivated by varied economic, ecological, and nutritional concerns, the diversity of their concerns is matched only by the diversity of their proffered solutions.

More Than Just Food highlights a promising movement from within this set of movements. What I refer to as the movement for community-based food justice has emerged in recent years—largely driven by locally focused nonprofit organizations, these groups work to breathe life into urban food deserts while promoting health, equity, justice, and sustainability. Importantly, this movement has taken shape not only in response to the failures of the industrialized food system but also in response to popular American progressive food activism, which has too often ignored issues of race, class, and injustice in its programming and organizing efforts. Advocates for community-based food justice insist that their organizing strategy offers the potential to catalyze social transformation, within historically marginalized urban communities and beyond. Critics of this approach, however— even those who are sympathetic to its social justice aims—have expressed concerns that it is not fully equipped to motivate social change in the age of neoliberalism

CSU and its South Los Angeles community of practice offer particularly valuable sites through which the possibilities and limitations of community-based food justice activism can be ethnographically explored. For one, the warm climate of Southern California offers nearly year-round opportunities for urban agricultural growth. In the early twentieth century, in fact, Los Angeles County was the top agricultural-producing county in the entire nation. While mid-century urbanization pushed intensive food production into other areas of California, Los Angeles remains a top urban agricultural producer today; in 2013, an estimated 1,261 urban agricultural sites existed across Los Angeles County, including 761 school gardens and 118 community gardens.[76]

This agricultural abundance, however, is accompanied by persistent food injustice across the region. Indeed, the "community food security" concept was initially pioneered by researchers and activists in Los Angeles after the widespread civil unrest following the Rodney King verdict in 1992. These events, in the words of a group of urban planning scholars from the University of California, Los Angeles, "shed harsh light on the disparity in services available to Los Angeles' many communities, a condition replicated in cities across the country," at the same time as they highlighted the "seeds of innovation which, if cultivated, could grow into a strong and stable base for community food security" (2).[77] In the intervening decades, countless progressive food projects were developed and deployed across the city, and the Los Angeles Food Policy Council was formed in an attempt to harness the collective power of these efforts. CSU's work is demonstrative of the community-based food justice organizing that has taken shape within this context. With this in mind, the next chapter ethnographically investigates the core of that organization's community organizing practice.

In a Community Like This

As I walked down the shady side of a residential South Los Angeles street one afternoon, I made eye contact with an older woman seated in a rocking chair on her front stoop. She greeted me in Spanish, and, despite my less-than-fluent proficiency in the language, I returned her pleasantries in kind.[1] I was working with an organization called Community Services Unlimited (CSU), I told her as best as I could, and we were opening a new weekly stand nearby that would sell organic produce. "Es muy necesario," she replied, speaking plainly and slowly while glancing at the multilingual flyer I offered, "porque no hay frutas o verduras frescas en el vecindad." A few steps later, I came across a young man pushing his baby daughter in a stroller, and we stopped for a moment as I handed him the flyer. He told me, in English, that he knew it was important for his child to eat healthy foods, but that it was not easy to find good, affordable options in the neighborhood. Check out the produce stand next week, I told him, and you'll see that folks in South LA are trying to make it easier for you to buy the types of foods you want for your daughter.

After a long morning of traversing the few-mile radius around the community center in which the new produce stand would be located, I and a handful of other tired staff and volunteers returned to our meeting place. There, Denise, a board member with CSU and a South LA public school teacher, reflected on the challenge that the organization faced in its work to motivate community action toward food justice. "Building a critical consciousness is hard," she said. "Critical consciousness takes years. It's grassroots organizing at its most fundamental. You try to start to talk to someone about how they see the world—it's not a one-shot deal. It's not even a two- or three-or four-shot deal. It's the kind of long-term work that requires money and it requires personnel."

As I detailed in chapter 2, groups engaged in the movement for community-based food justice across the United States have consistently emphasized grassroots organizing and localized program development as fundamental and influential components of their collective mission. In order to provide an ethnographic window into this strategic action, this chapter focuses on CSU's everyday efforts in this domain, analyzing how the organization worked to build a critical consciousness and develop alternative institutions within its South Los Angeles community of practice. Profiling CSU's popular education initiatives, its neighborhood agricultural activities, and the development of its entrepreneurial social enterprise, I explore the networks and narratives that came to characterize the organization's communication ecology that is devoted to community-based organizing.[2] These intersecting mini case studies illustrate several of the key community-based programs cultivated by CSU in their first full decade as a food-focused organization, although they are hardly exhaustive of the organization's catalog of activities. The pages to follow investigate how and why CSU worked hard to establish itself as an organization that spoke with and for *the community* to achieve its food justice goals. The chapter also interrogates what makes food a particularly viable entry point for this type of community development and considers the obstacles faced by CSU and other food justice groups who hope to incorporate localized activism into an agenda for sustainable community change.

By promoting local storytelling about food and justice, articulating how local food system struggles are the product of systemic inequities, and developing alternative community institutions through networked partnerships, CSU built a strong foundation through which community-based food justice could be realized. Working collaboratively with civic leaders and social justice partners from across South LA, the organization built capacity among youth and adult residents alike, encouraging them to assert their own rights to healthy foods, championing the validity of cultural knowledge, and providing opportunities for meaningful work. Together, these efforts actively strengthened the economic, environmental, and communication infrastructures of the local community, encouraging feelings of cultural empowerment and building collective efficacy in the process.[3]

At the same time, however, CSU also found itself embedded within various sets of philosophical, interorganizational, and demographic webs, which were spun through collaborations with partners and residents of diverse backgrounds and perspectives. Through this networked action, the organization engaged with a continuous set of challenges that complicated and constrained its ability to effectively advocate with and for *the community*. In this context, the community came to represent more than a space in which localized programs were developed. Rather, the community became a site of iterative and ongoing negotiation, one in which contrasting narratives of knowledge, expertise, power, and capacity development were put into tenuous interaction, all brought into conversation in the spaces and places of South LA. The intersecting case studies that follow, therefore, not only highlight the transformative potential of these activities but also point to the enduring limitations of community-based food justice encountered by activists working "in the shadow of the shadow state" within the globalized age of neoliberalism.

INJUSTICE AND JUSTICE IN SOUTH LA

Neelam Sharma, the executive director of CSU, spoke directly when describing the daunting challenges her organization—and its community—faced on a daily basis: "Whether it be illnesses related to the contamination of the air in our neighborhood, whether it be illnesses related to diet, whether it be health problems related to lack of access to health care, whether it be homelessness, whether it be the lowest-paid members of society, whether it be the unemployed—almost every single indices that you look at, its worst expressions are in South LA." Of Indian descent, Neelam derived her distinctive British accent during her formative years growing up in a community of immigrants in London. The last several decades of her life, however, have been spent in the South Los Angeles area, where she has raised two children—including Lawrence, also a staff member with CSU—and devoted herself to community organizing and youth development work. To understand any story about the work of CSU, she and other staff members would insist, one must first understand the South LA neighborhoods in which its work is situated. CSU was founded in South LA, is headquartered in South LA, almost all of its ten or so employees live or have once lived in South LA, and its programs were fundamentally constructed to advance justice in South LA.[4] "We fulfill our mission of serving the people, body and soul, by focusing on building a sustainable community here in South LA," Neelam told me, "using food as an access point to engage the community in that process."

For decades, South Los Angeles was commonly referred to as South Central Los Angeles, and the moniker had a historically negative connotation. In 2003, the Los Angeles City Council voted to change the designation, with the hopes that attitudes about the long-maligned community would shift along with its rebranding.[5] While the official name change was only associated with a sixteen-square-mile district centered around a once-bustling hub of African American businesses on Central Avenue, the geographic imaginary of South Central was actually much larger than that. Indeed, South Los Angeles has been described as a vast region of twenty-eight neighborhoods encompassing a population of nearly 900,000 people living in an area of over fifty-one square miles, including some areas that are part of the City of Los Angeles and others that are officially unincorporated areas of Los Angeles County.[6] It is a broadly defined community of communities that is undoubtedly best known in the American public consciousness for its history of poverty, instances of widespread civil unrest, and ongoing gang violence. Television coverage of the 1965 Watts riots, the civil uprisings that broke out after the Rodney King verdict was delivered in 1992, as well as John Singleton's classic film *Boyz n the Hood* (1991) and N.W.A's debut album, *Straight Outta Compton* (1988), are but a few of the media events that helped to solidify visions of South LA as a space of unceasing urban volatility and Black criminality.[7] The reality, of course, is much more complex than that.

Demographically speaking, in the first half of the twentieth century, South LA was actually made up primarily of non-Hispanic whites, along with a significant number of Japanese American residents and enclaves of African American populations. At the time, African American residence was restricted to a set of racially segregated zones—primarily in the Watts neighborhood—inhabited primarily by African Americans who had made their way to California from the Deep South during the First Great Migration of the early 1900s. During World War II, Japanese American families were forcibly removed from their South LA homes and businesses and placed into internment camps. Upon their release, many left the area for other sections of the city.[8] By the middle of the century, the movement of increasing numbers of African Americans to Southern California during the post-war period's Second Great Migration—combined with the loosening of restrictions on where African Americans could live and broader trends of "white flight"—meant that South LA was home to the highest concentration of African Americans in Los Angeles County.

From that point onward, South Central Los Angeles—a center of African American life, business, arts, and culture—became almost synonymous with the broader African American experience in Los Angeles. But new demographic shifts would radically transform the region yet again in the late twentieth century. An influx of immigrants from Mexico and Central America reshaped the community, as the highly concentrated African American population began to spread into other areas of the county. By the end of the first decade of the twenty-first century, the residential population of South Los Angeles was nearly two-thirds Latin@ and approximately one-third African American.[9]

Through it all, unfortunately, South LA remained a region of ongoing racially motivated economic marginalization and urban strife. For generations, local residents endured poorly functioning public institutions, systemic discrimination, police brutality, and high rates of gang-related violence. Today, decades after two of America's most infamous instances of civil unrest—the calamitous expressions of outrage and discontent that are commonly referred to as the Watts riots of 1965 and the Los Angeles riots of 1992—rocked South Los Angeles, poverty and unemployment in the community still far exceeded the city, state, and national averages. According to the Los Angeles County Department of Public Health, 31 percent of South LA residents have household incomes below the federal poverty level, a rate that is higher than any other region in Los Angeles County. Nearly 39 percent of adults residing in South Los Angeles did not graduate high school, the highest proportion in the county, while the percentage of adults who are gainfully employed is among the lowest.[10]

The local food system offers a case study for how the dynamics of social and economic deprivation played out over time. Several studies conducted in the 1990s and 2000s demonstrated that South LA residents lacked access to high-quality, affordable fresh foods, while the area was rife with unhealthy fast food restaurants, liquor stores, and corner markets.[11] Beginning with the movement of agricultural production out of Los Angeles County in the middle of the twentieth century, a persistent "grocery gap" gradually emerged. While other areas of Los Angeles developed strong food distribution and retail infrastructures in the years that followed, inequity in South LA was amplified by long-term disinvestment in the region, including a retreat of business that started after the Watts riots in 1965 and continued with a lack of reinvestment after the Los Angeles riots of 1992. A process of redlining—systematically denying ethnic minority communities a variety of vital services or charging them higher rates for these services—had come to define South LA's relationship to a set of necessary community institutions. Redlining had doomed the area to systemic food inequality and turned it into a food desert—or "food swamp," as some preferred to call it.[12] With these factors combined, it is no surprise that, in the 2010s, community health in South LA was worse than in any other area of Los Angeles County, as residents suffered disproportionately from a set of chronic health conditions that are related to diet and poverty, including heart disease, diabetes, obesity, and stroke.[13]

Despite all of these negative indicators, South LA has, throughout its history, proved to be a space of continuing resilience, artistic creativity, and collective resistance. The region has an impressive legacy of creative production and multiracial community activism on a number of social, economic, and environmental justice issues. Today, there are countless organizations engaged in efforts to improve the health and well-being of local residents through community organizing, advocacy, and institution-building.[14] While ever-cognizant of the downsides of the everyday social realities in their neighborhood, residents and community practitioners in South LA point to a number of past and present success stories that demonstrate the capacity of the area to thrive in the face of systemic injustice. CSU aimed to use the local food system as a site through which resistance, perseverance, and social justice in twenty-first century South LA could be pursued.

CONNECTING TO THE COMMUNITY

"It's not just food, but it's who you are as a person," Ruthie, a young Latina woman who had grown up in South LA and worked as a CSU intern before joining the staff, explained when asked about the focus of the organization. "Everyone uses food. *That* can build bridges." With food as an entry point, members of CSU insisted that they could make vital connections with the community. Only with this community-based grounding in place, they contended, could a collaborative agenda for food justice be effectively forged.

But what did CSU staff mean, exactly, when they repeatedly referred to connecting with "the community"? On account of the term's broad resonance, members of the organization usually found little need to explicitly state its actual meaning at all. Taken in context, however, their use of the imaginative concept had a clear set of intersecting geographic, economic, and racial implications.[15] First and foremost, they were referring to the lower-income people of color who resided in the general domain of CSU's South LA community of practice. Dyane Pascall, an African American man in his mid-twenties, served as CSU's financial and administrative manager. After a year of college in his home state of New Jersey, he had been looking for a fresh start when he relocated to South LA and began to work with CSU. It was this localized notion of community to which he often referred, and it was this concept that attracted him to the organization from the start: "Specifically, community is like, just people who I live amongst. The regular mother, father, son, daughter, you know, student, high school kid that I live amongst, that lives around here. You know, I'm walking down the street or whatever, and I hope that these are people we work with in the neighborhood."

CSU was committed to this geographic focus in its work, but the organization was also apt to point out that its local actions were embedded within a broader struggle that extended well beyond its own South LA neighborhoods. In their speech and actions, then, members of CSU constructed a more geographically fluid imagined community construct, one that emerged from the organization's historically oriented solidarity with other low-income communities of color that shared South LA's story of entrenched social and environmental injustice. In the eyes of CSU, systemic food injustice plagued communities of color across the nation—and also across the world—and it was time that those communities were able to have a bigger say in how these injustices could be remedied. Neelam explained this perspective in an interview:

> Unfortunately, the people who are most impacted by issues of food equity, you know, are people of color. That's just, you know, I don't need to tell you—I can give you 20 million statistics but you can find them yourself too, and that's just a fact, right? . . . Whereas most of the people who are the decision-makers and the power-brokers when it comes to decisions about food systems stuff are not people of color, right? And they're certainly not from the communities most impacted by those decisions, in the power structures as they exist.

Inspired by the community service arm of the Black Panther Party and Paulo Freire's methods of popular education (detailed in chapter 5), the staff worked to develop a series of community programs that would help meet the everyday needs of community members, provide an opportunity for residents to think critically about their social world, and build vital skills related to growing, cooking, and consuming food. "We do the 360 approach," Dyane explained as he outlined the components of what the organization called their Community Food Village Project. CSU constructed a diversified communication ecology devoted to community organizing, "serving the people, body and soul," through a life cycle strategy of community engagement.

It started with programs that brought preschool children into CSU's urban farms and continued with the building of school gardens and the integration of food and agricultural education into local primary schools. Staffers trained and paid a small stipend to high school-aged youth who served as interns and apprentices with the organization and then hired a number of standouts from these programs, along with other local community residents, as staff for their Village Market Place social enterprise. They partnered with a local senior citizen center and a nearby university, and they also led frequent free public workshops that covered topics related to gardening and cooking. The organization championed the idea that the local food landscape could only be transformed by bringing together local stakeholders into a sustained and common cause, as Neelam explained during a public event:

> The issues are not simple—they're systemic and a result of things planners have done, policies that have been made. . . . That's what our belief is. That it's systemic, there are systems-based reasons around why access to healthy and affordable food in our community is not as good as other places. . . . Just like the problem is systemic, we need systemic solutions to these problems. . . . So what we've created with community members is a series of programs to confront those issues systemically.

Youth Development—Growing Healthy and From the Ground Up

Engagement with youth became a primary component of CSU's community-building strategy in South LA. "That's who's going to lead the world. Those are the people that we have to impact," Dyane explained, reflecting on the food system challenges facing future generations. "They're the ones being sold this package of failure. Our community is literally dying because of food and all these other things. We've gotta change it, and they're the ones who are going to be around to do it." CSU's Growing Healthy program was the strongest representation of the organization's efforts to reach out to the youngest in the community. The initiative aimed to embed within young

FIGURE 2. A local resident of South LA purchases produce at a CSU market, which is part of the organization's Village Market Place social enterprise. Photograph courtesy of Community Services Unlimited.

FIGURE 3. Fresh fruit, vegetables, and flowers from CSU's mini urban farms and local farmers that have partnerships with the organization, being prepared to be sold at CSU markets. Photograph courtesy of Community Services Unlimited.

people an understanding of the intersecting importance of food, agriculture, and community prosperity from the earliest of ages.

As part of a partnership with a nearby preschool, CSU staff members could be seen on a sunny day in June parading around their mini urban farm with lines of a few dozen four-year-olds in tow. The children were tasked with helping the staff pick vegetables, which would then go into a salad that they would make together. As they marched, they chanted: "We are the salad pickers!" Other CSU staffers led the children in an art project under the shade of trees, and the preschoolers proudly held up their crayon-drawn works of art featuring flowers and plants for a group photo. When it came time for the salad taste-test, the results were more mixed. A few declared that it was one of the best things they had ever eaten, while others remained less enthused, leaving some fresh blackberries and greens to be dumped in the compost bin. The preschool teachers remarked that it was always an entertaining way to spend an afternoon and a great way to get the kids outside and active.

While encouraged and excited to interact with the little ones, CSU staff remained cautiously skeptical about the impact that an occasional salad pick would have on the kids. It was definitely a fun and useful experience, a valuable way to demonstrate to young children where food came from, why fruits and vegetables are important for their health, and how much they could enjoy the diverse feels, tastes, and smells of fresh produce if they gave it a chance. Yet CSU's systemic perspective told them that such an exercise was hardly enough to motivate social transformation on its own. They demurred, explaining that many community food programs ended their interventions at this initial stage. Getting one's hands dirty was of course an important part of building a critical consciousness, they insisted, but enduring racial, economic, and geographic barriers to health could not simply be overcome by a child spending a single afternoon in the garden. Instead, ongoing opportunities for dialogue and action were necessary.

Therefore, the organization's engagement with youth did not stop there. Growing Healthy also extended into partnerships with nearby elementary and middle schools. CSU's work at Normandie Avenue Elementary School, for instance, had been ongoing for nearly a decade. They had built a demonstration garden and orchard on school grounds, integrated food and agricultural curriculum into weekly classes, and collaborated with the directors of an after-school program to get kids working in the garden on a regular basis. CSU's work in this school alone brought the organization into contact with several hundred students each year. As the school's principal, Gus, described, the organization made an ongoing impact through its persistence and dedication. He compared CSU to a "stealth jet," as the organization's work of building gardens, beautifying the school, and working with children often remained out of his direct sight. But he saw the products of the staff's efforts all around the school grounds, and he was gracious for their contributions, which he described as "God's work—the giving of self."

Gus pointed to several concrete shifts in the food-related attitudes and behaviors of his school community, many of which he saw as directly influenced by CSU's work. "Kids don't really see healthy restaurants around here," he told me in an interview. "They don't see the need to eat healthy. CSU brings that education to say, 'we can plant our own things, we can feed the mind, the soul.'" In an attempt to champion a culture of health, he designated the school a "junk food-free zone," a noble, if difficult to enforce, institutional effort. "Kids still sneak it in," he said. "Across the street there are the guys at the ice cream trucks selling Hot Cheetos. Kids are kids, but we try to keep that stuff off and try to bring healthier alternatives." To counter the pervasive junk food vendors, he worked with CSU to sell locally grown fruits and vegetables at a produce stand in front of the school and initiated a bulk-purchasing program that offered produce giveaways for students and their families.

Still, as enriching as CSU believed its engagement with preschool and primary school students to be, the group saw an even greater opportunity to forge lasting relationships and build vital skills among slightly older South LA youth. The From the Ground Up program was developed with the intention to train mostly high school-aged teens in all aspects of CSU's operations—including agricultural cultivation, cooking and food preparation, retail and office work, community-based organizing, and participatory research. For two to three months, in seasonal rotations, youth interns train in cohorts of about ten. Standouts from the groups often stay on board to take part in organizational apprenticeships that last from one to two years, and some are later hired as staff members.

Lawrence, a product of an early version of this training himself, had stepped into the role of CSU's youth program coordinator by his mid-twenties. Of mixed Trinidadian and Indian descent, he was born in London, but moved with his mother, Neelam, CSU's executive director, to South Los Angeles when he was still a young child. A deep thinker but naturally soft-spoken, Lawrence's confidence and presence grew as he rose into a position of leadership. These newly acquired traits were necessary in recruiting South

LA youth into the internship program, a process that called for him to make presentations at local schools, build connections with other youth-based community programs, and work through the interpersonal networks of youth alumni's friends and family. Once in the program, interns are paid a small stipend, educated about the social justice mission of CSU, and expected to participate as contributing members of the organization. Importantly to CSU staff, the youth are not simply there to learn about the food system, although agricultural and food-related skills have always been a major part of the curriculum. Rather, they are also expected to develop the critical thinking skills that allow them to analyze the key cultural and social issues that shape their lives, as well as to build practical skills that make them more successful as students, workers, and community members moving forward. "Food is the vehicle to do things this organization has always been interested in doing," Lawrence described at a meeting with parents of youth interns. "We use it as way for self-improvement, as a way for youth to be improving themselves. It's about things like understanding what it's like to have a job and to be accountable."

Indeed, it is clear in the curriculum and activities of From the Ground Up that both critical thinking skills and basic work-related skills are seen as much more fundamental building blocks than developing the youth into some variation of a gourmet "foodie." Working with groups of teenagers has allowed CSU to delve deeper into a historical and cultural critique related to the underlying causes of economic exploitation and racial oppression in communities like South LA. In all of their efforts, CSU emphasizes how the cultural histories of diasporic communities of African Americans, Latin@s, and other people of color should inform the study and practice of food, agriculture, and health. If mainstream discussions about food and nutrition are consistently created and disseminated through a lens of whiteness, CSU is there to plant the seeds of dietary decolonization in the minds of South LA's youth.[16] "Talking about cultural food history is a very important component of everything that we do," Neelam explained. "And so we are able to build up, and we are talking about young people for example, their confidence around who they are, and their dignity around who they are, and what their ancestors have contributed to the world by talking about their ancestral foods."

Scholar Sheila Jasanoff coined the term *civic epistemology* to describe how public knowledge practices on issues of science and risk are produced through the dynamic relationships between history, politics, and culture. These social and cultural practices, she wrote, are played out through "story-telling by communities situated in particular times and places who are attempting to deal with unsettling or disruptive changes in their environment" (23).[17] This coarticulation of knowledge is displayed in the youth-centered work of CSU, highlighted by a heavy dose of storytelling between and among the youth and staff of CSU, an ongoing exercise in constructing a civic epistemology related to food justice. Through continuous "dialogue sessions" with the youth interns, the staff delves into the young peoples' everyday challenges, beliefs, misconceptions, and visions for change in the food system. Lawrence provided an example of what gets discussed during these sessions:

> Living a healthy lifestyle hasn't always been disconnected from their culture. . . . A lot of youth—their reality is that they do eat fries, burgers, eating unhealthy. But, ok—where do most of those things come from? Corn. Where does corn come from? Corn comes from the natives who were living on this land before it was taken from them. It's having them connecting with themselves, understanding where they're from. Healthy living is not something that's alien to them in connection to their history and who they are.

Lawrence hoped to stimulate the youth intellectually, offering a counter to the standardized tests and often dysfunctional environment of the South LA public schools he had struggled through himself: "What I'm trying to do right now is establish a curriculum that challenges youth, pushes them beyond the regular patterns in their environment, to more or less be aware of what they can accomplish in general." They explore from the outset what a youth's goals are in taking part in the internship—did they want to gain work skills, learn about food justice, get involved in the community, or simply get a paycheck? Anyone is welcome to participate, as long as they are serious about the commitment. A key part of the approach is to demonstrate that—regardless of their goals for taking part in the internship program—the knowledge and skills to succeed are located *inside* each of them, even in the face of an often-daunting social world. The collaborative efforts of the program are therefore an attempt to reclaim several key cultural and social competencies that have gradually diminished in the community, due to the area's history of racial, economic, and environmental injustice. As Neelam explained:

> It's really designed to get them to think about—What is culture? What is food culture? How does it relate to their history? And what is their food culture now? And why has it shifted so much from what it was historically to what it is now? . . . What has created that change? What are the things that

have acted upon it? And if they wanted it to be different, what's the reality, what can they do now to make it different?

Many of the interns were heartened by CSU's culturally and geographically grounded approach. The neighborhood has seen a fair share of service organizations, they told me, which had promised to come in and improve the quality of life for local residents. Few, apart from CSU, were founded in South LA and staffed by community members, however, and this authenticity is not lost on the youth participants. "Strategically, they're based in South Central. They're really working for food justice where we need it. In South LA *for* South LA," Ruthie explained. "It's taking place in my community, so why am I not a part of that?"

During my time at CSU, the organization was able to boast about several youth success stories of interns who made their way through From the Ground Up, gained valuable critical and practical skills, and went onto be productive and engaged young adults. This is not to say that the program proved to be a fully transformational experience for all involved. There were instances in which some youth interns were difficult to motivate, proved unresponsive to conversations about healthy food and social justice, and ultimately did not follow through entirely on their obligations. Still, in my conversations with youth interns, many pointed to a host of skills they gained related to agricultural work, public speaking, critical thinking, and more. I watched over years and months as once-shy teens developed the confidence to speak in front of groups of ten or hundreds, as they articulated the story of CSU's history, mission, and programmatic activity. CSU's work around food and agriculture, they explained, aimed to build a self-sufficient community in South LA, in the face of the struggles and hardships that always confront residents who live in a community like this.

Stephanie, another intern-turned-staff-member, who immigrated to Los Angeles from Guatemala in her early teens, pointed to her work with CSU as central to her success in a drastically new environment. "I learned a lot of things. I learned to plant my own food and to grow it. I also became, like, a lot more aware of the problems around my community. Like, the food issues and the food system, I didn't even know about it before," she explained. While many of her recent-immigrant peers at school remained isolated within Spanish-speaking groups of friends—and were subsequently held back from opportunities on account of this cultural and linguistic separation—Stephanie leveraged the communication and leadership skills she gained at CSU to test out of English as a second language coursework and gain acceptance into college. "If I was the person I was three years ago, I wouldn't even be talking to you right now," she told me.

Ultimately, through local storytelling and engagement with youth in activities that instill a strong work ethic, CSU hopes to change the story within the minds of South LA's young residents about who they are and who they can become. The organization sees youth as basic building blocks of new institutional formations—within the South LA area and beyond—that would promote greater justice and equity in the communities and organizations of the future. In their engagement with some of the youngest citizens of South Los Angeles, CSU staff worked to articulate a civic epistemology related to food injustice and aimed to integrate narratives of cultural empowerment and healthy living into the interpersonal networks of young people, their families, and their school communities. It was based on this storytelling foundation—rooted in cultural knowledge, grounded in grass-roots engagement, and connected to a systemic vision for justice—that the organization's work demonstrated a fundamental capacity to promote sustainable community change. Of course, in order for the seeds of long-term resistance and community development to sprout, conversations such as these must always be linked to the material foundations of everyday life.

Growing Good Food in the Heart of South LA

Despite the passage of time, residents of South Los Angeles still live with both the memory and the physical reality of the civil unrest that is commonly known as the 1992 LA riots. During the course of those events, over one thousand buildings were burned and destroyed across the city, with much of that damage right in the heart of South LA. Organizations like Community Build, "dedicated to the revitalization of South Los Angeles communities through investment in youth and commercial economic development," emerged from beneath the rubble to rebuild the area.[18] Two decades later, that organization's headquarters sat alongside two vacant lots, both of which had been burned out during the civil unrest and had lain dormant ever since. One lot was covered in concrete, soon to be developed into a skate park for local youth. The other was overgrown with grass and weeds, having been left untouched for two full decades. The space was fertile ground for a new partnership between Community Build and CSU, and a series of intensive workdays were scheduled to dig deep, reclaim the land, and build a new mini urban farm directly where ashes had once fallen.

On one such weekend workday, I pulled through a set of stubborn weeds that had attached to a fence, working alongside Anna, a native of South LA who was finishing up CSU's apprenticeship program and preparing to become a member of the staff. "I wish we just had a big machine that could turn this whole thing over," she said. Some heavy farm machinery would have made quick work of the initial stages of the project, but we had to make due with our hands. So, slowly but surely, over the course of several months, dozens of local residents, CSU staff members, interns, partners, friends, and volunteers put in the hard work that was required to turn the long-forgotten place into another of CSU's productive agricultural spaces.

When I asked members of CSU about the core values of the organization, several common terms emerged—such as community, cultural awareness, critical thinking, relationship building, hard work, and rigor, to name a few. The efforts that went into CSU's agricultural cultivation offered a prime example of these core values in action. Urban farming was continually conceptualized as a foundational building block through which the broader social-change goals of CSU could be realized. The creation, maintenance, and productivity of urban farm sites served as a pathway for programmatic sustainability, organizational viability, and community empowerment. This work provided a safe and peaceful space for community residents and partner organizations to gather, build skills, think critically about the contemporary food system, and advance environmental and economic vitality right in South LA.

Anyone interested in learning more about the work of CSU, or in getting involved more substantively, was generally first asked to lend a hand at one of the organization's urban farms. Depending on the time of year, a prospective participant would have several sites to choose from—including a few local school gardens, the reclaimed Community Build space, and the mini urban farm, adjacent to South LA's Exposition Park. While volunteers might get a brief orientation to the broader goals and mission of the organization, it was made clear from the start that the quality CSU most valued was an ability to put in a good day's work, just like everyone else involved with the organization. "You can't come in with an ego," Jason, at the time a relatively new CSU staff member, explained. "That's one reason why I think we start working out in the garden. Everyone weeds."

On any given day of the week, anywhere from a handful to a few dozen staff and volunteer workers can most likely to be found tending the soil at

FIGURE 4. Signs on the gates to CSU's Expo mini urban farm advertise upcoming workshops and produce stands. Photograph courtesy of Community Services Unlimited.

FIGURE 5. Volunteers join CSU staff for a garden workday at the Expo mini urban farm. Photograph courtesy of Community Services Unlimited.

CSU's primary agricultural site, the Expo mini urban farm. You can find them working in the shadow of one of the most traveled freeways in the city, directly below a large billboard that advertises the thirst-quenching satisfaction of a sugary soda product. A painted sign and an iron gate greet all entrants. At about an acre in size, the land is technically state-owned property, managed in conjunction with the City of Los Angeles, but CSU has full direction of its everyday maintenance. About fifteen rectangular plots hold dozens of different seasonal fruits and vegetables—tomatoes, several varieties of squash, leafy greens, carrots, strawberries, and more. Fruit trees donated by the TreePeople environmental nonprofit grow in the southeast corner of the garden, a large compost machine sits in the northeast, and a chayote gourd grows upon a shaded workbench in the northwest. Many of the foods grown have specific cultural relevance to the Mexican, Central American, and African American populations who live in the area. All the produce is grown without any petrochemical pesticides or fertilizers. They call it "beyond organic"—while CSU lacks the official USDA organic certification, which is costly and designed mostly by and for farmers that have larger economies of scale, the food grown by CSU is fed only water, sunlight, and other natural and environmentally sound products.

Like many other members of CSU, Dyane, the organization's financial and administrative manager, started in the garden, although he found his way there by an unlikely pathway—he got a traffic ticket while driving without car insurance. Given the option of paying several thousands of dollars or putting in fifty hours of community service, he did a Google search for community service opportunities in his South LA neighborhood and soon found himself putting in his time with CSU. While working in the garden for the first time, he listened as CSU staff members and other volunteers talked about their work: "It was kind of on the fly. While we were doing it, this is *why* we're doing it," Dyane recalled. "That's something we still do. We're not just here to weed, to do gardening. Here's the bigger picture, the bigger context." Through his time in the garden, Dyane became part of the first graduating class of the CSU internship program, and he has worked with CSU as a staff member ever since. The fact that volunteer work at the organization can be used to fulfill community service requirements for those convicted of a traffic court violation, of course, speaks to the hybrid connections between CSU's operations and official structures of power. At the CSU farm, these residents worked on state-owned property, alongside local residents of diverse demographic, cultural, and agricultural backgrounds, several of whom were there because they had been pulled over by the LAPD. Together, they created an agricultural, social, and economic space that would directly counter years of public neglect and police persecution in South LA.

Looking around the neighborhood, CSU could see that there was great potential agricultural capacity, not just in its own urban farms, but also in the backyards of local residents from within the community itself. Aware that not everyone would be interested or able to come directly to CSU's sites, the organization devised other ways to draw from the agricultural capacity of their local neighbors that involved going directly to *them*. This came to fruition most clearly in the Tree of Life program, an initiative to collect otherwise unused fruit from trees in the backyards of residents across South LA. The effort was initially created in partnership with another Los Angeles-based nonprofit group—Food Forward—whose entire mission focused on the gleaning and distribution of locally grown fruits from private homes and public spaces. That group had collected over a million pounds of produce in its first several years, but it had done most of its outreach through farmers' markets and in more middle-income and upper-income communities in Los Angeles. CSU expanded those operations into South LA, and the fruits of their labors, so to speak, were directly filtered into CSU's social enterprise or donated to another partner organization, which provided free, freshly cooked meals to the homeless and the hungry.

Jose was a part-time staff member with CSU when I met him. He was a loquacious young man, originally from the east coast, who also worked at a downtown homeless and poor-peoples' rights organization. For a time, he led the Tree of Life effort, putting in several hours per week canvassing the neighborhood to find willing participants. It was a little tougher to recruit in South LA than in some more affluent neighborhoods, he said, because folks in the area were more likely to actually be using at least some of the fruit that they grew in their backyards. On one Sunday morning in South LA, I made my way with Jose into the backyard of a small home. The homeowner was not there at the time, but had left the back gate open so we could enter. He was a patron of CSU's produce-bag sales program and was apparently happy to open up his backyard to the program. Otherwise, he had said, most of his oranges would fall and go to waste, as they had for years before.

We quickly went to work, standing on ladders and on a ledge and using a fruit-picking tool with an extended arm to grab fruit growing higher in the trees. Dirt and leaves came tumbling down on top of us as we rustled the branches, but the oranges also began to fall. It was not a huge picking operation, since only one tree was showing ripe oranges at the time, but within forty-five minutes, we had filled several crates to the brim, and we were able to bring in over sixty pounds of fresh, locally grown, beyond organic Southern California oranges. The produce would be trucked back to CSU's kitchens a few miles east, and soon it would be fed right back into the community, a valuable part of the organization's efforts to cultivate fresh food right within the heart of South LA.

Made possible through the construction of networked partnerships developed over time, the work of reclaiming and maintaining urban space for the purposes of growing food achieves multiple aims. It encourages a necessary measure of ecological vitality, ensures the reliability and dependability of localized food justice programming, and promotes neighborhood storytelling in places that would otherwise be silent. Some of that conversation is practical and mundane—for example, discussing the best methods to organize a row of squash plants, the ideal time to harvest a strawberry, or the proper way to pull weeds so they will not return. Even if these conversations remain at this basic level, as they often do, they still represent significant value within the neighborhood, as they pass along useful food- and agricultural-related skills and knowledge that residents can take with them and spread to their networks of family and friends. In many instances, however, these conversations reach a higher level of abstraction, as staff, volunteers, interns, and local residents dig into discussions about the history of South LA, the cultural traditions of its communities, the injustices of the industrial food system, and the politics of possibility that are being enacted through the work of CSU and its partners.

Community Workshops, Community Knowledge(s)

On numerous weekends throughout the year, CSU staff, volunteers, apprentices, and interns can be found in the organization's Expo mini urban farm, guiding a few dozen local residents through cooking and gardening activities as part of the Garden Gateway workshops. "On the face of it, the Garden Gateway workshops are very simply about coming and learning how to garden, and learning how to eat out of your garden in a very nutritional, healthy, and inexpensive way," Neelam explained. Consistent with the broader approach of the organization, however, the workshops are never simply about imparting useful information but also about building a critical consciousness to advance a community-led agenda for health and sustainability. "We really have to do everything that we can to create spaces where people can come together," Neelam continued, "so there is a way in which this gets people to start thinking about things." Interestingly, though, at the same time as the Garden Gateway workshops provided a space for the promotion of people-powered pedagogy, they also offered a lens through which some of the internal contradictions of community-based food justice organizing could be observed. Indeed, on account of the diverse networks of residents and partners involved, CSU found itself forced to navigate through complex fields of culture, power, and contrasting priorities, a reality that speaks to the ongoing challenges that face the broader movement for food justice today.

During my time with CSU, several of the most regular workshop participants were senior citizens who were recruited through an adjacent senior center; others were mothers, who would bring their young children along; and still others had simply been walking by one day and decided to drop in to check things out. Workshop topics ranged from ways to test the soil for toxicity to Mexican and Central American crop pairings to foods that served as natural bodily cleansers. Throughout the workshops, it was made clear that the status quo of the industrial food system—with its unsustainable practices in production, distribution, and consumption—put the world's health at stake. This was especially true in "a community like this," as both staff members and workshop participants often referred to the neighborhood. Together they would reflect upon a history of health challenges—related to poor nutrition, environmental hazards, poverty, and other intersecting issues—that they and their friends, family, and neighbors had experienced and call for action to help them rise above these threats.

The gathered residents were under no illusion, however, that their collective health challenges would be able to bring them any direct or immediate relief from government or corporate institutions.[19] What good would it do to simply wait for the powers that be to right the host of wrongs that had been systematically perpetuated upon them? Instead, the narrative that permeated the Garden Gateway workshops put residents in a position of significant control. If local and cultural knowledge systems could be activated, participants asserted, and community members were empowered with critical education and skills, personal and community health could become a reality, even in the face of systemic inequity. "They're the experts about it," Dyane articulated. "It just hasn't been asked, they haven't been asked. They haven't been in this conversation about what change can be or what change should be or what might be the challenges that you face."

FIGURE 6. A CSU staffer hands a mason jar bouquet of chamomile flowers, created during a Garden Gateway workshop, to a community participant. Photograph courtesy of Community Services Unlimited.

As with most of CSU's community-based programs, however, the workshops depend upon the cultivation of a variety of institutional relationships that engage with partners from outside of the organization's own community of practice. Grant-funded collaborations with a nearby university, for instance, allowed CSU to purchase workshop materials that participants could bring home and use to build their own garden projects. For the urban institution of higher education, the workshops represented a valuable community outreach strategy as well as a site of potential data collection for researchers and students interested in public health nutrition. However, tension ensued when the ideological standards of CSU and its partner groups differed. "I almost feel like we need to have an orientation with these groups to give them sort of the CSU worldview," Dyane lamented. Indeed, it was clear that such institutional conflicts were actually reflective of a broader epistemological challenge faced by CSU. Working "in the shadow of the shadow state," the group walked a fine line in positioning itself in opposition to mainstream public health and medical institutions—which often held many of the strings for funding local programs and whose expertise often contradicted the community knowledge the organization consistently championed.

A pertinent example of this conflict emerged during a workshop with the theme Foods that Cleanse. Neelam spoke to a group of a few dozen gathered local residents: "We live in an environment where there are toxins all around, especially in a community like this, which tends to be more heavily environmentally polluted." After the problem had been established, the focus of the workshop shifted toward the power of healthy food to intervene in this state of affairs. A youth apprentice began to read from a list that she had researched and compiled of foods and plants with the capacity to cleanse the soil and body alike. One by one, she described the chemical elements of bananas, mushrooms, hydrangeas, and other agricultural products that gave them specific antitoxic capacities. As she spoke, CSU staff members handed out a leaflet outlining foods that had been "scientifically proven" to be useful for medicinal purposes. At that moment, Neelam editorialized: "We partner with the medical school, and you can see aloe is not on your sheet there. What we can put in writing here is only the stuff that has Western science backing. So I can share with you verbally, but we can't put it in writing, aloe has been used for thousands of years as a medicinal and cleanser . . . I drink it every morning. I put it in a blender with some citrus."

What this interaction and others like it spoke to was a consistent and sometimes tenuous interplay that pitted mainstream medicine and Western ways of knowing against natural and embodied health approaches. Time and again, the language and metrics of nutrition science were used to guide CSU's nutritional advice to residents, while quantitative public health research helped them stake a claim about the inequalities faced by South LA's residents—the "20 million statistics" Neelam referenced earlier in this chapter. At the same time, CSU staffers and community members alike espoused the value of cultural knowledge that they saw as marginalized in dominant medical practice. Participants were eager to share their own natural remedies, describe tonics passed down from one generation to the next, and bond around a shared narrative that simultaneously recognized their embodied knowledge and called into question the authority of mainstream public health.

Ultimately, then, while CSU provided alternatives to perspectives from the public health establishment, the organization was hardly in direct and complete opposition. Instead, the diverse players embedded within CSU's communication ecology for community organizing meant that it was more often in conversation with these narratives than in irreconcilable conflict with them. In some ways, then, the contradictory storytelling that emerged during these workshops proved to be a generative force for ongoing community-based discourse. It was in this evolving mix of reflection and action—a hybrid praxis of food justice work—that civic epistemologies took shape.

I cite a plural notion of civic *epistemologies* here to underscore the fact that participation in CSU's Garden Gateway workshops does not present a single and unified experience for all who take part. Indeed, the workshops also demonstrate the ways in which the community-based food justice effort—situated as it is within a multiethnic and multilingual context—is compelled to grapple with the challenges and opportunities that globalization brings to its community organizing practice. Given that recent decades have seen a dramatic demographic transformation in South LA—such that the area has shifted from a majority African American neighborhood to majority Latin@ neighborhood—just how unified could community knowledge practices ever be? As chapter 5 will explore in greater detail, CSU has its roots in the struggles and experiences of African Americans, but intercommunal solidarity has always been a driving force of its Black Panther ethos, while the improvement of intercultural relations between African Americans and Latin@s has been central to its programming from the start of its food justice work. However, on more than one occasion during my time at the mini urban farm, I saw predominantly Spanish-speaking residents struggle to follow the conversations and hesitate to contribute their own voices. I also noticed several handouts of gardening and cooking information that had not been translated to Spanish and had therefore been left uncollected by Latin@ participants. Faced with limited staff, budget, and time, how could CSU tackle this obstacle that called into question its ability to speak with and for the community as a whole?

It was an issue that was clearly on the table for CSU, an organization whose longest-tenured staff members were all less than fluent in Spanish. The importance of cultivating connections both within and across South LA's dominant ethnic groups was put into relief for Neelam after she took a trip to Oaxaca, Mexico, to attend a two-week learning exchange and workshop. Almost all of the proceedings were held entirely in Spanish, a language she could not speak fluently, and when she returned, she felt compelled to make tackling this challenge an even greater priority than it had been in previous years. "It really showed me what it's like to be on the other side," she explained, a few days after the exchange. "Because most of our stuff is conducted in English. And now here I am, and I always knew it, I understood it. And I knew that we should have translation and all that. But here I could really feel it. I could feel it in here [placing her hand on her heart] and not just up here [pointing to her head]."

Over time, CSU has consciously worked to make sure interns, apprentices, and other staff members with Latin American heritage and Spanish fluency are integrated into the core of its activities and built strong partnerships with other Latin@-led food and social justice groups from around the region. Failing to take these steps would have seriously called into question the organization's ability to authentically represent the needs and interests of the community, whereas facing up to the task offers CSU a chance to make its community-based claims even stronger. However, CSU staff also insisted that simply flipping the script toward full-on engagement with Latin@ residents would not be appropriate. African Americans have suffered a history of being overlooked by the majority in society, they argue, and there is a real danger of this being perpetuated if community-based groups in South LA were to shift their focus outright to the new demographic majority. Instead, CSU has placed emphasis on attracting multilingual and, in particular, young Latin@ staff members and interns who can perform important bridging functions across linguistic and cultural divisions.[20]

Called upon to engage in dialogue with local residents—on both practical and conversational levels, as well as about the broader vision and ideals of the food justice organization—these young members of CSU were often thrust into unique roles of responsibility. Carlos, an intern-turned-staff-member, who had immigrated to the United States from Mexico as a young child, worked closely with his colleague Stephanie in their interactions with Spanish-speaking community members. Their conversations with local residents often went well beyond the task at hand, as shared language and culture opened up new avenues for personal storytelling. "Getting engaged in conversations about these issues in Spanish, it's really nice to hear what they have to say," Carlos explained. "Back in their hometown in Mexico, it was a lot of fresh foods, a lot of easy access to that," he offered as a particular example. "But now when they come to the United States it's a big shift, because there's not a lot of that. And they notice it's all a lot more expensive, and it's more easy to eat at fast food places." Stephanie continued on a similar tack, adding, "I think that's a connection that I have with people I speak to with our program. I think that, maybe when they see someone from their own culture or their own heritage, they think about, 'Oh yeah, it's really good to have some foods that I used to have in my country.'"

By cultivating mini urban farms not only as agricultural domains but also as contexts for communicative action, CSU works to build a foundation for sustainable community change. The Garden Gateway workshops offer an opportunity for participants to develop their gardening and cooking skills while simultaneously opening up spaces in which issues of systemic inequality, notions of embodied wisdom, and the nature of civic epistemologies in multiethnic communities could be explored. This storytelling about food and justice took shape in the face of—and, I would argue, partly because of—the complicated nature of the organization's networked action. One can follow how CSU's reliance on public health research and funding went on to inspire conversations about the limits of scientific authority and the value of cultural knowledge. Similarly, the obstacles faced in reaching out to mono-lingual Spanish speakers led to reflexive conversations and concrete actions that improved CSU's ability to represent the entire community. As subsequent sections of this chapter and book will continue to explore, navigating the inherent tensions of these types of networked partnerships remains a source of ambivalence for community-based groups seeking to make food justice a reality.

Earth Day South LA

I made my way into the auditorium of Normandie Avenue Elementary School for an organizing committee meeting of CSU's Earth Day South LA. While Earth Day events had long been common throughout Los Angeles, few, if any, had ever taken place in the South LA area before CSU decided to organize its annual festival. The theme for that year's celebration was P.O.W.E.R. (People Organizing With Each Other Resourcefully) Shift, and we were getting ready to transform Normandie Avenue Elementary School's playground into a site for musical and dance performances, gardening and cooking workshops, children's games, mural paintings, craft and art sales, and information tabling from dozens of local social justice and service organizations. I sat down alongside CSU staff and board members, a local high school teacher, staff from the elementary school's after-school program, the directors of a South LA arts program, and staff from Food and Water Watch, a national public interest organization that advocates for safe and sustainable food and environmental policies.

The conversation turned toward the team's strategy for publicity and outreach. Partners from Food and Water Watch had been tasked with media strategizing, and an intern with the organization said she hoped to get attention for the event from major city and state elected officials, as well as from big publications like the *LA Times*. She suggested that getting elected officials attached to the event could be a great way to generate media attention quickly, highlight the work of CSU for a bigger audience, and generate even more attention for future Earth Day events. Her idea, however, was not met with enthusiasm. A city councilperson had come to the first year of the event to do a ribbon cutting ceremony, a CSU staffer explained, but the media coverage that followed focused almost entirely on the councilperson, not on the work of CSU or the vision of the festival. Getting coverage from the *LA Times* might be nice, another staff member pointed out, but they would rather focus their efforts on getting attention from media that better understood food justice issues—that is, if media attention was important at all. It all came down to the vision of the event—a vision that was about building connections between and among local residents and organizations, providing a space for local artists and musicians, and advocating for collaborative organizing to shift the power toward justice and sustainability. If the Earth Day festival was really about motivating community-based action in South LA, they argued, their outreach needed to focus on connecting with that community.

Indeed, the organization had been somewhat disappointed with the turnout during the first year of the event—when the festival had more prominently featured public officials and had the attendant mainstream media coverage—not due to an overall lack of visitors, but because too low a percentage of them were local residents. In future years, they worked successfully so that upward of 90 percent of people who attended were from within a few blocks or miles of the school. As Neelam put it, "We are really happy that there is a good smattering and a good mix of folk from outside the neighborhood, from all over Los Angeles. And people of much more diverse backgrounds—South Asians, Caucasians, all kind of folk are there. And that's what we want to see. But if we are really serious about building in our neighborhood, then we need to preference the folks in it. And so if the stuff that we are doing doesn't speak to them and doesn't attract them, then it's not really inclusive."

In the weeks leading up to Earth Day South LA, CSU activated those connections from across its organizational network that it felt would best promote local storytelling about the event. Rather than aiming for the *LA Times,* staffers sought out interactions with a few local media producers, and news of the event made its way onto a local public radio program and into the online pages of a local news website. The staff also used an online newsletter and a Facebook event page to reach out to several thousand potential attendees. Ultimately, however, they felt that intensive media outreach often required more effort than it was worth. When staff members recounted previous interactions with the press, they insisted there was generally limited payoff. They showed little faith that journalists would be interested in covering Earth Day South LA and even less confidence that media coverage would provide an authentic reflection of the festival's broader vision for community change. "If you're not willing to do a real story about our whole team," Neelam explained, "about what this actually takes, I'm not interested."

Such a perspective of media coverage, I should point out, is actually quite common among community-based social justice organizers, particularly when previous experiences have left them dissatisfied with media representations of their local efforts. Still, the observations of scholars, and the experience of many activist groups, provide evidence to suggest that this kind of disconnect between organizers and media producers can significantly constrain the prospects for community-level change. Indeed, when the efforts of community practitioners are highlighted extensively in local and ethnic media, the coverage can provide a powerful force for energizing and sustaining community mobilization (chapter 6 explores these mediated dynamics in greater depth).[21] For CSU's part, though, the staff had mostly decided that they had neither the time nor the inclination to concentrate on actively changing their relationship with the media.

Therefore, when it came to really investing in a particular strategy for community outreach, it was not professional journalism or social media that the CSU staff deemed most worthy, but rather the very low-technology solution of a well-designed flyer and a host of personal conversations that emerged as central storytelling tools. In bold letters, the Earth Day flyer declared, "Spark the P.O.W.E.R. Shift," the words accompanied by images of windmills, bicyclists, and an electrified light bulb surrounding a vibrant tree, all superimposed upon an image of a South LA street. Names of key partners, sponsors, and supporters were inscribed alongside the date and time of the free family event. Thousands of these flyers were printed, at a substantial portion of the festival's budget, and distributed throughout the local community. Flyers were also sent home with students of Normandie Avenue Elementary, with the hope that local families from the school itself would make up a large number of those in attendance. On the weekends leading up to the festival, CSU amassed hundreds of volunteers to walk the streets of South LA, distributing flyers. I was one of many who canvassed in groups of six to eight, usually with a few bilingual English-Spanish speakers in each group, stuffing flyers in doorways, leaving stacks of them in the front windows of local businesses, and stopping to chat with local residents we passed along the way. This type of door-knocking strategy was key for CSU in much of its outreach work, but with staff and volunteers working across several square miles of South LA over the course of multiple weekends, the Earth Day flyer-distribution campaign was the biggest outreach effort of the year.

From the perspective of CSU staff, the intensive outreach paid off. The festival was considered a great success, with upward of 1,500 people in attendance. The key point CSU hoped to emphasize was that Earth Day South LA was not simply a one-off event, nor simply a showcase for a single food justice group. Rather, it was an effort to tell a bigger story of resistance, empowerment, and movements for change, articulated by a diverse set of South LA organizations, artists, and residents. From morning through the late afternoon during the event, attendees could discuss antihunger policy advocacy with staffers from Hunger Action LA, learn about the Housing is a Human Right campaign from LA Community Action Network, and connect with health care providers from the St. John's Well Child and Family Center. Children could participate in crafts and performing arts projects with the Center South LA, plant "seed bombs" with volunteers from LA Guerrilla Gardening, and enjoy a fruit smoothie made in a bicycle-powered electric blender. By organizing Earth Day South LA, CSU was working to establish itself as a central node within a larger ecology of organizations engaged in social justice work in the neighborhood, a collection of activists whose connection to the community could be strengthened when they came together in support of a common cause.

Gus, Normandie Avenue Elementary School's principal, could be seen on the day of the event leading kids in a jump-rope competition and organizing a basketball tournament. According to him, the event was well worth any support that he could provide. "I think Earth Day is so important for a school community like ours. Not just our school, but for all of South Central LA." He particularly appreciated the high-quality murals that were produced by artists during the event, which helped to beautify the outside of the elementary school, turning the drab tan exterior into a vibrant site of artistic production. "Certainly when people walk into our school they say—'Wow, we didn't expect to see such colorful and artistic work here.' And what's amazing to me is that people respect the artwork, so we have not had any of those murals get hit with graffiti. I think the community is inspired by them. There's a lesson there, they see themselves there."

FIGURE 7. A CSU intern standing in front of garden beds at the Normandie Avenue Elementary School. Photograph by Sahra Sulaiman.

Indeed, community members at the event continually remarked that Earth Day was an example of the positive community action that had always been present within South LA, even if it was a story rarely told in mainstream accounts about the oft-maligned neighborhood. A week after one of CSU's Earth Day festivals, an anonymous online commenter on the website of the *LA Times* responded to yet another negative story about South LA, this one highlighting homicides in the area around Normandie Avenue Elementary School. Going by the username "The Positive," she argued that other stories could be told: "You know, I clicked on the news for the South LA section of the LA Times and frankly I'm tired of this one sided story. Can you guys write about anything positive? I just went to an Earth Day fair two days ago in my neighborhood at Normandie Avenue Elementary School. It was an amazing event with artists, craft vendors and people of every color loving life, the event and a nice Saturday. How come I never see articles about things like this?"[22]

On one day each year, CSU worked to turn the blacktop of Normandie Avenue Elementary into a space of dynamic conversation, cultural education, and artistic production. As the event's vision statement outlined, "Together, we envision an annual Earth Day event where community residents in South

FIGURE 8. This painting of a tree and its roots was one of several murals created during Earth Day South LA celebrations at the Normandie Avenue Elementary School. Mural and photograph by Heng Leng.

Central come together in a safe environment to have fun, celebrate our foods and cultures, learn about and participate in sustainable practices, and connect with each other and organizations working to make positive change in our neighborhood." Alongside the organization's youth programs and agricultural activities, Earth Day South LA exemplifies a style of grassroots community organizing that considers connecting to the community to be the starting point for all future action. To realize these activities, the group drew from a host of interorganizational partnerships, depended on a person-to-person strategy of community outreach, and worked to boost the capacity of local institutions to serve as sites for community development and neighborhood empowerment. For a nonprofit like CSU—operating as it was "in the shadow of the shadow state"—the forging of these entrepreneurial partnerships was fundamental for achieving organizational sustainability when faced with ongoing fiscal and programmatic challenges. Expanding, sustaining, and funding this community-based programming signified an existential challenge and opportunity moving forward.

Creating a Sustainable Social Enterprise

Dyane and I returned to CSU's mini urban farm one summer afternoon, ready to unload the back of CSU's truck, which we had just filled with crates of mixed fruits and vegetables from a nearby farmers' market. Our next step was packing produce bags for subscribers, as well as setting aside some of the produce to be sold at CSU's Expo farm stand. Several years after the start of the Great Recession, CSU was starting to place a particular emphasis on building up these revenue-generating aspects of its operations. The organization was joining the ranks of a number of other actors in the "green economy" that saw engagement in the market as a powerful force for the grassroots promotion of social, economic, and environmental well-being.[23]

Indeed, CSU's strategic move emerged at a moment in which entrepreneurial and market-oriented models of community development were increasingly being incentivized by governmental policy and supported by funding agencies of various sorts.[24] As evidenced by the proliferation of Community Development Corporations (CDCs) starting in the mid-twentieth century and the introduction of newer social enterprise organizations in the twenty-first century, a movement for "community economic development" (CED) continued to gain momentum. At its foundation, this CED movement was grounded in a central narrative that, in the words of James DeFilippis, Robert Fisher, and Eric Shragge, "local economic development will create wealth and jobs, and thus act as a way to ameliorate inner-city problems such as affordable housing, unemployment and poverty" (69).[25] Initiatives in this vein have been touted not only by neoliberal ideologues, who advance market-driven programs, but also by left-leaning progressives, who tout the democratic potential of community-driven entrepreneurship.

For those with a commitment to social justice, CED initiatives offer both promise and peril. Writing in the late 1990s, the founding executive director of CSU—Kwaku Duren—outlined his belief in the potential of the strategy, but he lamented that it had heretofore lacked the political consciousness that would enable it to promote legitimate justice-oriented change. "Overall, the CED Movement has been able to improve the neighborhood infrastructure, housing, and services, but has seldom been effective in making the economy of a city work better for poor people," he wrote.[26] If social justice is to have any hope of being achieved through CED, advocates have long insisted, it must be driven by a social and economic critique of the status quo, integrated as part of a political vision in which local community members are empowered through direct participation and control of the process.[27] Branded as the Village Market Place (VMP), CSU's social enterprise hoped to do just that. The initiative was not conceptualized as being separate from the rest of the organization's food justice programming but rather was designed to be incorporated as a central aspect of CSU's community organizing strategy. The project was understood to offer a path toward programmatic integration, long-term sustainability, and organizational autonomy.

This shift toward the social enterprise began several years earlier. When CSU staff began to see their varied urban farm operations start to produce an excess of fresh produce, they opened a weekly produce stand in front of their Expo mini urban farm. The operations grew slowly over the next few years, expanding to include value-added products like dried herbs and jams, as well a subscription-based produce bag program. At the "neighborhood resident" rate, a small bag of mixed seasonal fruits and vegetables cost $10 a week, while the large bag cost $20 a week—the prices increased to $12 and $24 a week, respectively, at the "supporter rate," which was intended for those from other areas of the city. Bags could be picked up at the produce stand, delivered by bicycle, or dropped off to institutional buyers, which included a few social-justice oriented nonprofits in the South LA area. As demand began to grow, CSU worked to incorporate produce from other local farmers—including groups like the South Central Farmers' Cooperative—to supplement the food grown on its own urban farms.

The organization put additional effort into marketing and strategic business development as its operations expanded—new pop-up produce stands were opened; wholesale agreements with restaurants, schools, and corner markets were forged; and, eventually, CSU relocated its operations to a newly established storefront, catering center, restaurant space, and office in the Mercado La Paloma, a South Los Angeles community marketplace. Importantly for the community-organizing mission of the organization, CSU staff estimated that they reached well over three hundred families on a weekly basis through these various economic outlets alone. About seven out of ten of those were local residents who lived right in the South LA area, including many low-income residents, who used Supplemental Nutrition Assistance

Program (SNAP) benefits to make purchases. By the end of 2014, CSU had distributed over one hundred thousand pounds of beyond organic produce through the VMP, connecting with thousands of residents through the process. A social enterprise that had initially accounted for less than $10,000 in overall income for CSU, the VMP had grown, in just a few short years, into an operation that generated over $100,000 in revenue on an annual basis, and it was continuing to grow. In the broader context of the food service world, of course, these margins would be considered small, but with its revenue accounting for up to 30 percent of CSU's total operating budget, the VMP was undoubtedly reshaping how the organization structured its food justice work.

Like the owners of any other start-up businesses would, CSU's staff consistently evaluated the VMP's profitability and viability. Was the social enterprise fueling interest, meeting demand, and turning a profit? In what ways might the business model be retooled to increase its chances of sustainability while still meeting its goal of serving those community members in need? Staff members consulted with colleagues from organizations like the California Community Economic Development Corporation (CCEDA)—a group cofounded by CSU's founder, Kwaku. "I used to tell Neelam—small and funky is great, and I admire small and funky," Ralph Lippman, the director of CCEDA, told me. "But in community revitalization, the name of the game is still capacity. The groups you see prosper and have long tenure, it's not necessarily that they're relevant to the development of the community—it's that they have the capacity to attract money and attract attention." While CSU staff members pushed back against recommendations to minimize their social justice mission in favor of one with a depoliticized economic development focus, they also recognized that the capacity of their social enterprise was central to their community organizing strategy. Finding a balance between these potentially opposing forces was a challenge that they were willing to face head-on.

Indeed, after just over a year in the Mercado La Paloma, CSU found that the facilities were not fully meeting its needs. The organization opted for another shift and replanted its offices and the social enterprise into a nearby space with a commercial kitchen. "Our energies are concentrating on those outlets of the VMP that most effectively reach local South LA families," CSU offered by way of explanation in an online newsletter to friends and supporters. "We are up scaling all our Produce Stands to offer local eggs, baked goods and bulk items in addition to our delicious affordable produce and value added items; stepping up social marketing at stands, local corner stores and at community events and venues; expanding our Produce Bag program and wholesale to local stores, restaurants and other community agencies; and building our successful Soul Full Catering. And as is our core, all of this is driven by local youth, using and building their talents."[28] By early 2015, CSU was strategizing for another major move, kicking off a fundraising campaign to purchase the Paul Robeson Community Center in South LA: "The 5,000 square foot building and 10,000 square foot lot mean we can open the produce and grocery market South LA needs, create an on-site commercial kitchen and urban farm, and greatly increase our capacity to serve more local residents." By the time this book went to press, CSU had moved forward with the purchase of the building and continued to raise funds to support its renovation and buildout.[29]

The growth of CSU's social enterprise also allowed them to add new staff members to the team, employees that would be asked to contribute not only to the VMP but also to the other educational and agricultural programs that had long driven the social justice mission of the organization. To fill these roles, the organization's leadership sought out young men and women from the neighborhood. Cris, a twenty-six-year-old Central American man and lifelong resident of South LA, had bounced around from job to job before finding his way to CSU. "In the past, in previous jobs, there was something wrong," he described to me in an interview. "I didn't feel 100 percent great in selling a certain product to somebody if it looked like they didn't need it, if it looked like they couldn't afford it, if it looked like it was going to, in the end, if it was going to put them in a deeper hole. My conscience was just eating at me every time I would make a new sale or pitch or whatever it was." Looking for meaningful work, he sought out employment in the nonprofit sector, but was disappointed there too, this time by the tediousness of the jobs and the lack of broader purpose at the heart of the organizations. "The job I've had with CSU is completely different," Cris explained. "It's not to a point where my mind is blank and I'm doing the job. I'm thinking. I'm being aware of what's going on and what's next. I'm alive and active. It's sort of like I'm a plant that was uprooted and lifted from where I was at, and I settled into this new location. And recently I've felt like my roots have settled in and feel a lot firmer than what was before. I feel like I'm growing."

In addition to providing job training and employment opportunities to local young adults, CSU's VMP also represented a chance to support several other local businesses. The organization was on the leading edge, for instance, in bringing fresh fruits and vegetables to some of the many corner markets that dotted the landscape of South LA, many of which were owned by ethnic minority merchants. CSU partnered with a graduate student at a local university to conduct a feasibility study of potential corner market partners in the area. Groups of staff and volunteers went into dozens of these markets to interview store owners and managers, to get a sense of the types of produce, if any, that were being sold and to find out whether they would be interested in expanding the options that they gave the community by bringing some of CSU's beyond organic produce into their stores.

"These corner stores are like allies in this work. They're folks that have been in the community for thirty or forty years. Folks who have been able to withstand all kinds of stuff that's gone on over the years," Dyane explained. "For them to start selling fruits and vegetables, it isn't necessarily a plus for them. For a lot of stores, they're probably initially going to lose money, to get folks used to it in the community that they're serving." Recognizing the importance of these markets to the neighborhood, as well as the challenges of converting the stores' produce options, CSU did its best to facilitate the process—they sold the stores produce at a consignment rate, got youth interns involved in marketing and store design, and went door-to-door in the community to let local residents know about the markets' changes.

I arrived by bicycle at one such market—Mama's Chicken—one weekend afternoon, joined by a parade of seventy other cyclists, all of us taking part in the launch of the Healthy Food Map for South LA. A collaborative initiative between CSU, several of my academic colleagues at USC, and a local community development and sustainable transport organization called T.R.U.S.T South LA, the map highlighted safe pedestrian and bicycle routes that would connect local residents with healthy food access sites in the neighborhood.[30] "In this community, a lot of people come to the neighborhood stores more than they come to the big grocery stores. But the one thing that we didn't have was produce," the owner of the market, which had been in business since 1969, offered in an impromptu speech. "And they've been receiving it pretty decently, I must say. The more people that know about it, the more that's coming in. And it makes me really happy to know that they can come in."

The VMP's operations also provided support to a set of local farmers, those whose produce accounted for a majority of the total fruits and vegetables sold through CSU's retail and wholesale operations. The partnerships with local family farmers cultivating beyond organic produce began quite organically themselves, as Neelam got to know those selling produce at her local South LA farmers' markets years earlier. Those informal relationships developed into business partnerships, and over time CSU's purchases increased steadily—from around $4,000 in 2009 to over $35,000 in 2012; in total, the organization bought some fifty thousand pounds of produce over those three years, and the amount is consistently rising. Throughout the process, CSU was explicit about the type of farmers they were dedicated to supporting. Production methods mattered, as CSU worked only with those who produced organic foods, although they did not require that the farmers had been granted the official, and sometimes prohibitively expensive, USDA Organic certification. Furthermore, the organization's emphasis remained on seeking out partnerships with ethnic minority farmers, groups that had historically been marginalized and discriminated against in the broader food production system. This effort, at times, did not always represent the path of least resistance—CSU had to help several of these farmers build up their managerial and technological infrastructure to ensure that the ordering and delivery process would be smooth and consistent. Such efforts, however, were in line with the organization's broader strategy to build skills, promote economic development, and advance social justice within the people-of-color community of which CSU was a part. As Dyane described:

> We prioritize these small farmers and farmers of color because a lot of them are being run out of business. . . . A lot of these farmers don't make a lot of money there, but with our model, they can at least come to a farmers' market and they'll know we're earmarked for $500 or something. That makes their trip worth it. . . . With our mission, as far as folks that need it the most, farmers of color are folks that really need the support and the business. That's attached to our mission, not only when we're doing our programmatic work, but also when we're doing our purchasing. We try to purchase from the guys that really need that support.

As the VMP social enterprise took shape, CSU's community-organizing networks incorporated new partners from the community economic development landscape. The organization's food justice narrative was put in conversation with the language of business models, profit margins, and economic development partnerships across the private and public sectors. It was a strategic move that would likely draw the ire of radical, left-leaning critics of the alternative food movements, those who have argued that community-based food initiatives have placed too much emphasis on neoliberal values of entrepreneurialism, self-improvement, and community-based economic development.[31] Such critics have called for food justice activism that works outside of capitalist frameworks, promotes autonomy in low-income communities and communities of color, and champions sets of alternative cultural values that illuminate the fundamental flaws of neoliberalism.[32] Was CSU blinded to the fact that its strategy of community economic development was playing into the hands of a hegemonic system, or were critics of the green economy missing something about the political possibilities that were actually available in the age of neoliberalism?

These questions were hardly lost on the leadership of CSU, as staff members actively grappled with these considerations, took criticism from their radical-left friends, and considered the best ways to continue to advance their mission. "I think at this point, the stage of society and capitalism, I don't see another way yet," Dyane described. With this system so strongly entrenched, what other options did CSU have if it wanted to make a difference in the everyday lives of the community that it served? CSU staffers were deeply critical of certain aspects of capitalism, but ultimately, they found that reluctant capitalists like them were uniquely positioned to make a difference, as Dyane explained:

> It's much more beneficial to the community for us to be that actor, because we have a longer investment. And our bottom line is not dollars, our bottom line is for the better of the community. So we're more suited as an actor in that place, because any other actor is not really going to care about the community in the way that we do. . . . People are going to buy the stuff somewhere, so they might as well be buying into something that is for their benefit. Not only for the food that they eat, but for the community that they live in.

When CSU staff described the difference that they brought to the local food system through their entrepreneurial efforts, they once again put a central focus on neighborhood storytelling. When folks interacted with the dominant structures of the food system—the industrial farmers, the mass-market grocery chains, the fast food restaurants—so many stories went untold. There was no discussion of toxicity, or of workers' rights, local economic development, cultural knowledge, racial exploitation, or long-term community health. CSU changed that story. Lawrence recounted an interaction with a youth intern who remarked—in front of a produce stand customer—that CSU's price for peaches was too expensive. The market exchange proved to be an object lesson:

> Yeah, those peaches are expensive. But the reason the peaches are so cheap at Ralph's or at Von's, at the grocery store, is because the farmers who picked that stuff, they get paid pennies, they're like slaves. A lot of them are Mexican

and Central American immigrant workers who don't get paid anything at all. They work in harsh environments and the food doesn't even taste good. All these things—the transportation of the food, the pesticides that are sprayed on it, how it gets from the farm. Our pricing on the food has to do with that, and it pays for your participation in this internship program. You've got to think about those things.

The bottom line for CSU's Village Market Place was the same as that of all its programs: to serve *the community*. A powerful way to do just that, staffers had concluded, was to build a market-based model that would serve as a form of community economic development, support minority farmers and local business owners, and create jobs and build skills for the youth of South LA. Engagement in the local food system meant engagement with markets, and part of the civic epistemologies CSU cultivated among youth and residents of South LA included knowledge about using business models for good. Money talks, of course, but its story is malleable within the contexts of exchange. In South LA's dominant structures of food distribution and consumption—the poorly equipped grocery stores, the fast food restaurants, and the corner markets—stories of systemic injustice and the possibilities of equity and sustainability were muted, if they were even present at all. But by cultivating alternative institutions within the community and thereby shifting the networks with which local residents interacted on a daily basis, CSU found that they could work collaboratively with the community to build sites of ongoing conversation and constructive action toward food justice. Did they depend upon some of the logics of neoliberalism to push this forward? They undoubtedly did. Yet they were willing to work through these tensions, aiming to find the generative possibilities that existed in a community like this.

. . .

By offering intersecting snapshots of several of CSU's key community-organizing activities, this chapter outlined the networks and narratives that characterize the organization's localized food justice work. The ethnographic research detailed in the chapter highlights the strengths of community-based food justice organizing, a movement that has successfully identified food as a powerful vehicle to build cultural bridges, start critical conversations, and develop the grassroots basis of community development. In its efforts to "serve the people, body and soul," CSU worked hard to use local action as a way to build a critical community consciousness. By promoting neighborhood storytelling about issues of food and justice and contextualizing how and why food injustice reverberated well beyond South LA, the organization insisted that its strategy could serve as an effective antidote to inequity and discrimination.

With that said, in my months and years participating with CSU, I never got the sense from staff and volunteers that they saw their handful of mini urban farms, garden workshops, or even their social enterprise as *the answer* to meet the material nutritional needs or environmental justice concerns of hundreds of thousands of South LA residents. Instead, CSU staff and community partners spoke of starting a conversation, cultivating sets of skills, and building a model for change that could be refined, expanded, replicated, adapted, and connected to diverse geographic and cultural contexts. Each weed picked from a once-vacant lot, each conversation that championed cultural wisdom, and each meaningful job created for a young adult in South LA was considered a contribution to this mission. "For CSU, the thing is, people are right here," Heather Fenney Alexander, CSU's associate director for development, told me. "They have the opportunity to create something for themselves, to realize their hopes for their own future right here. So why wouldn't you support and cultivate that to happen?"

Several of the key foundations for sustainable community change were ingrained in CSU's strategy. The organization used storytelling to articulate the challenges of local food inequity and situated those efforts within broader legacies of resistance and justice. The group developed a "360 approach" that used networked partnerships to transform both social values and structures, cultivating places and spaces in the community that could build community-based capacity over time. However, embedded in this approach were a set of undeniable limits, contradictions, and lingering questions about its long-term viability. CSU struggled, for instance, to build productive relationships with local and ethnic media producers that could boost the organization's capacity for neighborhood storytelling and motivate community action. Furthermore, the organization was compelled to alter its community engagement practices in order to better reflect the multilingual composition of the diversifying South LA region. Staffers and community participants faced an additional set of challenges when they endeavored to integrate the priorities of public health funding agencies with their commitment to holistic and local knowledge. These difficulties speak to the need for community-based groups like CSU to continually evolve, reflect upon, and improve their practices. As subsequent chapters of this book will continue to explore, honest and direct engagement with organizing obstacles such as these is necessary if the movement for community-based food justice hopes to expand its reach and impact in the years to come.

Nonprofit groups working "in the shadow of the shadow state" are consistently confronted with challenges to autonomy and the purity of their mission. A community-based food justice organization undoubtedly relies on varied sets of network partners and philosophical perspectives—emerging from both within and outside of its local community—that collectively shape its communication ecology for community organizing. New and evolving civic epistemologies are borne out of these interactions, as the visions and experiences of community members, organizational staff, and institutional partners are put into tenuous conversation. For CSU, the development of the Village Market Place social enterprise, in particular, was characteristic of these dynamics, as it brought a host of diverse and sometimes divergent partners, strategies, and philosophies into a unified purpose. CSU staffers were reluctant capitalists, yes, but they saw value in a capitalistic economic model for promoting their bottom line of community empowerment. It was through this hybrid praxis of community-based activism—situated in public, private, and reclaimed spaces of South LA—that storytelling about food and justice could commence, connections to the community could be forged, and the networks and narratives of the local food system could ultimately be transformed.

The Youth Food Justice Movement

As the lines began to form, I grabbed a ladle and took my place behind a large serving dish of black-eyed peas, made fresh in the kitchen of Community Services Unlimited (CSU). I was one of six CSU staff and volunteers—each of us wearing an apron and holding a serving utensil in hand—standing in front of well over one hundred teens and adults, their faces and body language exhibiting a mix of exhaustion, anticipation, and excitement. One by one, they stepped up to survey the dinner selections, all of which, we emphasized, were made with local beyond organic produce and other locally sourced ingredients. "Where are you coming from?" I asked each one with a smile as I scooped a hearty portion of beans onto their plates. Despite having traveled for many hours and miles throughout the morning and afternoon, our guests were eager to enthusiastically represent their hometowns and organizations. The youth of Food, What?! made the drive down from Santa Cruz, several members of the Urban Nutrition Initiative had taken their first plane ride out of Philly, and the folks from Grub had traveled a thousand miles due west from the flatlands of Lubbock, Texas. As the representatives of these and dozens of other groups sat down to enjoy their meals, we all knew that the long day was hardly complete. The dinner was just the beginning of the opening ceremonies for the annual Rooted in Community network summit—hosted that year in collaboration with the staff, interns, and volunteers of CSU.

Soon after participants finished their meals, the rhythmic sounds of drums and dance rumbled throughout South LA's Mercado la Paloma community center. The crowd gathered around as an intergenerational group of traditional Aztec dancers, dressed in colorful indigenous garb, complete with long feathered headpieces and lavishly designed vestments, stepped into the center of the room. As I looked around, I could begin to see the seemingly strict boundaries of dozens of locally focused youth groups start to give way, at least in part, to a broader networked identity. Rooted in Community—often shortened by its members to the acronym RIC—represented the only national network of organizations working explicitly at the intersection of food justice and youth development.

Over the next four days and nights, youth members and adult staff alike shared ideas, built skills, and forged a host of new relationships across generations, ethnicities, and regional identities. Through conversation, education, artistic production, and direct action, the summit offered participants an opportunity to collectively articulate the priorities, possibilities, and practices of a youth-led movement for change. "You know, youth are the future," Lawrence, CSU's youth coordinator, told me as he reflected on the value of the RIC gathering. "Creating a space where they can come together and go back to their communities and continue doing this work and increase knowledge in their community and amongst their peers—that can have a major impact on the ways in which we live our everyday lives."

As I discussed in the previous chapter, much of the strength of community-based food justice organizing rests in its ability to achieve community-level successes, catalyzing critical consciousness and building alternative institutions at the local level. Still, this book remains steeped in the recognition that, for those grassroots food justice organizations that pursue their goals "in the shadow of the shadow state," the capacity of community-focused action should be neither diminished nor overly romanticized. Indeed, there is ample evidence to demonstrate that community organizing has the power to promote health, equity, and sustainability in historically marginalized communities. However, given the deeply entrenched and systemic nature of injustice, broader movements for change are still required, and community organizations must actively engage in partnerships that expand their local horizons in order to make this happen.[1] Through the lens of the RIC network, this chapter ethnographically describes and empirically assesses the benefits gained and challenges faced when community-based food justice groups engage in networks that extend beyond their respective localities. What role might a group like RIC play in parlaying localized action into a more expansive, collective, and youth-led agenda for sustainable change?

For CSU's part, from its early days as a food-focused, community-based organization, it had maintained an interest in building relationships and constructing partnerships that would situate local organizational efforts within broader flows of social justice activism. The RIC summit and other activities like it offered opportunities to disseminate lessons learned in South LA to new geographic and ideological arenas, to integrate outside knowledge into CSU's own community of practice, and to work collaboratively with other social justice groups toward shared goals. Exchange programs and conferences, for instance, brought staffers to sustainable agriculture initiatives in sites as diverse as Boston, Detroit, Oaxaca, and Johannesburg. CSU's longstanding engagement in issues of community economic development led to interactions with a host of local, regional, and national nonprofit groups; with policymakers and government representatives; and with community-minded corporations and foundations. In recent years, the RIC network had proved a particularly useful avenue through which members could connect with other young activists from across the country, building skills and strategizing about ways to put the youth food justice movement on the map. Collectively, this communication ecology for broader movement-building proved vital to advancing CSU's food justice goals.

However, this process of extension did not come without its own set of complications. Many of the food justice advocates I encountered were still processing and theorizing about the ways in which engagement in national networks could best serve and be served by their grassroots actions. Should they be doing more to tell their collective story and promote societal-wide change? Or could a push in an extra-local direction actually endanger the strides they had made while focusing at the local level of their own communities?

With a focus on the networks and narratives of RIC, this chapter aims to investigate these and other questions. It highlights the strength of RIC as a networked organization, one that encourages youth activists to recognize the systemic and geographically widespread nature of food injustice, while also building capacity among the staff of community-based groups to build collective cultural and institutional resistance. In addition, the research continues to demonstrate the hybrid praxis that has come to typify contemporary food justice organizing. Tracing ongoing efforts to balance youth leadership with adult priority-setting and exploring the tensions that characterize discussions related to media storytelling and policy advocacy as part of the food justice toolbox, the pages that follow illustrate the evolving nature of the food justice agenda. Through an interrogation of the meanings, possibilities, and constraints faced by CSU and other members of the RIC network, the chapter offers insights into the capabilities, limitations, and potential futures of a youth-driven movement for food justice and community change.

Enshrined in the names of both Community Services Unlimited and Rooted in Community—as well as in the titles or mission statements of nearly all of the other organizations involved in the RIC network—is "community," that foundational but elusive term, the one that advocates of varied political perspectives have seized upon as being fundamental to social change in the age of neoliberalism. "It seems never to be used unfavourably," social critical Raymond Williams wrote, while the sociologist Nikolas Rose insisted that "society is to be regenerated, and social justice to be maximized, through the building of responsible communities, prepared to invest in themselves" (136).[2] As the ethnographer Nina Eliasoph described, from every direction lately, "we hear summons to volunteer, to participate, to build grassroots, multicultural community, and to become empowered." From within this context, she continued, "youth programs are ideal places to witness those transformations" (ix).[3]

Indeed, groups involved in RIC were among the countless contemporary organizations that, in recent years, had situated a call to community action directly alongside a vision for positive youth empowerment. From this optimistic perspective, organizers have identified young people as potentially powerful actors who can—and, in many cases, must—lead the way toward community health, sustainability, and civic revitalization. As a recent report by the Funders' Collaborative on Youth Organizing insisted, "Grassroots youth organizing is alive and well, and it is changing communities, as well as the lives of young people who are leading campaigns for social justice" (i).[4] Scholar-activists Shawn Ginwright and Taj James share a similar sentiment, arguing that "community organizing around local issues of direct concern to youth and their communities is the most central strategy that young people are using to create systemic change" (38).[5]

Most of the scores of youth participants attending the annual RIC summit in South LA brought with them a localized, largely geographic understanding of what community was and how it could be activated to encourage social justice. It was taken as a given that this collective understanding of community would serve as a foundation upon which all subsequent activities of the network could build. Yet, part of the mission of RIC focused on expanding young peoples' conceptualization of what, exactly, "community" could mean, what capacities youth could bring to community-based activism, and how the linking of these dynamic elements could be leveraged into a movement for food justice. By uniting young people of diverse regional and cultural backgrounds for a common cause, organizers aimed to build a community of community-based actors, constructing a new collective identity for groups of youth leaders who are all committed to bringing about social transformation through food.

As RIC participants explained, this process began by giving young people the space to lead their own way. This was the sentiment expressed by Celeste—a high school senior from East New York who was a youth member of RIC's advisory committee—when I asked her if anything was special about RIC for the young people who took part in its gatherings and events. "Inside Rooted in Community, I feel like definitely our opinions are heard," she told me. "At other conferences that I usually go to, there's a lot of adults. So, when we talk, we talk and they kind of hear us, but it goes out the other ear." At Rooted in Community, by contrast, "we have the stage for the youth to talk. So we actually get a chance to talk and kind of figure out what *we* want."

More than fifteen years before this conversation—and not long after Celeste and the other youth participants of RIC were born—these same sentiments were being expressed by the young people attending the 1998 conference of the American Community Gardening Association. As the story is told, a group of young people from the Boston-based youth development program The Food Project were in attendance at this national event, but they were disappointed to find few other teens or people of color represented. Working with leaders from the American Community Gardening Association and the San Francisco-based Literacy for Environmental Justice organization, The Food Project served as the host for a youth-focused food and agricultural conference held in Boston in the summer of 1999. Shortly thereafter, RIC became its own organizational entity, operating as one of over sixty projects under the fiscal sponsorship of the 501(c)(3) nonprofit Earth Island Institute, the California-based incubator founded by the renowned environmental activist David Brower.

Described as a national network of groups of youth and adult mentors working for food justice, today RIC connects upwards of one hundred community-based organizations. Members of the loosely identified collective all work on issues related to agriculture, nutrition, and youth development, and nearly all of the groups are centered in low-income communities and/or communities of color. As its website explains, "RIC provides a unique opportunity for young food leaders from marginalized communities around the country to connect with other youth like them, acknowledge their shared experiences and struggles, and build community to address and change the injustices in our food system." Through an annual conference, regional gatherings, curriculum sharing, organizational consulting, an e-mail Listserv, and social media, RIC has aims to shift both the culture and structure of the contemporary food system toward justice and equity for all, with youth voices leading the charge.[6]

The hallmark initiative of the RIC network is its annual summer gathering. Since the first event in Boston in 1999, the network summit has been held across the United States in such locations as San Francisco, California, in 2000; Milwaukee, Wisconsin, in 2003; Olympia, Washington, in 2005, Philadelphia, Pennsylvania, in 2007 and 2011; and Aimes, Iowa, in 2012, to name a few. Each year, planning for the gathering is led by that year's host organization in conjunction with RIC staff, and the event is supported primarily by registration fees, supplemented by a few foundation grants, seed money from RIC, and substantial amounts of in-kind donations.

Rallying around the theme of Reclaiming Our Land, Reclaiming Our Roots, over 120 youth and adults—coming from almost thirty different organizations based in cities and towns across the nation—attended the midsummer RIC summit in South LA in 2013, hosted by CSU. What followed were four days of participatory workshops, shared meals, tours of local historic and agricultural sites, a plenary session featuring Will Allen of the Milwaukee-based Growing Power, breakout dialogues for youth and adults, spoken-word poetry, hip-hop performances, and other outlets for artistic and creative expression. The summit culminated on Saturday evening with a Day of Action, which featured a march through South LA in support of food justice, youth-led presentations, a press conference at the Mercado La Paloma community center, and a celebratory dance party.

As the codirector of RIC, Gerardo Omar Marin, who goes by Gera, explained, the RIC gathering itself had evolved substantially from the time of its inception. The first several years had been heavily focused on food, farming, and agriculture—a noble and valuable pursuit, but one that seemed to be attracting mostly youth who were already invested in those topics. When Gera, a Mexican-American practitioner of holistic healing arts, took on a leadership role in the organization, he looked to build upon this foundation by expanding RIC's scope of action: "We brought on the arts and the artivism"—a term he defined as using "the arts as tools for social awakening and transformation." He continued: "We did the food, the farming, the permaculture. And now we're all going to culminate together to use this art to inspire each other and to use these tools to go educate our people that are under a spell." Representative of the always intentional, reflexive, and culturally rooted practices of RIC as a whole, Gera stopped himself, adding, "and I would be very critical of the way I use the word 'educate.' I would say [the Spanish word] *educar*, which is 'to pull out.' Basically, to use the arts to inspire and awaken our peoples to give a shit about themselves." With a blend of hands-on food and agricultural learning, artistic activism, and youth-of-color-led dialogues on cultural awakening, Gera told me that the youth of RIC no longer wanted to refer to the annual event as a conference, as they did in its early years. "It's a summit," he said. "It's at the top."

Gera's remarks pointed to what might be described as the other hallmark of RIC: the narratives of deeply held conviction and the strong sense of spirit that permeated the network. RIC operated with a skeleton crew of paid staff—Gera; Kate Casale, the codirector, who supported program planning for local, regional, and national summits; and Maya Salsedo, the youth organizer. Everyone else—from members of RIC's advisory committee to the hosts for its national and regional gatherings—were volunteers, operating based on a commitment to the cause alone. Lacking the type of clearly delineated nonprofit organizational bona fides that major funding agencies tended to prefer—such as an official board of trustees, a certified strategic plan, and evaluated replicable models for success—the fiscal health of RIC was, unsurprisingly, not its strongest asset. Although the RIC advisory committee was thinking through ways to build a more sustainable organization in the future, they were not fearful of any existential threats. Indeed, as Ari, an adult member of the advisory committee, explained, "the spirit is so strong that we never miss a conference, and I don't think we ever will. Because there's such a will for it to happen." For RIC, the basis of that spirit, it was consistently emphasized, was centered in the youth themselves.

YOUTH LEADERS AND COMMUNITY CHANGE

Doron Comerchero, founder of the Santa Cruz County-based FoodWhat?! organization, began attending the RIC annual gathering in its second year of existence and remained integrally involved in the network from that time onward. "I was in this weird phase, where I think I was twenty-one or twenty-two," he explained, describing his initial experience at the RIC gathering. "So, in that space, I was going as an adult, but I was actually much more aligned with youth, both in my energy and my culture at the time." At the 2013 summit in Los Angeles, I listened to a number of adult mentors—a multiracial group, the majority of whom were themselves only in their twenties or thirties and could easily be considered youths in other contexts—work through the meanings, challenges, and opportunities that were embedded in the network's style of organizing. While members of RIC had decided that their focus remained primarily on high school-aged young people, they were reflexive and committed to investigating the foundations of their youth-led approach. They explored many issues: What, exactly, does it mean when we refer to "youth" or a "youth-led movement"? What is the value of placing youth at the center of food justice organizing processes to begin with? What purposes does RIC serve in linking together these youth-focused programs into a national network? What role should adult mentors play as part of this approach, and in what ways can different generations ultimately work together to collectively advance an agenda for food justice transformation?

The experiences and perspectives of Maya, RIC's youth organizer, provide insight into how these questions have been actively pursued and built back into the practices of the network itself. She grew up in Santa Cruz, California, the daughter of a single mom who worked at a farm-to-table restaurant and had a culinary degree but still struggled to provide her child with anything other than inexpensive fast and convenient foods. As a teenager, Maya started working as an intern and junior staff member with FoodWhat?!, and the experience helped her understand the systemic imbalances faced by her mother and others in similar situations. "She knew about nutrition—it wasn't just poor decision-making on her part," Maya said, referring to the food choices that society pushed her mother to make. "And I think that's why the kind of food justice and access lens resonated with me—recognizing that my family or my mom wasn't to blame for our poor nutrition." When the RIC summit came to the Bay Area in 2008, Maya took on a major role in the organizing process. Shortly thereafter, RIC brought her on board as its first paid youth organizer, a position she held while she pursued her college education. A few years later, she became a staff member with the Oakland-based organization Planting Justice. "She and I are now peers," Doron, who had introduced Maya to food justice work years before at FoodWhat?!, reflected. "That's part of the model."

Maya was a leading and devoted advocate for RIC, an entity that she believed helped construct a shared and expansive community-based identity for lower-income young people, youth of color, and the organizations with which they worked on food justice issues. "We help youth to see their role in their local organizations as part of a bigger movement of youth," she explained. The efforts of RIC helped solidify an understanding that, in Maya's words, "it's the same system that's affecting our community in West Oakland as [the one that's affecting] the youth from Raleigh, North Carolina." It was this systems-based framework of analysis—one that emphasized widespread and common histories of social injustice—that validated RIC's purpose. "Sometimes in our local level, we're looking at just our local community," Maya continued. "It's easy to see lots of different reasons, or locally specific reasons, for injustice in the food system. But I think when we look at it in the national framework, it helps youth to really understand the root causes more."

The geographic and cultural contextualization of food injustice provided RIC participants with a connection to common legacies of discrimination and resistance. The network's emphasis on unearthing the knowledge and capacities of its participants—an imagined community of historically marginalized youth activists—was seen to be fundamental to the broader vision of the movement. But accomplishing this offered its own unique challenge, especially because the stories told about youth in general, and specifically youth of color, often remained grounded in stigmatizing assumptions. As civic media scholar Sasha Costanza-Chock articulated, although "young people are often key actors in powerful social movements that transform the course of human history," they "are often framed in the mass media as, at best, apathetic, disengaged, and removed from civic action. At worst, youth (in the U.S., particularly youth of color) are subject to growing repression" (1).[7]

In order to advance a youth-focused vision of community development, members of RIC consistently emphasized the youth-led nature of the network as an intentional and elemental part of its approach. "A lot of programs that talk about youth leadership and things like this, they can also be tokenizing for youth. It's really an adult planning everything," Doron explained. But, he continued, "when you look at the nature of the RIC conference, there may be 150 people, and the ratios are one adult for every four youth. That is a youth-dominant space." Zoe, also a member of the RIC advisory council, was among several other adult staff members who expressed displeasure with the tokenizing nature of many youth-oriented programs. RIC, by contrast, took seriously the knowledge practices of young people themselves, institutionalizing this belief by placing youth in positions of leadership and consistently integrating methods of peer-to-peer and popular education into their practices. "It really felt like it was this place where there were other youth organizers who understood how youth empowerment really only happens by helping to facilitate them doing things," Zoe explained.[8]

To hearken back to a concept articulated in the previous chapter of this book, RIC offered an outlet for youth to develop what might be termed a *civic epistemology* related to food injustice and organizing for social change.[9] RIC provided low-income youth and youth of color—who were often the "target" of health-related interventions, but who rarely had the chance to guide such initiatives themselves—with a space for storytelling and strategizing. With that said, just as my observations in chapter 3 led me to declare that it was a plural notion of *civic epistemologies* that best described the community-based work of CSU, my analysis here suggests that the youth-led nature of RIC was not quite as clear-cut as it might seem from the outside. As I came to understand, a term like *youth-led* did not fully encapsulate the complexity that characterized the intergenerational, iterative, and sometimes contested process of knowledge production that was really at the heart of the RIC network.

I saw ongoing tensions between youth-led activism and adult priority-setting play out in a variety of ways during the preparations for the RIC summit in South LA and the event itself. I was present, for instance, at a meeting with CSU staff and board members several months before the summit, when we began to brainstorm ideas for the theme. In that moment, our conversation moved toward a focus on the importance of having access to and control of *land* as a fundamental building block for any effort to advance social, economic, and environmental justice. From colonial expansion to contemporary processes of gentrification, communities of color have long been exploited through unconscionable acts in which local residents are divested from enjoying the full physical and cultural benefits of their own homelands.[10] As our conversation continued, several permutations of a potential tag line for the summit were offered before Reclaiming Our Land, Reclaiming Our Roots was selected as the guiding theme.

Flash forward several months to the opening ceremonies of the RIC summit. A group of CSU interns were center stage, facing the hundred-plus youth and adult participants and backed by a large projection screen displaying a PowerPoint presentation. They explained the theme of the conference, and in doing so they explored historical and contemporary instances of "land grabbing" in communities of color across the globe. The screen flashed maps and photos of the loss of Palestinian land to Israeli development from 1947 onward.

The youth interns continued with examples from India, explaining how the Monsanto Company's aggressive patenting of seeds had brought forth a rash of indigenous farmer suicides. Next, they described land grabbing in their own backyard, criticizing the University of Southern California—an institution that, quite interestingly, was hosting the visiting youth in dorms and serving as a site for a full day of RIC workshops—for its development practices in the community, which were forcing out long-tenured residents on account of rising rents.[11]

As I listened and watched these youth give testimony to the assembled RIC community, I could not help but ponder the implications of the presentation for the youth-led ethos of both CSU and the RIC network. The topic of land grabbing was one that had undoubtedly resonated with both the CSU interns and the other youth who had come to South LA from around the country. Indeed, it was a theme that became woven into many of the workshops, conversations, and field trips that would follow in the coming days—some of them collaboratively led by youth participants—as members of the collective shared their experiences facing issues of land access and power within their own communities. However, the theme had not initially emerged from the priorities of the youth themselves. "I didn't even know about it before. I didn't even know what land grabbing was," Stephanie, a youth-intern-turned-staff-member of CSU explained to me. "I didn't even know that people were making plans to build something that wouldn't benefit the community, only for people who had money." Yet Stephanie and her youth colleague Carlos both expressed to me that the experience of conducting research and developing an interactive workshop—all under the collaborative guidance of adult mentors, myself included—was conceptually and pragmatically valuable. "It taught me how to lead a conversation," Carlos explained, "and how to help a group that I'm facilitating reach that point that I want them to reach."

Another example of this process of intergenerational negotiation comes from the RIC advisory committee, which was created under the fiscal sponsorship of the Earth Island Institute. RIC's bylaws stipulate that its advisory group must include a majority adult membership, although several spaces are reserved for youth. On a recent organizational vote, however, all of the adult members found themselves aligned on the opposite side of the youth. Because adults were in the majority in the committee, it was ultimately their perspective that held sway. In this particular instance, the issue at hand was procedural in nature and did not hold a great deal of import for the broader strategic action of RIC. Still, the conflict pointed to an underlying tension at play. "We say we're a youth-run organization and we say we care about youth voices," Ari, an adult member of the committee, explained. "How are we not tokenizing their voice when we go against what they're telling us?" Consistent with the always-evolving and ever-intentional practices of the network, the conflict itself served as a point for internal critical reflection. "It was a good conversation," Ari continued. "I think it's not done. I think it's a conversation we'll continue to have and continue to be a part of what we process."

Did these iterative processes of knowledge production and contestation call into question the youth-led nature of CSU, RIC, and the broader movement for youth food justice? Or did they simply call for a more nuanced understanding of what youth-led really meant, of how youth leadership could best be engendered, and what the optimal relationship between adult mentors and youth leaders should ultimately be? To the credit of both CSU and members of RIC, these questions were actively considered and debated. As Doron explained: "Part of how RIC lives out the youth empowerment piece is that there is a youth team with really strong adult—or let's call it intergenerational—partnership to help realize that vision. And I think if we were to do any kind of movement theory analysis, we would see there was no one generation who did anything in isolation. . . . Whatever it may be, it was always in concert and in allyship with many, many other generations."

Discussions about these exchanges were part of a broader ethos of intentionality and reflexivity that characterized the core of RIC. It was a process that was not always the most efficient. As several adult staffers of RIC pointed out, for example, if their aim was to grow as much food through urban agriculture as possible, a youth development program was not necessarily the way to do it. But while growing food was important, cultivating indigenous leaders who could envision a just, equitable, and sustainable future was the real goal. By linking localized groups together into a networked common cause— through collaborative storytelling about food and justice and engaging in intergenerational discussions of social movement history—several of the core philosophical foundations for sustainable community change were put in place. "Youth have a voice," Celeste, a youth member of the RIC advisory committee, explained to me. "Even though we're kind of young compared to others, we still have knowledge, and the knowledge that we have can benefit everyone. And through the work of being intergenerational—working with teenagers, working with kids, working with people in their thirties and ranging all through there—we can make the job that we all want to do better." In

FIGURE 9. Neelam Sharma, CSU's executive director, serves dinner alongside other staff and volunteers from CSU and Rooted in Community during the RIC summit in Los Angeles in 2013. Photograph by Sahra Sulaiman.

practice, what came to the fore at RIC gatherings were sets of dynamic and interrelated civic epistemologies that combined the voices of youth and adults of varied ages, ethnicities, and geographical backgrounds. While at times a source of contestation and debate, this hybrid praxis of youth-oriented food justice activism was actually a fundamental piece of RIC's emergent collective identity, providing a foundation for a movement that hoped to scale up its cultural and institutional impacts in the years to come.

BUILDING A MOVE-ENTITY

If creating a networked vision for change among youth participants was step one of RIC's organizing process, step two focused on building the actionable capacity of those youth leaders in order to develop and sustain a movement agenda moving forward. Participants hoped that their local and national organizational efforts could simultaneously change the stories youth told about themselves, change the types of stories that were told about youth by others, and give youth practical tools to reshape the institutions around them

FIGURE 10. This flyer advertised the Day of Action events held during the final evening of the Rooted in Community summit in Los Angeles in 2013. Flyer by Community Services Unlimited and Duce.

to achieve greater justice and sustainability. "People don't really see youth as being engaged or being passionate about something. They just see them as just, kind of like, just there," CSU intern-turned-staffer Carlos observed. "But when they're actually fighting for something, I think it sends an impact."

Making this leap, however—from vision to sustained action—should not be considered an easy task. Notably, the fact that the burgeoning movement for food justice is characterized by significant diversity—both the geographic, ethnic, and economic diversity of its membership and the diversity of its basic organizing strategies—complicates its ability to develop consensus. Indeed, among scholars and practitioners engaged in food justice work today, the only consensus seems to be an agreement that the movement stands at a pivotal moment of opportunity. Actions taken in the next few years will help determine whether food justice will emerge as a substantive force for large-scale social transformation or whether its impacts will be limited to localized alterations to the status quo.[12]

As I detailed in full in chapter 1, RIC was one of several networks that has been formed since the early 2000s with an aim to help push the food justice movement forward. RIC's belief that young people must play a prominent role in expanding the movement was shared by many of the groups in this networked field of activism, even if actual youth involvement was more substantive in RIC than in many of the other organizational initiatives. Anim Steel is a well-known food justice activist who once served as the director of national programs for The Food Project, was on the ground floor of RIC, and later launched the Live Real community and founded the college-focused Real Food Challenge. "To become a strong, national force, the food justice movement needs a youth-led organization that unifies and amplifies these disparate efforts," he argued in an essay. "Such an organization should celebrate and encourage the diversity of local work; the best local solutions come from local communities. But it should do what local organizations often have a harder time doing: focus the national spotlight, spread innovation, involve masses of people, and harness our collective political and economic power" (120).[13]

As I spent time collaborating with and speaking to members of the RIC network, I asked myself whether it would ever be able to develop into the type of organization that Steel and others saw as necessary for systemic change to take place. I also wondered whether any single entity could ever live up to such movement-building expectations and what consequences expanding food justice activism in this manner would have for the work of community-based practitioners. What I found was that these very questions were being actively explored by organizers involved in the network. "We've got all this power, all this potential," Gera, one of RIC's codirectors, explained. "And we're actually really just aligning right now and strategizing how to channel it." The organization was concerned with shifting the institutional and policy-related dynamics of the food system, on one hand, and transforming societal mindsets related to food and culture, on the other. They sought to develop plans for a youth-led movement for food justice that could be scaled up to achieve more widespread influence but that would also stay true to its community-based ethos of empowerment from the ground up.

In its early days of existence, RIC certainly did not clear this high bar for movement-building. As Doron explained, "when RIC started, it was more of a straight, old-school—we are a collective. We are all these different organizations who come together and share something, and our youth get something out of it." Yet RIC shifted and broadened its scope and practices over time—its conference became a summit, it incorporated artivism in addition to food and farming, and it expanded its membership to connect with more youth from across the nation. These extensions demonstrated that the local member groups involved in RIC were developing a greater willingness to grow their community-focused activities into something larger. In the eyes of members like Doron, RIC had evolved into an institution that was part movement and part entity. "If I were to try to encapsulate RIC in one word, I would think of it as a move-entity," he explained. "Because it's not quite an organization, and it's not only a collective. It's a space, and it's a way of interacting with youth, and a way of interacting with the food system, and a way of interacting as humans. And that is newer—and it's unique and powerful."[14]

This organization of organizations—the move-entity, if you will—was very much still in the process of figuring out what type of structure could best move its aims forward. "There hasn't been a ton of investment made in an organizational infrastructure for RIC," Zoe, an adult leader on the RIC advisory committee, explained. "Which, on one hand can be seen as, well, that's great—it just means it's grassroots-led and volunteer-led. Which is great, but it also means it has capacity issues." Consistent with the reflexivity and intentionality that characterized RIC as a whole, adult mentors were torn regarding the costs and benefits that came with further institutionalization. Some wondered whether this would simply be a first step toward integration into the growing "nonprofit industrial complex" of food activism. Many also expressed deep concern about what might be lost if community-based groups—those that had been leading the food justice charge for years, developing localized strategies for change and cultivating youth leadership from within marginalized communities themselves—were pushed to channel their efforts through a national-level bureaucracy.

I clearly saw these tensions in the work of CSU, an organization that had been involved in a number of national and international collaborations over the years but had scaled back to the point that RIC was now the primary avenue through which it connected to organizing outside of South LA. "We felt like we needed to take a step back," Neelam explained, "because we were building all of this in our community. We needed to be able to have this all be set up, have people who are skilled to be up and running this. And from there I think we can step back in." Leaders of RIC were struggling to figure out the best way they could productively engage with these dynamics. "Do we want to cast a wide net and be the kind of supportive network that hosts leadership development conferences and gives support at the local level to our network of organizations but really puts the local organizations center stage in terms of proactive stuff?" Zoe wondered. "Or, do we want to be the kind of body that has a kind of core of staff and infrastructure that allows it to be a little more proactive and kind of centralized?"

Even with these fundamental questions and their possible solutions still open for debate and experimentation, RIC did demonstrate several characteristics that suggested it was, indeed, helping to push forward a nascent national movement for change. As I have already illustrated, RIC served first and foremost as a space in which young people from diverse backgrounds could come to see their work playing a role in a broader youth-led agenda. The benefits of participation, however, were not isolated to the youth participants alone. The annual summit, coupled with smaller regional gatherings throughout the year and online spaces for resource sharing, also allowed the insights of localized groups to spread and be adapted by community-based staffers from across the nation. This networked strategy helped local groups develop, fund, and sustain their community-based programming over time. Lawrence, CSU's youth coordinator, was one of many adult mentors who pointed to RIC events and the RIC Tool Shed—an online compendium of curriculum materials—as providing a variety of practical benefits for their youth development work. "CSU has always been involved in working with youth, but I've learned a lot from RIC, specifically a lot more in the programmatic area," he shared. "As far as relating to youth, and little things, like playing games with youth, getting them excited about the program, how to recruit youth."

This collaborative knowledge sharing also provided a route through which a diversity of models for youth and community development programs could be introduced and championed. At the RIC gathering in South LA, for instance, Growing Power's Will Allen took the stage to discuss his vision of the future of food justice. He argued that it was *jobs* that young people of color needed most, and it was jobs that community-based food projects like Growing Power and others could provide. Once given a steady paycheck, he suggested, youth could continue to build their critical consciousness and become more engaged in the broader movement. Allen was joined on stage by several young activists, each of whom told the story of their own model for community-based change. Several of the speakers were committed to direct action and popular education techniques, skills that they had honed while advocating with and for the rights of immigrant farmworkers. Others echoed Allen in providing outlines of models that encouraged local economic development through food-based social enterprises. Taken together, the intent was to demonstrate the different forms that activism could take, communicating to youth and adult participants alike that there were multiple strategies that had the potential to bend the structures of the food system toward justice and sustainability. "I want to see twenty-five models throughout the nation," Gera explained. When other organizations heard the stories of Growing Power, CSU, and other successful initiatives that had been building capacity for years or decades, the hope and expectation was that this storytelling would, in Gera's words, "inspire other youth programs nationwide."

RIC also aimed to strike a chord in the cultural heart of food system activists. Indeed, the group was dedicated to a style of organizing that took racial and social justice seriously, a quality that set them apart from much of the mainstream in the alternative food movements, not to mention the often conflict-averse and colorblind world of youth empowerment projects.[15] The conceptual framework that was built into the core of RIC's activities attracted like-minded organizers who were guided by similar justice-oriented commitments, and it had the potential to shift the practices of community-based groups that were still struggling to understand the place of racial and social justice issues in their everyday work. "I was one of those youth organizers who was going to environmental conferences and not finding people of color," Zoe explained to me. "I mean, there were a lot of white affluent folks who were talking about our community, but I was just not finding our community there." Through RIC, Zoe and other organizers discovered that there were indeed others with a similar dedication to a people-of-color-led style of food justice organizing. They were able to build relationships with new friends and collaborators from across the nation and were energized by a sense of cultural empowerment that helped motivate them to deepen their community-based activism. "As a youth organizer, I needed RIC to succeed and flourish."

The culturally rooted, people-of-color-led approach that characterized RIC had a primary aim of cultivating and sustaining leadership within those communities that had long been marginalized by food injustice and other systemic inequities. At the same time, members of the network also saw that they could play a key role in reshaping the perspectives of white allies, potentially shifting the dial toward greater social justice from within the "nonprofit industrial complex" itself. Conversations about race, privilege, and collaboration were embedded in the gatherings and tools of RIC, and RIC staff members were increasingly being asked to lead antiracist trainings and provide support for white organizers who wanted to improve their understandings of the issues at hand. "That means talking about white privilege, white supremacy, talking about what it means to be an ally and a mentor," Maya explained. She recounted an instance in which she had presented the work of RIC at a conference on food activism and was approached by a white staff member from another organization that worked with African American youth. "He took us aside and asked us, specifically, like, 'I want to be able to relate to the youth I work with more. And I see it as a barrier to the work that I do.'" Maya saw the conversation and other interactions like it as an example that RIC was helping to shift a culture of food activism that had been dominated in the United States by the voices and perspectives of privileged whites. "It's just another affirmation around the work we're doing with antiracist training and mentor training that the social justice lens in this national work is so important for us to do," Maya concluded.

Through its evolving structure and practices, the RIC move-entity showed signs that its vision of community-based food justice might grow into a larger force for change. By building a national community of local youth leaders, sharing programmatic knowledge across organizational forms, and placing racial justice concerns onto the agenda of white-led nonprofits, the contours of movement-building were taking shape. However, if the organization was to clear the lofty bar set by some of the leaders of its own movement—that is, in the words of Anim Steel, being able to "focus the national spotlight, spread innovation, involve masses of people, and harness our collective political and economic power"—clearly more work needed to be done.[16]

POLICY ADVOCACY, STORYTELLING, AND THE YOUTH FOOD BILL OF RIGHTS

Sympathetic critics of food justice organizing insist that, like other community-based alternative food movement efforts, the approach too often works around the edges of entrenched food injustice. Alternative food organizations have been chided for focusing too much on local initiatives, reinforcing neoliberal market-based strategies for change, and shying away from the types of major policy initiatives that might ensure long-term health, equity, and sustainability across the entire food system.[17] At the same time, a number of scholars and practitioners have expressed hope that the emerging food justice movement might be able to provide a productive counter-force to these trends.[18] Scholars such as Alison Hope Alkon and Teresa Mares, for instance, have argued that food justice groups that incorporate a more radical perspective of food sovereignty into their practices—a perspective that is deeply critical of contemporary capitalism's role in perpetuating racialized food injustice—might be able to connect networks of local projects "to build power and eventually mobilize for a broad-based transformation of the corporate food regime" (358).[19] In critically analyzing the overall effectiveness of RIC, these questions of scale and impact always lingered. Operating as it was, largely "in the shadow of the shadow state," could RIC ever have the power to shift the narratives and networks of the industrialized food system? Could it encourage community-based food justice organizers to develop the willingness and capacity required to lead an effective movement forward?

RIC participants pointed to several developing avenues for policy advocacy and media storytelling that they hoped would do just that. The Youth Food Bill of Rights (YFBR)—created at the 2011 RIC summit in Philadelphia—was consistently offered up as a primary example of such an initiative. As a living artifact and a call to action, the YFBR was seen as encapsulating the youth-driven ethos of RIC as an entity at the same time as it provided a central set of principles around which a broader youth-led movement for food justice could coalesce. Composed in the same city in which the Declaration of Independence and the US Constitution were signed, the initial idea was spearheaded by members of the host organization for that summer's summit—the Agatston Urban Nutrition Initiative—and was conceptualized in part as a response to the federal Farm Bill that was set to be introduced that year. While adult mentors waited in a separate room, the more than 125 youth in attendance gathered to craft the contents of the YFBR themselves. The young people broke into small groups to discuss the work of their own local organizations and to come up with a set of guiding statements upon which they could all agree. Consistent with RIC's intergenerational spirit of collaboration, the adult mentors were then brought back into the room to help refine the document's language, but as Celeste, a participant in the process, explained to me, "the foundation was from the youth," and only minor alterations were made after the adults provided feedback. "In order to reshape our broken food system," the final version of the YFBR opens, "we the youth have come together to name our rights." The list of seventeen demands and attendant descriptions each begins the same way: "We have the right to . . . " The document calls for the right to culturally affirming, sustainable, poison-free, and fair food; the right to nutritional and leadership education; the right to cultivate unused land and to save seeds; the right to good food subsidies; and the right to support farmers through direct market transactions.

Sent out as part of a press release, distributed digitally to friends and colleagues of the RIC network, and accessible online at www.youthfoodbill ofrights.com, the YFBR concludes: "This is only the beginning step in many to come to make our visions, our dreams, and this bill a reality."[20] In the years since the YFBR was created, the staff and mentors of RIC have actively woven the principles of the document into the network's activities. At subsequent summer summits, for instance, the YFBR has been used as a way to guide conversations, build collective identity among participants, and engage community-based groups in projects that are linked through networked action. It has functioned as an antidote to a common criticism of youth summits like RIC's—that is, that three or four days in the rarified air of youth solidarity and relationship-building is a nice experience, but not one that is parlayed into sustained action outside of that venue.[21] "The Youth Food Bill of Rights is this set of goals that we all agreed to, that youth came up with, and that we can all work together to move forward on," adult mentor Ari explained. She described how her youth returned from RIC to their hometown of Camden, New Jersey, energized to follow through with a YFBR-inspired project involving corner markets: "When my youth came back after the conference, they were so psyched. They shared that with other youth, all of them worked on the research project and we did it. And part of the reason they were excited to do it was because they knew they were part of this bigger effort. And even though ours was just about corner stores in Camden—it wasn't about corner stores everywhere—but if other groups were doing corner stores in their own neighborhood, then we could be part of this bigger thing."

The YFBR was also seen as providing a potential tool through which RIC could better tell its story of food justice to larger and more diverse audiences. The initial launch garnered some media attention in the local Philadelphia area, and the principles and a short YouTube video about the process were digitally shared by a number of friends and allies involved in food, agriculture, and youth development work.[22] Furthermore, youth were encouraged by their adult mentors to use the demands of the YFBR as an inspiration for their own creative and artistic expression. "When it's presented with art, it gets them excited. They want to get into it. They recognize this is revolutionary," Gera explained. "There's a big thing coming through with the hip hop culture piece. We're asking people what do they want—in the arts, in the celebration? Because it's got to be fun, it's got to be dope, it's got to compete with other shit going on in the streets." This attitude was on full display at the 2013 summit in Los Angeles as dozens of youth took to the stage on the final night of the conference at the conclusion of their Day of Action to present their perspectives through skits, spoken-word poetry, and other performances. Participants held court with their hip-hop stylings, which were recorded by other RIC participants and later uploaded to YouTube. One young man rhymed: "We in the midst of changes / We need better education / 'Cause this ignorance is dangerous. / No thanks to corporations, / Or your local petro-stations, / We're facin' incineration. / Let's prepare this generation."[23]

While it is easy to be inspired by the energy of this youth activism, it is important to note that the ultimate influence of RIC and its YFBR initiative have remained quite limited. Indeed, while artivism and performance was increasingly being built into the activities of RIC and its youth participants and members of RIC were increasingly being asked to speak about their work and lead antiracist trainings for food movement groups, it was still a struggle to get these stories told to wider audiences and throughout popular culture. Participants were disappointed by the fact that their on-the-ground and social media activity did not get picked up by mainstream media that could help shape a national discussion. "The people who are getting media coverage are the people who are already getting media coverage," Maya reflected. Too often, she said, the conversation at the national level was dominated by folks like Jamie Oliver and Michelle Obama—who, although they were potential allies for the movement, were hardly authentic voices of youth food justice themselves, and whose influence could potentially overshadow community-based social justice activism because it represented a "safer" type of food politics. RIC was faced with the task of trying to navigate in this space while staying true to its principles. As Ari explained: "None of us are celebrities. So I think there's this weird struggle of, how much is it worth using these celebrities we have connections with to try to bolster RIC in this national lens, a media lens? Is that a benefit? Or is the grassroots-ness of RIC so important to its identity that it's kind of selling out to use celebrities and their status to get our message and idea across?"

Notably, the skeleton crew of RIC's organizational structure lacked an effective infrastructure devoted to media relations—a topic I touched on when describing the localized work of CSU in the previous chapter and will explore in more detail in chapter 6. With this in mind, in the lead-up to the 2013 summit in South LA, I offered my own services to help craft a press release, working in collaboration with the staff of RIC, CSU, and the other partners involved in the event. Ultimately, however, our push to grab media attention was constrained by a combination of the generalized disinterest of the media in the story and a lack of intensive follow-through on our part. With so many other things we needed to accomplish in the days leading up to the summit and without dedicated staff members with expertise in media relations, it was easy for media storytelling to fall by the wayside.

This was clear on the final day of the summit—the Day of Action—when youth participants led a march through the streets of South LA. "Ain't no power like the power of the youth, cause the power of the youth don't stop!" they chanted, dressed in matching T-shirts, some banging on drums and others holding signs that highlighted the principles of the YFBR. The march began at a local Wendy's fast food restaurant, where a member of the Student/Farmworker Alliance announced that the participants of the summit were standing in solidarity with the Coalition of Immokalee Workers, a Florida-based farm labor group that was demanding the corporation do more to protect their rights.[24] Later, the marchers delivered a press conference at the nearby Mercado la Paloma, where energized young people stood on a make-shift stage to express the demands of the YFBR to a crowded room of inter-ested and eager listeners. Members of the press itself, however, were hard to find during the Day of Action. A single profile of the event was written by a South LA–based journalist with a deep commitment to social justice issues in the area and a history of collaboration with CSU.[25] While compelling and appreciated, the lone article hardly had a reach that could match the enthu-siastic goals RIC had set out to achieve across the broader culture.

Paralleling their struggles to get media attention, RIC faced additional challenges in the policy domain. As the food justice perspective has gained resonance within communities across the United States, many scholars and practitioners have seen commitment to the policy arena as the logical and necessary next step for action. What has taken shape, in large part, has been engagement in policy conversations and actions at local institutional levels. Youth-led food justice groups have successfully lobbied for menu changes in schools, for instance, and food justice organizations have increasingly become involved in food policy councils at the municipal or state level.[26] In practice, however, even these initiatives have been critiqued for not tackling the fundamental policy issues that create risk and injustice in the contemporary food system. Instead, they tend to bolster the types of entrepreneurial and community access oriented programs and strategies for change that have become increasingly common in these domains.[27] In the words of scholar Julie Guthman, this community-based food justice approach "still does not fundamentally challenge the dynamics that cause the vast majority of Americans to eat vacuous food and to be exposed to appreciable amounts of toxins by dint of the way most food is produced" (141).[28]

Members of the RIC network had hoped to make the demands of the YFBR a reality, and they understood that engagement in policy—at local and national levels—offered a key avenue through which such principles could be institutionalized. Importantly, however, they did not want their move-entity's agenda to provide an overdetermined characterization of what food justice activism could and should be in the years to come. "Policy work is a natural evolution of where folks could go, but it's not the defining one," Doron explained. "I think it's just about allowing for more sophistication within our community of organizations, and within the youth community, to engage in politics." Heather Fenney Alexander, CSU's associate director, who worked on local and national food and agricultural policy issues before coming to the organization, reflected, "I think, at different times, me personally, I've been on both of those sides. I don't have that personal feeling of, like, it *has* to happen on the ground, or it *has* to happen in policy. I think both are important."

CSU had chosen to largely retreat from direct policy engagement in order to focus its attention on community-based initiatives. This is not to say that policy was entirely outside of the organization's purview. Neelam, for one, was a key member of the coalition that pushed forward a "soda ban" that was adopted by the Los Angeles Unified School District in the early 2000s; Dyane had served for a time as a member of a South LA neighborhood council; and CSU had occasional interactions with the newly established LA Food Policy Council and had built relationships over the years with a host of Los Angeles City councilpersons, state senators, statewide policy advocates, city planners, and other elected officials. Kwaku Duren, who founded CSU as the nonprofit arm of the Southern California chapter of the Black Panther Party, had long advocated for policy engagement that might advance community organizing and economic development. In an interview, he insisted that a group like CSU "cannot separate itself from the political realities, and it has to be engaged in one way or another with those political realities." But he added, "I think it takes a different type of vehicle to ultimately bring the political change that's necessary."

Over the years, CSU staffers got frustrated by the tedious and time-consuming nature of policy advocacy as a whole. Having worked on food justice issues for over a decade, they had seen various local and city policy initiatives related to food production, procurement, and access come and go, often accomplishing little, in their estimation, to impact the daily lives of local residents. CSU suggested that, rather than spend all day sitting in a meeting near City Hall, they would be happy to have folks come to *their* South LA headquarters to see the progress they had made and to talk about ways that policy changes could boost their efforts. Heather explained that policy change was no panacea in communities like South LA: "No matter what the policies are, if people don't have the knowledge, the skills, the resources, they're not going to realize the benefits from that."

In the minds of CSU staff and many other members of the RIC network, the key strategic move was not to jump in fully at either the local or national level of policymaking but rather to be sure that their base of community-based action was developed before their organizational activities fully evolved into those areas. Only with this foundation in place could they be able to tell their story in such a way that would meet the demands and expectations of the contemporary social, political, and economic climate. That is to say, in order to shift cultural narratives and structural networks on a broader scale, these community-based food justice activists believed they first had to clearly demonstrate that goals had been achieved in their local community of practice. "People will not support you unless they see what you're doing is actually making an impact," Neelam argued. "If you're going to move into the political system, you better be damn sure you're coming from a place of real strength. From a place of community support, with the community really understanding what you're about. Because when we go into the political system, we ain't coming to lose. We'll be coming from a place of political strength."

In a landscape of community-based food justice, in which local action predominated, the RIC network represented a valuable medium through which a broader agenda for change could be advanced. And, while staff and youth participants alike were proud to champion the productive possibilities and outcomes that had taken shape through RIC's activities in recent years, they were also cognizant of the fundamental challenges and tensions they faced as they endeavored to scale up their impact. Like the food justice movement as a whole, RIC was a work in progress in a moment of growth, opportunity, and evolution, and participants remained consciously reflexive about the potentials and perils of their efforts. It is this type of reflexivity itself that alternative food scholars such as David Goodman, E. Melanie DuPuis, and Michael Goodman identified as central to the contours of a just food movement: "What reflexivity does, as a process, is to ask groups to go beyond their own shared visions, values and carings and to participate in larger, cross-solidarity, collaborative modes of social change."[29] Based in this process-oriented perspective, RIC hoped and expected to bring the stories, programs, and policies of community-based and youth-led food justice activism into ever larger and influential domains in the years to come. At the same time, they remained guided by a set of principles and perspectives that simultaneously energized their actions and, in some ways, constrained their very viability as an effective counterweight to systemic injustice. "There's a spirit to Rooted in Community, of multicultural community and love and inspiration," Gera offered. "And we have to combine forces now—the youth with the elders and all of these generations together."

· · ·

For the dedicated food justice activists of CSU and the RIC network at large, there was no shame in focusing their efforts at the level of the local community. The community offered a space in which civic epistemologies related to food and justice could be cultivated, supportive institutional structures that encouraged healthy lifestyles could be constructed, and historically stigmatized youth of color could build the skills of empowerment needed to lead the charge for community development—now and in the future. Yet the organizations involved in RIC recognized that conceptualizing their activism as isolated within their local communities alone would necessarily abstract their efforts from the systemic social inequity that they aimed to counter.

Part of a broader field of organizational networks that had begun to channel community-based action into collective power, RIC hoped that it could operate as a move-entity to build momentum for political and cultural change. Involvement in RIC allowed both youth and adult practitioners to see that their own community-based struggles were connected to histories of systemic inequity that went well beyond their respective cities and neighborhoods. Engagement in RIC granted CSU and the other community-based organizations involved in the network an opportunity to spread their local models for change, learn from like-minded activists, and ultimately reshape the cultural and structural dynamics of broader society toward social justice and sustainability.

Participation in the network also brought to light several enduring tensions that were inherent in the community-based food justice organizing process. The navigation of challenges such as finding the right mix of youth leadership and adult priority-setting, balancing the demands of localized work with the potentials of national coalition-building, and influencing cultural storytelling and policymaking on broader scales was fundamental to the evolving hybrid praxis that characterized food justice work. Members of the RIC network saw these tensions as productive forces that called for reflexivity and careful consideration. "We do everything with intentionality and from the heart," Ari, a RIC advisory committee member, explained.

At the time of this writing, RIC and its membership continue to balance these various tensions, and the network has not emerged as a powerful collective voice in media or an influential actor in policy circles. This could be read as confirmation of some of the central critiques of community-based food justice. The ethos of the movement has been criticized for lacking both a willingness and a capacity to challenge the dynamics of social injustice beyond the local community and across multiple sectors of the food system. Evidence from this chapter suggests that this critique certainly carries some weight, and the practitioners of CSU and RIC themselves are aware of the limitations of their own approach. Still, it remains important to recognize that widespread changes to cultural norms and national policymaking cannot simply emerge on their own. As the media studies scholar Timothy Gibson has argued, there is a tendency among those who advocate for macro-level approaches to cultural and policy change to overlook the years of hard work required to build grassroots movements, as they assume that "these subaltern groups are always-already organized, always-already unified around particular policy proposals, and thus ready to bend the ear of the policy-making vanguard using the powerful tools of mainstream, polity-wide media coverage" (61).[30] Ultimately, for enduring and unjust food system networks and narratives to be shifted, the efforts of activists and advocates must be grounded in the interests, needs, and desires of local community constituents, whose voices must be recognized and energized to demand that a change is needed. It is work that requires time, commitment, funding, and expertise.

From the perspective of RIC and member groups like CSU, the voices and energy of young people can lead this charge toward food system transformation.

Of course, with low-income youth and youth of color facing such entrenched injustice on a daily basis—in the food system and beyond—one could easily write off this youth-led community activism as merely working around the margins. One could also overstate the liberatory power and potential of these programs, overlooking the enduring constraints that will undoubtedly take years or generations to overcome. The truth that I found in my explorations of these initiatives was somewhere in between—activists were both optimistic and realistic, focused on community action but always cognizant of the broader dynamics at play. Neelam explained the goal of CSU's youth programs: "Using food as a lens to get them to think critically, get them to look at the world critically, to see the power in themselves—if we do that, and we succeed in doing that, then all is good."

Youth-led food justice organizing was never billed as a cure-all or offered as a magical solution to structural inequity or enduring stigmatization. As this chapter has demonstrated, there is still significant progress to be made if a youth-led strategy is to play any major role within a long-term agenda for sustainable food system change. Yet its advocates remain committed to the notion that, if the movement has any opportunity to sprout and to thrive, the *community* offers the most fertile soil in which its seeds could be planted.

From the Black Panthers
to the USDA

It was a busy Saturday morning in April for the staff, youth interns, and volunteers of Community Services Unlimited (CSU). Out on the playground of South LA's Normandie Avenue Elementary School, over one hundred college students stood in small groups, waiting for some direction as to what they would be doing during their university-organized day of service. In a small trailer-turned-classroom, five high-school-aged interns sat, ready for their first day of training with CSU leadership. For the college volunteers, a brief orientation and explanation of the history and mission of CSU was in order before they were sent out to canvass the neighborhood with flyers publicizing CSU's upcoming Earth Day South LA event. The interns were in line for a more in-depth conversation. They would be expected to learn enough in the coming weeks about CSU's values, visions, and activities to become qualified youth staff members for the community-based group.

At the center of these parallel but distinct orientations were two key stories. First, CSU staff explained that South Los Angeles had historically experienced significant racial and economic discrimination and disinvestment. That legacy was quite clearly illustrated by the countless fast food restaurants lining the streets, the lack of healthy food options that were available to community members, and a host of other troubling social, economic, and health-related indicators. All of these injustices had long been acknowledged to exist in the neighborhood, but CSU had systematically confirmed them when they conducted a Community Food Assessment in the early 2000s. Importantly, however, such enduring historical inequities had never been acceptable to community members. There was a second, equally significant, story to be told about those neighborhood residents who, for decades, had actively and collectively worked to overcome the challenges faced by their community. As staff members described, CSU itself was created as the non-profit arm of the Southern California chapter of the Black Panther Party. Today, the organization still carries on the party's legacy of "serving the people, body and soul," through the development of community-based programs. Neelam, CSU's executive director, spoke to the group of youth interns: "You barely know about them, but at one point there were five thousand full-time organizers working for the Black Panther Party. That's a pretty big deal, and it's been sort of washed away from the history books. When you do hear about them, it's usually about guns or violence. But the party was about much more than that."

When CSU described the mission and practice of its work, these two tales were almost always prominently featured together in the introduction. I found the pairing of these narratives a telling and, initially, somewhat confusing example. References to the Black Panther Party (BPP) stirred up notions of Black Power, revolutionary activism, and political controversy. On the other hand, mentions of the Community Food Assessment—a governmental strategy of community-based evaluation that I had learned about while reading urban planning literature—made me think of wonky urban policy discussions and the fastidious audit requirements of contemporary funding agencies. As I would come to understand, however, these complementary, and in some ways contradictory, stories of origin were actually fundamental to CSU's organizational development. Indeed, the BPP's political ideology and legacy of community-based programming provided a historical foundation for CSU's organizational identity, helping to solidify CSU's status as a social justice organization committed to the people and places of South LA. Yet the BPP's influence hardly told the entire story of how CSU had come to conduct its food justice work in the present day. References to the Community Food Assessment, therefore, were evidence of the multitude of other external forces, embedded into the organization over years of practice as a nonprofit group, that had helped to shape its strategy, philosophy, and actions in the twenty-first century.

This chapter focuses on these hybridized cultural and historical dynamics. Previous chapters of this book have used ethnographic research to provide insight into the everyday practices of community-based food justice organizers and explore how networked connections between local food justice groups might extend the impact of the broader food justice movement. Here, I take a longer view, returning to discuss the work of CSU in depth to uncover the path through which its strategic action was shaped over time.

Every community-based food justice group has its own unique history, of course, but by examining the communication ecology that forms the basis of CSU's nonprofit identity, the pages to follow not only speak to that group's individual complexities but also underscore the inherent challenges faced by other food justice groups working "in the shadow of the shadow state" today.

What follows is a genealogical story of evolving ideas and practices in changing social, political, and economic contexts. Starting with a brief history of community-based programming in the BPP, I go on to trace CSU's emergence from within the Southern California chapter of the party, describe how its foundational Community Food Assessment integrated the organization into the logics of nonprofit organizing, and situate the organization's current strategic fundraising practices within this sociohistorical context. The analysis remains in conversation with the book's working principles for sustainable community change, introduced in chapter 1, demonstrating how, through the course of CSU's journey, elements of this evaluative framework were not only present, but actually quite often in conflict. Notably, the group's desire to ground its local activism within a community-driven vision of social transformation has not always been easy to reconcile with its need to develop networked partnerships that provide programmatic and fiscal sustainability. The research here ultimately shows that tensions between revolution and reform, autonomy and alliance-building were central to CSU's prehistory, history, and present. Understanding the ambivalent landscape of opportunity and constraint that emerges from these networked interactions, I argue, is central to conceptualizing the past and future of food justice in the age of neoliberalism.

THE BLACK PANTHER PARTY: ALL POWER TO THE PEOPLE

First—a caveat. It is well beyond the scope of this chapter to tell a decisive and all-encompassing history of the Black Panther Party. Even book-length treatments and documentary films that claim to tell the party's full story necessarily fall short of the task. In truth, the Black Panthers meant many different things to many different people. To some they were revolutionary freedom fighters, to others they were dangerous subversives. To some they were innovative and devoted community builders, to others they were violent and out-of-control misogynists. For many, of course, the legacy of the BPP includes some combination of these and other seemingly conflicting qualities. Ultimately, the BPP was an organization with a philosophy and action that evolved significantly over time and a membership and community-based praxis that differed between geographically distinct contexts. My interest in the pages to follow is to tell an abbreviated history of this complex phenomenon—guided by the perspectives of my research collaborators in conjunction with the historical record, this chapter uncovers specific networks and narratives from within the party's history that proved central to shaping the community-based identity of CSU into the twenty-first century.[1]

In the diverse historical retellings, the story always begins in Oakland, California, where the Black Panther Party for Self-Defense was founded by Bobby Seale and Huey Newton in October of 1966. The organization took shape at a time when police oppression against the Black community was the norm in Oakland and in other cities across the United States, young Americans were routinely being sent to fight and die in Vietnam, and skyrocketing urban poverty rates prevented many African Americans from securing the basic necessities of modern life. The Black Panther Party for Self-Defense's original Ten-Point Program, first publicized in May of 1967, delineated what the group wanted ("What We Want") and explained what they believed ("What We Believe") in that moment. The call to action listed a host of social and economic demands, including freedom and power for the Black community, full employment, exemption from military service, an end to police brutality, the end to the robbery of the Black community, and "land, bread, housing, education, clothing, justice and peace."[2]

In the early days, dressed in their trademark leather jackets and black berets, Seale and Newton were joined by a small group of devoted followers in Oakland. Together, they took an aggressive stance to counter persistent police brutality, employing a strategy of "policing the police" through armed self-defense that was distinct from the nonviolent civil disobedience that had characterized mainstream Civil Rights organizing. Several events in the late 1960s became catalysts for the party's growth, including the assassination of Martin Luther King Jr., the murder of Panther member Bobby Hutton, the imprisonment of Huey Newton for the murder of an Oakland police officer, and the "Free Huey" campaign that persisted through his trial. Reflecting an evolving sociopolitical ethos and a developing community-based strategy, the organization shortened its name to the Black Panther Party in 1968. During its heyday in the late 1960s and early 1970s, the BPP opened up chapters in cities across the United States and enjoyed widespread support from African

Americans nationwide. Its diverse set of community programs provided necessary services in African American neighborhoods. Its official membership grew into the thousands and its newspaper—*The Black Panther*—grew to a circulation of approximately 250,000. The BPP emerged as a leading national voice for the rights and interests of African Americans, built relationships with allies from across the spectrum of radical left politics, and advocated for international and intercommunal anti-imperial coalition-building.[3]

Key ideological influences on the work of the BPP included Malcolm X's Black nationalism; Mao Tse-Tung's revolutionary organizing principles; Frantz Fanon's call for revolutionary violence; and a Marxist-Leninist commitment to socialism, class struggle, and dialectical materialism.[4] Over time, the BPP underwent significant ideological evolution—moving from Black nationalism to revolutionary nationalism and then to revolutionary internationalism before coming to what they called revolutionary intercommunalism. That final ideological stage was defined by Newton as, "the time when the people seize the means of production and distribute the wealth and the technology in an egalitarian way to many communities of the world."[5] Several amendments to the BPP's Ten-Point Program demonstrated the organization's conscious ideological progression. In 1969, for instance, the call for "an end to the robbery by the White man of the Black community" was changed to "an end to the robbery by the capitalist of the Black Community," and the demand for "freedom for all Black men held in federal, state, county, and city prisons" was changed in 1972 to a demand for "an end to all wars of aggression."[6] The BPP's evolving intercommunal spirit was exemplified by its inspiration for and interaction with similar groups that extended well beyond the African American community, including the Southern California-based Chicano leftist Brown Berets, the Black Beret Cadre in Bermuda, the Black Panther Party of Israel, the college-based White Panther Party, and the electorally focused Peace and Freedom Party.[7] As Joshua Bloom and Waldo Martin detailed in their political history of the organization—*Black Against Empire*—the BPP framed its efforts as part of a global anti-imperialist struggle, an ideological positioning that made it possible to draw support from racially, geographically, and socially diverse groups of allies who were key to its growth and effectiveness.[8]

Due to these evolving philosophies and practices, the late 1960s and early 1970s saw a significant internal struggle within the BPP. With Newton in prison and Eldridge Cleaver—a top-ranking official in the party, who remained a strong proponent of armed defense—in exile to avoid a parole charge, Panther leaders Bobby Seale and David Hilliard emphasized that the development of community programs was central to advancing the revolutionary mission of the BPP. When Newton was finally acquitted and released from jail, he supported this shift away from armed insurrection and toward a demilitarized process of "survival pending revolution." Cleaver levied intense criticism against the BPP's bureaucratic establishment, and many of those who shared his more militant perspective went underground or opted to leave the party around 1971.[9] As these internal tensions mounted, the groundswell of support that the BPP had enjoyed from across the African American community began to wane. In an effort to consolidate its resources, the BPP decided to close many of its local chapters and shifted its emphasis toward gaining local political power in Oakland. Almost a dozen BPP members and supporters gained seats on community development and local planning councils in Oakland in mid-1972, prompting the organization to gear up for a political push in 1973. However, shortly after both major Panther candidates—Bobby Seale for mayor of Oakland and Elaine Brown for Oakland's city council—lost their bids, the organization started to decline significantly in membership and influence.[10]

Through the mid- to late 1970s, Newton further consolidated organizational power, often through autocratic means, while deep-seated factionalism led to an intense and dangerous rivalry with Cleaver and other BPP members who were in exile.[11] Drug and alcohol abuse, misappropriation of funds, and violent behavior against members of the community and other party comrades on the part of Newton's security squad signaled the demise of BPP, which officially ceased operations in 1982.[12] Not to be understated, the BPP was, throughout its existence, under significant stress from police repression, government infiltration, and retribution from groups like the FBI's COINTELPRO program. Indeed, the deconstruction of revolutionary Black Power groups like the BPP was a concerted aim of US authorities during this time, and it is unclear exactly how the organization might have developed differently had their efforts not been consistently undermined by external forces.[13] Ultimately, as scholar Ollie Johnson described, the unraveling of the BPP can be attributed to a host of intersecting factors, including "state political repression, ideological errors, an inexperienced and youthful membership, intraparty strife, strategic mistakes, and the cult-of-personality phenomenon" (391).[14]

Today, the significance of the BPP is often minimized and its constructive contributions downplayed. Popular depictions generally suggest that it was an antiwhite, ultraleftist organization of thugs and criminals whose importance was overhyped by the media. Yet scholars of the BPP insist that, while the so-called dark side of the party—which undoubtedly included a history of violence, misogyny, and outright organizational malfeasance—should not be dismissed or excused, focusing only on that issue is unfair and marginalizing. Indeed, during the BPP's prime, its philosophy and actions had significant impacts in global communities of color, and the party left a significant legacy—related to the notion of armed resistance, a tradition of community service, a commitment to self-determination, and a model of political action for the oppressed—that in many ways endures.[15] When members of CSU told the story of their Panther roots to introduce their organization, they acknowledged that armed violence was a characteristic element of the early BPP, but they suggested that this strategy was in many ways an appropriate response to the aggressiveness of a racist police state in the late 1960s. Still, CSU derived its own organizational history from an understanding that this perspective was significantly countered, even then, by a part of the Panther ideology that considered fostering community development through local "survival programs" and critical educational to be equally representative of the spirit of the party as its militancy.

SERVING THE PEOPLE, BODY AND SOUL

From BPP's early years of organizing, the party's emphasis on community programs became a central piece of its broader approach to social change and served as the primary focus for many of the local BPP chapters in cities across the United States. Referred to as survival programs, the initiatives aimed to, "meet the needs of the community until we can all move to change the social conditions that make it impossible for the people to afford the things they need and desire" while serving "as a model for all oppressed people who wish to begin to take concrete actions to deal with their oppression" (3).[16] The BPP sponsored nearly two dozen types of community-based programs, with initiatives that included health clinics, housing advocacy, sickle cell anemia testing, safe escort services for senior citizens, legal defense, political petition campaigns, the publication of the *Black Panther Intercommunal News Service,* and the Liberation School/Intercommunal Youth Institute, among many others.[17] As former BPP member JoNina Abron described, fostering self-determination among oppressed African American communities was at the heart of these efforts: "Institutional racism relegated a disproportionate number of African Americans to deplorable housing, poor health care services, an unresponsive criminal justice system, inadequate diets, and substandard education. The Party's survival programs aimed to help black people overcome the devastating effects of racism and capitalism" (178).[18]

As scholar Alondra Nelson recounted in her in-depth look at the health care survival programs of the BPP, in the face of health crises that disproportionately affected them, "black communities had little choice but to provide their own solutions to what ailed them" (26). Through the building of alternative institutions, the BPP linked its service provision in health, safety, and education to a grander project for racial justice and social transformation.[19] And, within this community-based context, *food* emerged as a particularly salient and necessary tool for the movement-building capacity of the BPP. Indeed, in the face of governmental negligence related to hunger in African American communities, the Free Breakfast for Children program was among the party's first and most effective initiatives—the BPP claimed to have fed at least twenty thousand schoolchildren in the 1968–69 school year alone.[20] Initiatives like free food giveaways had multiple aims, conceptualized on one hand as providing a basic service within the impoverished and often malnourished cities in which BPP chapters operated and on the other as a space in which a discussion about the broader social transformation goals of the BPP could be initiated. Even then, food was put to use as a vehicle for more than just nutrition, as BPP leader David Hilliard explained: "Food serves a double purpose, providing sustenance but also functioning as an organizing tool; people enter the office when they come by, take some leaflets, sit in on an elementary PE (political education) class, talk to cadre, and exchange ideas" (58).[21]

Not all Black Panthers, however, championed the transformative power of food giveaways and other community-organizing programs. Critics within the party felt that the organization was moving too far in the direction of reforming present institutions, promoting "sissy stuff" as opposed to focusing on revolutionary procedures that they believed could only be advanced through armed defense and aggressive militant action. Defenders of the community-based strategy argued that the survival programs were indeed a vehicle for radical political socialization.[22] The philosophy behind the actions was, as David Hilliard articulated, "survival pending revolution—not something to replace revolution or challenge the power relations demanding radical action, but an activity that strengthens us for the coming fight, a lifeboat or raft leading us safely to shore" (31).[23] Bobby Seale similarly rejected the label of "reform": "They're not reform programs; they're actually revolutionary community programs. A revolutionary program is one set forth by revolutionaries, by those who want to change the existing system to a better system. A reform program is set up by the existing exploitative system as an appeasing handout to fool the people and keep them quiet" (178).[24]

Despite the internal strife and the significant external pressure placed on the BPP, the community programs continued through the late 1960s and well into the 1970s. During this time, however, the BPP also confronted existential challenges related to building and maintaining organizational capacity— challenges that served to motivate the group's ongoing ideological and action-oriented evolution. There was an increasing recognition within the BPP that, if the organization was to be optimally successful in promoting social and economic revolution in the African American community, it could not do so in a fashion that was completely autonomous from the white power structure or from the dynamics of capitalism. In its legal advocacy, medical provisions, political initiatives, and other community-based program development, the BPP consistently constructed networked partnerships with established white professionals, leftist radicals, and other institutions that it considered legitimate allies of its cause. Tens of thousands of dollars in donations were acquired from wealthy artists, philanthropists, and other members of the liberal establishment, and partnerships were also forged with African American businesspeople, those who had previously been the target of BPP scorn.[25] While still opposed to the exploitative structures of capitalism, the BPP began to recognize that its socialist agenda of economic redistribution necessarily required engagement with capitalism itself. In a 1971 essay, Huey Newton outlined this change in purpose:

> In order to carry out such programs we have always needed money. In the past we received money from wealthy White philanthropists, humanitarians, and heirs to the corporate monopolies. At the same time we were engaging in a blanket condemnation of the small victimized Black capitalists found in our communities. This tactic was wrong.... When we say that we see within Black capitalism the seeds of its own negation and the negation of all capitalism, we recognize that the small Black capitalist in our communities has the potential to contribute to the building of the machine which will serve the true interests of the people and end all exploitation.... We will do this through our survival programs, which have the interest of the community at heart.[26]

Some BPP chapters went so far as to actually secure minor governmental funds to support their community-based initiatives, although this came with some trepidation. Ultimately, party membership concluded that, as long as this funding did not go against their ideology, it made sense for them to take available philanthropic and government money and make good use of it. What they might not have expected, however, was that many of their survival programs—including Free Breakfast for Children and those programs providing sickle cell anemia testing—would come to be mimicked and eventually overtaken by a host of government and nonstate actors, including the Nixon White House. The BPP saw such actions as an unfair co-option on the part of establishment actors who looked to minimize the BPP's importance and to move the control of community program development and management away from low-income Black communities themselves.[27] Such co-option represented another factor that led to the slow demise of the BPP's influence in communities across the nation.

Still, both the survival programs and the BPP's forays into electoral politics demonstrated that the forces within the party calling for outright separatism, characterized by an underground movement of guerilla warfare, did not hold sway. The political context that had made armed self-defense a rallying cry for an intercommunal, anti-imperial revolution had shifted in just a few short years. Instead, after a more militant early stage, the practices of the Panthers moved toward a style of changing cultural values and reshaping institutions from within. To some, this symbolized the end of the revolutionary capacity of the BPP, but to others, it was more a reflection that changing times and new contexts always called for evolving strategic action.[28] As Huey Newton explained: "You can't very well drop out of the system without dropping out of the universe. You contradict the system while you are in it until it's transformed into a new system" (63).[29]

THE SOUTHERN CALIFORNIA CHAPTER OF THE BPP

"Community Services Unlimited was formed as the nonprofit arm of the Southern California chapter of the Black Panther Party." Those words rolled off of the tongues of CSU staff, volunteers, board members, youth interns, and partners alike, usually repeated verbatim, a testament to the centrality that those historical roots played in CSU's own narrative of itself. While the BPP was national and international in its scope and mission, each local branch of the organization came with its own unique history. The Southern California chapter was formed in 1968, with Alprentice "Bunchy" Carter at the helm. In the early 1960s, Carter had been a leader of the Renegades, the hardcore element of the Slauson gang, the largest street force in Los Angeles. Incarcerated in Soledad Prison in the mid-1960s, Carter read the works of Malcolm X, joined the Nation of Islam, and met radical intellectual and future Panther leader Eldridge Cleaver. Upon his release, he became the deputy minister of defense for the BPP and worked to organize former gang members and ex-inmates toward a revolutionary consciousness under the auspices of the party.[30] Just a few years after the 1965 uprisings in Watts and throughout South Los Angeles, many in the Southern California region were responsive to the revolutionary perspective of the BPP, and the chapter's membership grew quickly. Facing brutal repression by the Los Angeles Police Department (LAPD), Carter developed a strong martial defense force, and working with BPP member and Vietnam War veteran Geronimo Pratt, he also cultivated an underground militia that was kept separate from the rest of the organization.[31]

Carter's leadership, however, was short-lived. He and fellow Southern California BPP member John Huggins were murdered on the campus of the University of California, Los Angeles, in January of 1969. The murder was the result of an altercation with members of the US organization, a Black cultural nationalist group with whom the BPP had been engaged in an intense rivalry. Years later, it came to light that conflict between the groups was stoked by the FBI as part of its COINTELPRO effort to impede the efforts of Black radicals.[32]

Still, the Southern California Chapter persisted, and BPP members built up the social and community-oriented aspects of the organization, working under the leadership of key players like the writer, singer, and activist Elaine Brown and the politically minded Raymond "Masai" Hewitt. The Los Angeles office became one of the largest in the nation, anchored by the development of several key community survival programs, including community policing of the police, health care services, educational programs, legal aid, and three different Free Breakfast for Children programs. Facing violent attacks by the LAPD and persistent threats from the FBI, the chapter partnered with churches to host its food and clothing giveaways. These collaborations provided a safe space for BPP programming and also helped build relationships within the local community. The membership also found allies within the left-leaning white establishment of Southern California. The

"Friends of the Panthers" organization, for instance, founded by playwright Donald Freed, included a host of Hollywood players, including Elliot Gould and Elizabeth Taylor. Not surprisingly, the FBI's COINTELPRO program went to great lengths to target those celebrity friends and attempted to destroy their collaborative relationships with the BPP.[33]

The most visible display of police repression against the Southern California BPP chapter came in late 1969. Days before members had planned to open the Bunchy Carter People's Free Medical Clinic, which was to be fully staffed with volunteer doctors and nurses, at 3223 South Central Avenue, the chapter's headquarters at 4115 South Central Avenue came under heavy attack by a police raid. After several hours of exchanging gunfire, the Panthers surrendered, leaving the facilities destroyed, a host of party members injured and imprisoned, and three police officers wounded. Although they were forced to delay the anticipated inauguration of the clinic, members found a way to open the Bunchy Carter PFMC just a few weeks later, a testament to the organization's commitment to community service in the face of great adversity.[34]

Mirroring what was happening to chapters across the nation, however, as Newton consolidated power and Los Angeles-based BPP leader Elaine Brown relocated to Oakland in the early 1970s, the Southern California chapter's operations eventually came to a virtual standstill. It was around this time, though, that the contours of what would become Community Services Unlimited began to take shape. CSU's future founder, the twenty-seven-year-old Kwaku Duren, was granted parole after serving nearly five years in Chino and Soledad Prisons for an armed robbery charge. Introduced to and inspired by the works of W. E. B. Dubois and Malcolm X during his imprisonment, he studied anthropology and sociology, took on what he termed a "conscious Black perspective," and began to look for an opportunity to engage in activism.[35] By the time he was paroled, there was no longer a vibrant Panther movement in the Los Angeles area that he could join. So, in 1973, he partnered with his sister and other community activists to form the nonprofit Intercommunal Youth Institute, an alternative school modeled on the BPP's Oakland Community School. Two years later, his sister Betty Scott was wrongfully shot and killed by California Highway Police Officers during a routine traffic stop. Her boyfriend, George Smith, a passenger in the car at the time of the incident, was accused of attempted murder of a police office, a trumped-up charge that was later dismissed after Duren and other supporters formed the Scott-Smith Justice Committee to apply pressure on authorities. In response to these events and other instances of criminal injustice in the region, Duren worked with several other Black and Chicano community advocates from Southern California to form the Coalition Against Police Abuse in 1976.[36]

In early 1977, a trip to Oakland with other Southern California activists to meet with Elaine Brown—who had by that time become the chairwoman of the BPP—led to the reformation of the Southern California BPP chapter and Duren's official initiation into the party. For several years, he led a small but devoted group of BPP members in the region. They worked out of an office on Central Avenue in South Central Los Angeles and developed community-based programs that they hoped would continue to raise community consciousness and serve the needs of the disenfranchised. They also officially established Community Services Unlimited Inc. in 1977. It was classified as a 501(c)(3) nonprofit structure to help the organization properly solicit donations and provide fiscal sponsorship for a variety of community-based efforts. "It was formed for that purpose," Duren explained in an interview, "to obtain resources for what we were calling at the time survival programs, that ran the gamut of free food programs, free shoe programs, safe program for seniors—Seniors Against a Fearful Environment—bussing to prisons programs, an array of community programs. Any time we saw a need, we tried to develop a program around it."

Even with these revitalized efforts in Southern California, however, the walls of the broader BPP were falling down. Elaine Brown resigned from the party in 1977 as Huey Newton's increasingly erratic and dangerous behavior destabilized the organization. The Southern California chapter of the BPP was formally closed in 1981. Reflecting years later on his official letter of resignation to Newton, he wrote: "With revolutionary criticism, love, and undying hope for the eventual liberation of oppressed peoples, we remained dedicated to the revolutionary ideals of the Black Panther Party but accepted the fact that the Organization was no longer viable."[37]

THE NEW PANTHER VANGUARD AND COMMUNITY SERVICES UNLIMITED

While the BPP, including its Southern California chapter, ceased operations in the 1980s, the nonprofit Community Services Unlimited remained intact, providing tax-exempt services and fiscal sponsorship for several community-based efforts in the area. From the late 1970s to the early 1990s, Duren worked with the Los Angeles Legal Aid Foundation, pursued an independent legal study, and enrolled in classes at the Peoples College of Law. He was also active as a member of the Peace and Freedom Party, and even made a few unsuccessful bids for local political office. He received his JD in 1989 and began to practice civil rights and community-based law. As he said in an interview, "I've been criticized by loved ones that I don't have the economic model that most lawyers have. My practice has always been sort of a community-based practice. I couldn't practice up in the corporate world. I don't have the heart for that."

It was after the civil unrest of 1992 in Los Angeles, in the wake of the Rodney King verdict, that Duren began to engage in discussions about organizing a new "Panther-like" group in South Central Los Angeles. Working with other former members of the Southern California BPP chapter as well as younger activists from the area, he aimed to develop a principled grassroots organizing force that understood both the values and mistakes of the original BPP. Calling themselves the New African American Vanguard Movement, the group was launched during a community festival in 1994. "We are learning in LA that just as other communities are coming together, so must we," Kizzy Brown, a member of the coalition, was quoted as saying at the time.[38] A name change followed shortly thereafter, and the group became the New Panther Vanguard Movement (NPVM), in part reflecting its commitment to an intercommunal ethic of action.[39]

Meanwhile, across the Atlantic, Neelam, the future director of Community Services Unlimited, was engaged in her own social justice organizing among historically marginalized people of color in London. Neelam had grown up in Southall, a low-income community with a majority of residents from the Indian subcontinent and others of African heritage. As a young activist, she worked to combat spousal abuse within her own community of immigrants, engaged in campaigns against fascism and police abuse, and helped to create a successful legal rights center that still operates to this day. In the 1980s, Neelam and other activists were inspired by the anti-imperial, intercommunal model of the BPP, and they went on to form an organization called PANTHER. "We felt that the Panthers in the US were a representation of the highest political level of thinking," she explained in an interview. "In terms of their ideological development and their political theory, we felt like they really spoke to who we were and what we were trying to do."

One of the first initiatives of PANTHER was to create a newspaper. With the lead headline on the first issue declaring, "Fight the Power," the publication quickly sold out, and membership in the organization grew rapidly. Soon, PANTHER was organizing rallies and events in the Southall area—some of the largest political rallies of ethnic minority residents in the history of England—and doing community work on the topic of gang intervention and gang truces. They began to build relationships with some of their inspirations from the American BPP, bringing former leaders like Bobby Seale over to England to take part in events. In the 1990s, an exchange program of sorts commenced, as PANTHER leaders began to travel from England to the United States, taking part in meetings and observing the activities of newly reconstituted groups like the NPVM. Neelam eventually participated in one of those exchanges, and it was there she first met Duren, with whom she began a personal relationship. Although she had little plans to do so when these exchanges began, she moved to Los Angeles in the mid-1990s, bringing along her young son, Lawrence. At that point, Neelam became a central volunteer in support of the activities of the NPVM and CSU.

The NPVM remained active through the late 1990s and into the early 2000s, with CSU serving primarily as the economic arm of the organization, continuing to raise resources and provide fiscal sponsorship for its other groups. Neelam and Duren worked with volunteers to publish a newsletter on a somewhat-less-than-quarterly basis—*The Black Panther Intercommunal News Service*—which featured writings on the history, philosophy, and current activities of members and allies working to advance racial justice and social transformation. Although deeply committed to eliminating the oppression and exploitation of communities of color, the NPVM did not include armed resistance as part of its strategy. The coalition looked, instead, to the community service arm of the original BPP as a source of inspiration. Calls for "Peace, Justice and Reparations" and "Food, Housing, Medical Care and Quality Education" led the list of demands on the NPVM's own Ten-Point Platform and Program.[40]

South Central Los Angeles, the neighborhood that was once the home of the Southern California chapter of the BPP, was in the midst of rapid demographic change. As the previously predominantly African American community became, within a few decades, majority Latin@, the historically African American NPVM focused much of its local organizing on forging intercommunal bonds and building joint projects with new partners in the Latin@ and indigenous communities. In the late 1990s, Duren and his colleagues went to the pages of the *Black Panther Intercommunal News Service* to outline the people-of-color-led plan for "Education in *Our*

Interests," a strategy NPVM had been implementing through a number of after-school programs in South LA. "Forcing the public schools to teach the truth will be the hardest part of any educational effort. The lies and distortions are deeply imbedded in the consciousness of our people and will not be easily dislodged or discredited," the collaborative editorialized. "The choice lies between a genuinely new and radical approach and maintaining the ineffective, often paternalistic, often self-destructive, violence-breeding public school life as it exists today. . . . From the point of view of conscious African Americans and people of Mexica ancestry, the road to 'education in our interest' is the path we choose to take."[41]

The narrative put forth by the NPVM as a guide for its community-based action was consistently grounded in two intersecting propositions. First, there was an insistence that solutions to historical inequities must emerge from within the very communities that have been historically oppressed. Second, there was an assertion that significant *investment* in those traditionally marginalized communities of color was necessary if the cause of social transformation was to be successfully advanced. Showing shades of strategic thinking that would later shape the methods undertaken by CSU in its food justice work, the NPVM emphasized the importance of encouraging economic development and reparations for communities that had long been subject to slavery, discrimination, and exploitation. "There are populations worldwide that need economic assistance," Duren explained in an interview. "Not as a handout, but as an effort to pay for the past acts—call it genocidal acts against people."

The emerging philosophy of the community economic development (CED) movement—a foundation for CSU's social enterprise in the 2010s, discussed in chapter 3—was identified by Duren in the 1990s as offering a pathway toward change. Writing in the *Black Panther Intercommunal News Service* in 1999, Duren offered his interpretation of the roots and possibilities of the CED strategy. He reached all the way back to the work of Booker T. Washington and Marcus Garvey, explored the economic justice arms of the Civil Rights movement, and found insight in contemporary social justice responses to the policies of Ronald Reagan and his successors. "Then, as now, CED advocates continued to point out the fact that the private, market-driven economy of the US is, at best, *blind* to the notion of equitable distribution of economic benefits and actually fosters concentration of wealth in the hands of individuals and families," he wrote (18, emphasis in original). He argued that government must play a pivotal role in stimulating economic development but that previous efforts to improve conditions in low-income urban and rural places had been both temporary and shallow. A sustainable and effective initiative, by contrast, would encourage partnerships between the private and public sectors, individual entrepreneurs, community development corporations, and community-based organizations with genuine interests in promoting economic development for the entire community, not just the already well-capitalized.[42]

This embrace of a market-engaged model of community development, one that could look to the BPP's rethinking of its own relationship to the structures and fruits of capitalism during the heyday of its survival programs as a precedent, was part of an evolutionary process for the NPVM. As the historian and former BPP member Paul Alkebulan has argued, a key reason the party's survival programs did not have longer staying power might be found in the fact that the BPP did not think nearly enough about sustainable economic development. That is to say, while the BPP committed great time and resources to redistributing goods to the community—through, for instance, giveaways of food and other basic necessities—its membership failed to conceptualize how they might transition to a focus on production, ownership, and control. "Despite its advocacy of socialism, the central committee missed the importance of establishing an economic base (especially in a capitalist society)," Alkebulan argued (44).[43] Former BPP member Jimmy Slater offered a similar sentiment, suggesting that rigid ideology prevented the BPP from long-term community-based sustainability. "We had buildings and homes. We owned property. We should have learned how to control the economy and to manage those things," he argued. "Instead we wanted to fight against capitalism, and now we know that we should have established an economic base. In order to keep the movement going you've got to have capital" (152).[44] For Duren, the philosophy of community economic development offered a political and economic pathway for community transformation based on the recognition that "the traditional flow of economic benefits must be *fundamentally* transformed in order for these benefits to reach minority and poor communities" (18, emphasis in original).[45]

If a market-engaged philosophy of community economic development was to be pushed forward in South LA into the early 2000s, however, the NPVM was not the entity that would be leading the charge. For several years, it continued to remain active in community organizing, publishing its newsletter, hosting community events, facilitating weekly community forums, engaging in critical intercommunal education, and working toward gang truce interventions. Yet as Duren focused more of his attention on his civil rights law practice and the NPVM's membership became engaged in other forms of activism, the organization's activities began to recede. A few years into the new millennium, the NPVM was mostly defunct, but the spirit and the legacy of the BPP did not disappear with it. Indeed, it was around that time that Neelam began to take on a more active role in consciously cultivating the work of the decades-old entity Community Services Unlimited. She saw great potential in expanding its operations, breaking from its history as a mostly tangential economic tool put to use by Panther-affiliated groups and developing it instead as an independent organization that could more thoroughly promote critical education and community economic development throughout the South LA community.

Given the historical conjuncture—it was a time in which the "shadow state" of third-sector nonprofit organizations was proliferating—it certainly made sense for this 501(c)(3) legacy of the BPP to emerge as a viable avenue for community-based social justice organizing. And while this was a new stage for the operations of CSU, the group was hardly starting from scratch. CSU's organizational identity was built on a networked foundation that started with the original Black Panther Party, stretched across the Atlantic to the activism of the London-based PANTHER organization, and returned to South LA under the auspices of the New Panther Vanguard Movement. Its communication ecology was characterized by a powerful set of guiding narratives of change—the organization's identity was founded in the intercommunal revolutionary philosophy of the BPP, grounded in an engaged style of community organizing amongst low-income people of color, and committed to a plan of community economic development that promoted community ownership and sustainability. In the years to come, CSU began to shift its focus toward food and worked to build its profile as an independent nonprofit organization working toward food justice. The organization was faced with the challenge of maintaining a historically grounded, community-based mission for social transformation while at the same time meeting the inherent demands that beset nonprofit organizers working "in the shadow of the shadow state."

THE COMMUNITY FOOD ASSESSMENT AND FOOD JUSTICE ORGANIZING

For years, food had played a role as an organizing tool in both the BPP and the NPVM. Food giveaways had long served a dual purpose, as Duren explained: "One, to let the community know we could take some initiative to make sure people had access to food. Two, we needed to get them onto things. To rally, to get recruits from people, to get them involved and active." In the late 1990s and early 2000s, while Neelam was volunteering with the NVPM after moving to the United States, she began to take stock of the poor quality of meals her young son, Lawrence, was being served in his South LA public school, and she became increasingly concerned about the food environment in which the children of her neighborhood were being raised. "Lawrence started going to the schools here, I moved to South Central," she explained. "And you know, you couldn't get decent food. I mean it was that simple. Lawrence started complaining about it. So I, literally for the first time in my life, started to grow my own garden. You know, like not just for fun, but for food."

Guided by an activist's commitment to social justice and a gendered ethic of motherly care, Neelam began to meet with other dissatisfied parents and engage in conversations with school administrators and cafeteria staff. She then connected with researchers from nearby Occidental College who were looking for parents interested in getting involved in improving school food.[46] Together, they formed the Healthy School Food Coalition, a still-active consortium that has focused its advocacy efforts on changing food policies and practices throughout the Los Angeles Unified School District, both in individual schools and within communities. As a founding member, Neelam was particularly active in the group's early years, helping to lead efforts to institute a district-wide Healthy Beverage Resolution that came to be known colloquially as the "soda ban." Her work on the Education in Our Interests after-school program with local African American and Latin@ young people further intensified her interest in exploring the links between youth development and food. While she and other volunteers involved in that effort saw students making great strides in their critical educational process, the initiative seemed to be hamstrung by the youths' limited attention spans, their inability to focus, and their propensity toward erratic behaviors. There were clear connections, the organizers felt, between the food the kids were eating and the possibility for advancing their educational goals. Neelam and her colleagues began to investigate:

> We started to have the kids document what they were eating, what they were consuming. We started having them document when they were getting into trouble on graphs. "Oh, I had a soda and here, twenty minutes later, I did this

crazy thing which I have no idea now why I did it." . . . I was really horrified to see that these kids were being given these stupid messages about eating five [vegetables] a day, but no kind of like—why does sugar do this, what's the impact it has on you, what does it make you do, how does it affect your chemistry, and how does that then affect your physical reaction? . . . And what we found was that when you actually talked to kids on that level and you treat them like they're intelligent, they get it.

It was around this time that Neelam and her activist and educational colleagues—made up solely of volunteers working out of Duren's cramped legal offices—began to think explicitly about the ability of food to serve as a powerful medium for exploring the key issues with which the BPP, the NPVM, and CSU had always been engaged. They began to develop ideas around programming—at this point, fully under the auspices of the CSU nonprofit designation—in which they would use food, agriculture, and culturally oriented nutrition education as primary methods to advance social, economic, and environmental justice in South LA. They realized, of course, that significant funds would be required if they were to make any legitimate impact in the local food environment. Fundraising and governmental grant applications, however, hardly represented an area of expertise for CSU leaders, who were ultimately community organizers at heart. At this moment, they were faced with some central questions: Could CSU successfully transform itself into a "fundable" nonprofit organization while still maintaining its long-held commitment to a historically situated vision of social justice transformation? Could the organization productively tell its story of revolutionary, community-based cultural empowerment while also speaking to the interests of those external allies whose support was necessary if it was to have the capacity to proceed?

CSU's Community Food Assessment (CFA)—led by the organization in collaboration with a coalition of South LA–based residents and organizations in 2003 and 2004—was the exercise in food justice organizing through which the group began to develop answers to those critical questions. The concept of the CFA, broadly speaking, emerged at a moment in which community economic development strategies, community assessment projects, and "asset-based" approaches to community building were being trumpeted as valuable tools by a host of voices from across the urban planning, policymaker, and practitioner communities. Policy trends in the age of neoliberalism that called for the devolution of social programs to the local level, combined with the development of new digital communication technologies and the rise of geographic information systems, created both a need and a strategy for the deployment of methods that collected community-based data and devised evidence-based strategies to improve localities.[47] At the same time, many practitioners engaged in community development were lamenting the dominance of externally directed and deficit-oriented strategies of assessment in which low-income communities were often conceptualized as "problems" to be "solved." Instead, advocates like John Kretzmann and John McKnight called for assets-based approaches that involved community members in the process and identified local strengths to build upon: "In a community whose assets are being fully recognized and mobilized, these people too will be part of the action, not as clients or recipients of aid, but as full contributors to the community-building process" (6).[48]

From within this environment, the CFA began to take hold as a key mechanism to advance community food security in the early twenty-first century. Institutions like the United States Department of Agriculture's Economic Research Service and the Community Food Security Coalition were eager to publish how-to guides for this food system audit, trumpeting the benefits of the process. "Community food assessments promote community food security by increasing knowledge about food-related needs and resources, by building collaboration and capacity, by promoting long-term planning, and by facilitating a variety of change actions including policy advocacy and program development," the Community Food Security Coalition articulated (6).[49]

As CFAs came into wider use among community-based groups, common threads emerged. The projects tended to focus on the needs of low-income residents, demonstrating concerns about the environmental sustainability of the food system, showing a commitment to the local community as a strategic unit of action, emphasizing community assets in the appraisal process, and using multiple data sources and categories of information in the research process.[50] Many CFA projects also assessed the differential access to healthy and affordable foods that was associated with socioeconomically advantaged as opposed to disadvantaged areas. This strategy allowed researchers and activists to draw comparisons between different locations, support arguments regarding the existence of food deserts in specific areas, and parlay this comparative evidence into demands for action. Importantly as well, while government was never granted a central role in the conceptualization of the CFA process, there remained an underlying understanding that the CFA itself could open up the door for governmental funding of community-based alternative food programming.[51]

At its core, the CFA process matched the philosophical interests of multiple actors involved in contemporary food movement action, including grassroots community-based organizations, scholars and practitioners of urban policy and planning, and funding agencies, among others. Importantly, the CFA process emphasized the power communities themselves had to lead the development and deployment of research, analysis, and action. This philosophical ideal was attractive to both the devolution-oriented advocates of neoliberal ideals and the community organizers who championed the need for self-determination in historically marginalized communities of color.[52] By carrying out a CFA, organizations engaged in food-related work would be able to demonstrate to potential funders that they were serious nonprofit groups equipped to competently design and carry out programmatic activities and evaluative research. At the same time, the initiatives were inherently shaped within a community of practice, as they fundamentally reflected many of the concerns, interests, and historically situated lived experiences of low-income communities that consistently endured food injustice.

It is no coincidence that these networked practices took their form in the late twentieth and early twenty-first centuries, a time when the rise of digital communication technologies facilitated the emergence of geographically dispersed partnerships. The hybrid praxis that took shape through these efforts was bound by the communicative possibilities that these digital technologies brought to the fore.[53] Rather than minimizing the importance of local action, as some might suspect new media technologies would, the tools served to reinvent the nature of place-centered activism as locally focused but digitally connected.[54] Digital communication tools helped to collapse distance between USDA bureaucrats in Washington and activists in California, linking community-based organizing with traditional centers of social and political power. In ways that would have been unfathomable in the time of the BPP, for instance, new technologies opened up the possibility for consistent and rapid communicative interaction among diverse partners, allowing for ongoing evaluation procedures to be collaboratively deployed and monitored over time.

It is in this context, then, that the CFA played an integral role in shaping CSU's food justice action. As staff member Dyane explained, "CSU basically started as a facilitator for the people to change, to create change, to change whatever they feel might be problems in their community. And I think that process started in 2003 with our assessment, and we saw that there's no getting around food." The initial recommendation to conduct the CFA, however, did not actually emerge from within CSU itself. Instead, energized by an interest in food in the early 2000s, members of CSU looked to expand the organization's programming by applying for a grant that would allow them to grow an "edible schoolyard" at a local South LA elementary school, one that could be used for both nutritional and educational purposes. Their application was rejected, and they were given a recommendation that they should first conduct a CFA and then reapply. CSU attempted to get funding for such an assessment, but one funding proposal and four letters of intent were rejected by different foundations. Despite these setbacks, the organization and its partners decided to move forward, even without any real budget or dedicated paid staff to devote to the project.[55]

Writing in its 2004 report on the process, the team reflected on the push to conduct a CFA after the edible schoolyard proposal failed to get funding: "We took this to heart, but decided that from its inception it was going to be an educational process for all involved and not simply an academic exercise to gather information."[56] With this in mind, in 2003 and 2004, CSU marshaled resources from across its network of interorganizational connections. To lead the CFA effort, the group brought together partners from the Healthy School Food Coalition, the NPVM, and other community-based social justice organizations, including the youth-focused Blazers Safe Haven and the Mexican rights group Atlachinolli Front. Several other local community residents, high school interns, and college students studying public health played integral roles in the research and analysis process. Furthermore, the Community Food Security Coalition provided support and training throughout the initiative, including partially funding the work of a professional program evaluation consultant. Together, the team went by the acronym ACTION—Active Community to Improve Our Nutrition. As guidelines for their research approach, they pointed to Brazilian educator Paulo Freire and his method to "get learners to question the root causes of oppression and create their own solutions," as well as the Participatory Appraisal model, which was "designed to engage community members in describing their own situation and preferred changes in ways that help them and decision-makers determine the best solutions for sustained change."[57]

The CFA process employed by ACTION largely followed the roadmap of common threads that had come to typify these assessment projects. It focused on the local community as a unit for change, highlighted community assets where possible, collected data through multiple methods on a variety of intersecting topics, and used "an ongoing dialogue . . . throughout the assessment to ensure community members' ideas and beliefs were continuing to be important in shaping next steps of the assessment." Working from May of 2003 to January of 2004, the ACTION team engaged with over 750 community members at eighteen different local sites, including schools, markets, and grocery stores. Their CFA survey included traditional survey questions and a community mapping of available food resources as well as more nontraditional practices that included taste-tests of healthy food products and photo journals of youths' daily food consumption. In the eyes of CSU staff and volunteers, this multimethodological effort stood in stark contrast to most traditional research on health and nutrition in their South LA community. Not only did the CFA measure aspects of the local food environment that had never been focused on by public health or planning researchers, but the participatory nature and nontraditional methodologies employed in the effort staked a claim about the legitimacy of local knowledge gained from residents' experience. Not having been filtered through the blunt and disengaged approach of mainstream public health and medical research, the CFA gave residents of South LA a chance to exercise their rights to food justice through their own words and expressions.

The conclusion of the 2004 report clearly implicated the local food environment as a key player in perpetuating health disparities in South LA. Focusing primarily on a grid of ten by fifteen blocks that were home to approximately 500,000 residents, the authors declared the neighborhood was rife with fast food restaurants and liquor stores, lacked high-quality restaurants and full-service grocery stores, and had only a few local farmers markets that remained inadequately promoted and underutilized by local residents. Faced with the widespread availability of junk foods and sugary drinks, community members expressed a strong desire for better access to fresh, healthy products. Consistent with the broader ideological perspective of the coalition, however, the issue of food injustice was not isolated from other important issues. In their descriptions of the problem and recommendations for solutions, the authors of the CFA consistently pointed to the ways in which concentrated poverty, racialized inequities, and imbalances of cultural and political power were at the heart of the food injustice they were assessing. ACTION included messages to the Los Angeles City Council, the California State Legislature, the LAUSD Board of Education, and the USDA, calling for them to improve zoning laws as a way to restrict the proliferation of junk foods, to invest in initiatives that would promote the distribution and consumption of healthy foods, and to incorporate greater community-based voice in order to set culturally appropriate policies moving forward. In terms of their own community action, the team added that "programs resulting from the assessment address multiple factors of a strong community including health, economics, the environment, hunger, sustainability and self-sufficiency."[58]

With its multimethod and participatory findings as a guide, the completion of the CFA served as a foundational moment in which CSU decided it would focus almost exclusively on projects that provided nutrition education, agricultural training, fresh local produce, and food-based job creation for the youth and adults of South Los Angeles. The resident-led and participatory nature of the exercise, the collaboration with other social justice oriented groups, and the integration of experts and researchers from outside of the community were reminiscent of BPP community programs, but they were also a signal of what was to come as CSU grew into a viable player in the food justice world. The effort also went a long way toward incorporating CSU into the contemporary landscape of nonprofit organizing, as it established the organization as a "fundable project" in the eyes of grant-making agencies. The process of organizing and executing the CFA demonstrated that CSU was capable of mustering the necessary resources to construct the types of networked and collaborative partnerships—between and among residents, community organizations, and professional researchers—that funding agencies valued as successful models to promote sustainable change.

At the dawn of the CFA process, members of CSU faced the key question of whether they would be able to transform the organization into a "fundable" nonprofit while still maintaining their long-held commitment to the ideals of social transformation. After the CFA, although they were still at an early stage of their development, they seemed capable of telling an affirmative story, keeping local community knowledge and resident participation at the forefront of their efforts. Yet the challenge would only grow more daunting as the organization's scope and reach increased. What new challenges would they face as they worked to balance the myriad of sometimes conflicting influences that would come to characterize their expanding organizational network?

SEEKING FOOD JUSTICE IN
THE NONPROFIT INDUSTRIAL COMPLEX

In the years that followed the Community Food Assessment, CSU went onto develop a wide set of food justice projects, which included setting up gardens at schools and community centers, initiating educational programs with local residents, and founding a growing social enterprise—the Village Market Place (VMP)—through which they sold organic produce and value-added products. The organization looked at the VMP as a pathway toward self-sufficiency, a model for community economic development that could be an independent force for the creation of local jobs and the distribution of healthy foods throughout the area. Yet achieving self-sufficiency was still years away, even if the share of the organization's operating costs that was covered by the VMP increased significantly in the years following its launch. Like the vast majority of nonprofit organizations, the ongoing viability of CSU's food justice work depended in no small part upon the fiscal support of others, both through the donations of supporters and, primarily, through the acquisition of competitive grants. CSU had been rejected for funding for its initial CFA effort, but after completing the collaborative assessment, the organization found itself in a much stronger position to assert its fundability moving forward.

Organizational and program development through grant acquisition was consistently guided by CSU's historical vision of social transformation, its strongly rooted philosophical view of social justice, and its ongoing relationship with its community of service. At the same time, situated as the organization was in the contemporary nonprofit landscape, the strategic action of CSU was also consistently shaped by the audit-oriented demands of funding agencies, by the governmental thrust that called for the incorporation of diverse sets of partners into funded programmatic activity, and by the broader contours of a media and cultural environment that deemed community-based food justice a problem worthy of being solved. These dynamic interactions began to take shape with the CFA process, and they became ever more central to the praxis of CSU as it sought out greater support to operate and expand its food justice programming in South LA.

Finding a path toward fiscal sustainability required vision, reflexivity, and discernment. "When we go out and ask for money, we do it in the context of a whole story," Heather, CSU's associate director for development, explained. "That isn't just this year's story; it's a thirty-year story of how CSU got to where it is. That's what's compelling. That's what raises the money." CSU staffers resisted what they saw as a common urge within what they consistently called the "nonprofit industrial complex" to simply shape organizational programming in direct response to the calls of certain funders. "One thing we don't do when it comes to fundraising is be like—oh, there's this money, how do we mold ourselves into their talk to get that money?" Heather continued. "It's staying really true to who we are, why we do it, how we do it."

Sticking true to this principled approach was not always easy. Money did not necessarily come rolling into CSU's coffers, and there were times in which funds to support staff and programming were tight. Yet its staff and volunteers persisted, committed to their mission and confident that their strategy would ultimately be recognized as fundable by the right types of partners. Even in times of austerity, the community programs would not cease. "There's not many organizations doing food work where that could happen," Neelam asserted. "There's a way in which we have been very, very careful to distinguish between going after money if it can serve you to do what you're doing, and being reliant on that money to do what you're doing." Anjali, a long-time CSU board member, argued that it was a steadfast and politically imaginative approach that set the organization apart from many of the other progressive organizations with which she had worked in the past. "So many other organizations get caught up in the nonprofit industrial complex," she explained. CSU, on the other hand, had a view of what the future of food justice could hold, and it was up to them to connect with the funding agencies that had the ability to see that long-term goal. "I feel like there's a way [CSU is] very flippant towards power, and it's like, we're just going to do our own thing" Anjali continued. "So I think that refusal of the terms, refusal to engage in the conversation in the way that it's been given to us, is one of the reasons that I have just consistently gone back to CSU."

Indeed, some key economic and fundraising advisors had repeatedly encouraged CSU to focus *less* on the story of its Black Panther Party legacy, its political ideology, and its long-term vision of social transformation. Downplaying these abstract ideas, some suggested, and focusing more directly on how CSU's programs would fit the strategic interests of potential funders, could prove useful in attempts to garner significant and long-term fiscal support. As one expert with a background in fundraising and economic development told me, for the politically moderate community of funding agencies—such as banks, the government, and major foundations—the natural reaction would *not* be, "Golly, you're a Panther—let me go get my checkbook."

There were, however, certain strategic moments when CSU did indeed minimize its Panther history—certain federal grant applications, for instance, went without a mention of the BPP legacy, with CSU opting instead to focus on their organizational history since the early 2000s.

Vacating this historical and ideological positioning entirely, however, would be antithetical to CSU's approach and would cause the organization to lose credibility in its community of service. Without that foundation, the work would lose all meaning, vision, and purpose. So, while CSU did de-emphasize its Panther connection in selected instances, the organization still opened many of its public appearances, community workshops, and youth education programs by telling the story—in other words, its connection to the BPP was no secret. For those holding the funding cards, did the risks of being associated with a BPP-inspired food justice group outweigh the benefits of supporting an organization with deep community roots and a strong potential for local impact? Undoubtedly, for some, the potential publicity damage this might do to their philanthropic or corporate brand was too much, but CSU opted to reject maximum fundability in favor of staying connected to its ideological roots.

With a set of hybrid philosophical and pragmatic foundations in place, CSU, over time, went on to construct new sets of networked relationships, catalyzed by a host of public and private grants that supported the organization's evolution. Some were narrow in focus and scope, intended to support a specific event, project, or collaboration. Others were substantial grants attached to significant program development, job creation, and partnership-building. Key funders of CSU's work included private foundations, such as the W. K. Kellogg Foundation, the Foundation for Sustainability and Innovation, and the Aepoch Fund. They found modest support from corporate partners, like Bank of America, as well as from private institutions, like the University of Southern California. Public funding came from regional and local sources, including the Network for Healthy California, part of the California Department of Public Health; the City of Los Angeles Office of Community Beautification; and the offices of local city council members. The most expansive support tended to come in the form of major federal grants, with CSU owing much of its organizational growth to the help of funds from USDA's Community Food Projects Competitive Grant Program and the US Department of Health and Human Service's Community Economic Development Program.

This list of funders might read like a hodgepodge of somewhat surprising—and potentially dubious—supporters of food justice. How could a group like CSU seriously advance its mission of social and racial justice while needing to placate the interests of these diverse groups, which include several public and private funders who have a history of supporting interests and practices that are anathema to its stated vision? Is this not an example of the pernicious influence of neoliberalism at its worst, characterized by well-capitalized interests who devolve responsibility to individuals and community groups in the name of empowerment and then co-opt any radical social justice goals by institutionalizing an imbalanced dependency relationship? What prevented CSU from becoming just another cog in the "nonprofit industrial complex"? It is an easy and understandable narrative to construct, and one that CSU was acutely aware of from the time the organization entered the food justice field. Still, staff and board members generally maintained that they could persevere within this landscape—so long as CSU's grassroots participation and social justice vision remained intact. Paying constant attention to the risks and benefits involved, CSU believed that the opportunities these funding relationships offered represented a necessary pathway that would lead toward greater autonomy and impact in the future.

In the process of building and maintaining key partnerships and funding arrangements, members of CSU routinely checked in with themselves and with each other to see if their current work was advancing their broader mission. They recognized that not all partnerships would be perfect, but they nonetheless looked for opportunities to educate partners about the importance of the organization's community-based and race-conscious approach. In other instances, they put up a heavy guard, concerned about being used as a tokenistic prop or marketing tool, especially in a popular cultural context in which food system issues had recently gained a salient broad-based appeal. Ultimately, different funders were met with different levels of scrutiny— CSU rejected some outright, while they considered others as potential partners even if the gut reaction was negative. In order to handle this ambiguity, CSU staff engaged in a deliberative process of interrogation. "We've had lots of conversations where we're like—hmm, I don't know," Heather explained. "Especially when it's corporate money. If we take their money, is it a dirty money kind of thing?" Difficult decisions such as these were beginning to permeate the broader landscape of food justice organizing. This was highlighted, quite controversially, by the decision of Milwaukee-based Growing Power to accept a major donation from the corporate behemoth Wal-Mart in 2011.[59] "As soon as you start to play the game on any level, you're making a compromise," Neelam explained. "As soon as you become a nonprofit, you're already compromising. But it's like, to what extent? Everybody has a place where you will go and won't go. You just have to navigate that very carefully." It was an inexact science, most certainly, but not an unthinking one, even if its consistency could be questioned.

One domain with which CSU seemed particularly amenable to building partnerships was the public sector. Despite their many critiques of governmental policy in the agricultural, social, and economic domains, staff and board members tended to see government funding as a social good. These sources offered an opportunity to demonstrate the proper role of local, state, and federal support, as taxpayer funds could be put to use by and for the people the government was intended to serve. Public partnerships were, in many respects, the type of ideal collaborations that Duren had outlined when writing about community economic development in the pages of the *Black Panther Intercommunal News Service* well over a decade earlier. The success of the movement, he declared, depended in large part upon the ability of governments to "generate, legislatively, significant additional resources to assist in formulating a comprehensive plan to support community-based economic development" (19). If, as Duren advocated, these partnerships were approached by involved parties as a *political task,* they offered the chance to contribute to fundamental institutional change as opposed to being a "symbolic gesture" that provided no tangible contribution to development in low-income communities.[60] Such a political perspective, in other words, made it possible for community-based initiatives to maintain a connection to a broader movement for societal change.

Years after Duren had written about this, Heather offered a similar explanation when asked why CSU would want to partner with an entity like the USDA when the organization is fundamentally opposed to many of that agency's central policies: "Why not take [USDA funding]? And then you can be in a position to say, 'Look at what you can do that is *good.*' That's what the money should go to . . . So we're going to take it and we're going to show that this is what the government can do, and this is what the government can be investing in and creating."

Key to this ongoing *political* task, however, was that funding from an organization like the USDA could never preclude CSU from criticizing that partner institution. Indeed, especially in the case of a government operation such as the USDA, which was far removed from the grassroots work of a group like CSU, speaking out against it while simultaneously taking funds from it was both conceivable and necessary. In many ways, CSU staff saw the ability to speak out against systemic inequality as a central organizational priority, one that went back to the organization's very foundations. "We're not going to shy away from saying that the [USDA] commodity programs are whack," Heather emphasized. "We're going to say it. I guess that's one thing—the money doesn't silence us. I think CSU, the people who are part of it, who have been a part of it, and the history of where it comes from, is rooted in a righteousness. So your money doesn't buy our silence, or it doesn't buy going along with some craziness."

It was always made clear that fundamental to that historically rooted righteousness was CSU's ongoing engagement with issues of race and ethnicity as part of its broader social justice vision. Indeed, when CSU believed its race-conscious approach to food justice organizing had been undermined—be it by funders or by other groups engaged in collaborative environmental or agricultural activities—the organization was not afraid to initiate what it believed to be productive conflict. CSU's members saw themselves as being on the front-lines of ensuring that people of color had a major say in the political task of community economic development through food movement activities. The staff was acutely aware of the statistics regarding the dearth of philanthropic investment in minority-led and minority-serving nonprofit groups.[61] Without continued pressure from groups like theirs, members argued, such disparities would remain, and with such disparities in place, the organization's broader social justice and social transformation goals could never come to fruition. "I just fundamentally believe that, for any movement to have validity, it has to be led by [people of color] and defined by [people of color], even more so," Neelam explained. "Really, it's more than even people of color, but by the needs of those who most need to be served by that movement."

Ultimately, CSU staff insisted that they were eager to work with funding agencies and other partners who were sincerely interested in coming into the community from the outside in order to facilitate long-term and sustainable change. But when a partnership did not proceed in a way that respected the community-based and people-of-color-led approach that CSU prioritized, critical interventions were put into action. Some funding agencies specifically included space for conversations like these to take place, and CSU staff took advantage of the opportunity to speak their minds when they felt it needed to be done. With their broader social transformation goals in mind, they felt compelled to do so—not just for CSU but for the broader social and racial justice movements. Heather, herself a white ally, described the process:

> There's been many times over the years when we've had foundations who've worked with us or done things with us in certain ways that were just not the right way to do it. And we've come back and said, "No, that wasn't right."

And I think a lot of people don't. They just say, "I don't want to say anything, because hopefully next year we'll get to do it." And that's not how we roll. If we're going to say something that is true, it's not just for us, but for other organizations, in terms of how you work with nonprofits. And if you decide you don't want to give us money because of it, okay.

All the while, CSU remained strategic in its initiation of conflict-oriented discourse, always weighing the benefits of such an intervention with the time, effort, and potential risks that the action would entail. While strong and principled in their approach, members were also pragmatic about the possibilities for change that existed when some of their partnerships did not proceed optimally. Ultimately, they found themselves asking whether CSU could still pursue the ideals of its broader mission while working in a less-than-ideal situation. Could they find ways to work around divergent approaches rather than ending a partnership and losing funding for an important community program? Could they stomach suboptimal circumstances as long as such circumstances did not negatively impact their work in the long term? These context-specific questions were representative of the key tensions that defined CSU's activities in the age of neoliberalism, tensions whose roots extended in many ways back to their Black Panther Party beginnings. The fundamental question was always: could they still serve as an authentic voice for community concerns when tied up in these networks of power and dependency?

CSU's answer seemed to be an uneasy mix of yes and no. Members relied on a central set of value priorities to guide their decision making, and they constructed a related set of organizational boundaries and cautions to preserve those values over time. With history as a guide, the organization always stood on guard, aware that its mission could be constrained by larger forces. A commitment to community and youth participation was necessary to resist outside expertise that failed to integrate local knowledge. A belief in critical education, free speech, and racial justice allowed the organization to avoid co-optation by groups whose practices did not embody similar value systems or include people of color in positions of leadership. A long-term vision of social, economic, and environmental sustainability pushed members to avoid short-term partnerships that ultimately detracted from their long-term mission of social transformation. Yet outright rejection of *all* potential partnerships that are not entirely ideologically pure—if an ideologically pure partnership were even possible—would doom the organization to fiscal bankruptcy and resultant programmatic ineffectiveness. However, a simple and universally applicable guide to navigating these waters was not in place, had never been in place, nor would ever be in place. Duren spoke to this ongoing give-and-take in an interview: "I think it's a tightrope walk, it is. You can be easily co-opted. They have a history of co-opting. So you have to be true to your mission and your spirits. But it's not impossible. . . . You're fighting a system that just naturally attempts to co-opt and dilute any kind of revolutionary fervor in terms of real change. So there's a tension there. And it's just part of the environment. So we just have to recognize that."

In its long-term planning, the organization resisted the idea of always remaining reactive and instead developed a plan for self-sustainability, which members saw as the ultimate outcome of their efforts in South LA. It would be through the Village Market Place social enterprise, they hoped, that CSU could more proactively work to achieve their goals of building "a sustainable food system from the ground up in South Central LA while training local youth, creating real jobs and building the local economy," as the organization explained in its promotional materials. Somewhat paradoxically, though, although the VMP was designed with an intention to minimize the importance of external funding, the initiative actually proved to be a major selling point to funders. It was one of the first projects to be funded, for instance, by the Obama Administration's Healthy Food Financing Initiative, which considered it to be worthy of governmental investment that was earmarked for promoting local economic development through community food entrepreneurship. Ultimately, though, as proud as the organization was to be able to bring in substantial grants to support its programs, members looked forward to the day when their operations were completely sustainable—socially, economically, and environmentally.

For some left-leaning critics, of course, this ongoing interdependent relationship with structures of governmental power, coupled with a commitment to community-based entrepreneurship, is seen to negate the transformative capacity of food justice activism. Instead, they wonder, where is the decommodified and independent food justice action that fundamentally opposes the marginalizing practices of neoliberalism?[62] Hearkening back, however, to an overly romanticized version of fully autonomous social justice activists of yore as a model for action fails to reflect the past, present, and future in an accurate light. Although the Black Panther Party, for instance, was "radically opposed to capitalism" in its rhetoric, in reality, its survival programs were deeply dependent on redistributing the fruits of capitalism itself.[63] Furthermore, the BPP's lack of organizational sustainability was attributable, at least in part, to the party's long-term failure to handle the means of production and manage a resource base of capital through which they could advance their social transformation goals.[64] "In this society, unfortunately you need to have funding to be sustainable," Dyane, CSU's financial and administrative manager, asserted. "You need to be able to support yourself." These words were as true for the BPP over forty years ago as they are for CSU today.

In CSU staffers' eyes, their fundamental goal remained a revolutionary one, even if their programmatic activity might at times suggest otherwise. "A revolutionary program is one set forth by revolutionaries, by those who want to change the existing system to a better system," Bobby Seale once declared. "A reform program is set up by the existing exploitative system as an appeasing handout to fool the people and keep them quiet" (178).[65] Members of CSU believed that, given the political and economic realities that characterized the history of South LA, it was indeed revolutionary to be at the leading edge of a community-based, people-of-color-led agenda for food justice. And, they insisted, maximizing organizational autonomy was central to turning community activism into a broader force for a revolutionary food justice movement. "It's about creating income that ultimately isn't dependent on any foundation or any funder or their whims," Neelam explained. "It's about self-determination." As my analysis has shown, however, even with increasing autonomy and self-determination, CSU could never be fully independent of the logics, strategies, and partnerships that characterize the age of neoliberalism. These elements were inscribed into the genetic code of the group's organizing strategy, and they will surely adapt and change *with* the organization as its networks and narratives evolve with the times.

. . .

While CSU's model for social change differed in many ways from the vision proffered by the original BPP, the organization still saw its practice as a transformative act. Members were inspired by those Panthers who shifted away from armed self-defense toward a strategy of developing programs for "survival pending revolution" as they recognized that new times brought with them new types of revolutionary pursuits. Following the ideas of Huey Newton, who argued decades before that you must "contradict the system while you are in it until it's transformed into a new system," CSU aimed to develop its own ideas of revolutionary action within an evolving sociopolitical context. Grounded in a philosophy of cultural empowerment and community economic development, the organization worked to build a model for social transformation that used food as a primary vehicle for change. Operating in relation to the "nonprofit industrial complex" in the age of neoliberalism, and in a new era of digital communication technology, CSU's actions were embedded within broader networks of fiscal support, organizational partnerships, and auditing techniques. Over time, the organization combined a set of philosophical knowledge practices with community-based experiences, consistently reshaping its activities to thrive within the existing political and economic landscapes. The stories members of CSU told, therefore, about the aims and scope of their mission, incorporated central aspects of the very systems that they looked to transform.

With CSU imbricated in complicated and sometimes contradictory relationships, the organization's work was hardly reflective of a pure and simple community-based authenticity. Did the nature of grant funding and the threat of co-optation from above call into question CSU's stated mission to "foster the creation of communities actively working to address the inequalities and systemic barriers that make sustainable communities and self-reliant life-styles unattainable"? CSU's work was certainly influenced by the priorities and expectations of grant funding agencies and other external partners. However, in devising a plan for programmatic activity, the organization kept its mission as a guide, with its members setting priorities and constructing boundaries that allowed CSU to keep the organization's long-term goals at the forefront of their efforts. It was the interaction of these practices over time—a hybrid praxis of food justice organizing—that gave way to the political imagination that would come to define CSU's community-based advocacy.

Of course, this chapter told the story of one specific organization, its history, and its challenges in balancing a social justice vision with the demands of nonprofit organizing. When one explores the backgrounds, philosophies, and practices of other food justice groups, however, it becomes clear that, while CSU's story is definitely distinct, it is not wholly unique. The food justice movement is filled with leaders who have deep connections to legacies of radical organizing for racial justice and social transformation. Today, they are often working as part of nonprofit organizations and developing social enterprises, meaning that they too have been pushed to consistently evaluate the prospects for revolutionary activism while operating "in the shadow of the shadow state."[66] Ultimately, though, the mixed feelings that emerge from these types of dynamic interactions are not only part and parcel of food justice activism in the contemporary moment but can also serve as a potentially productive force for change.[67]

In the case of CSU, the hybridity of the organization's communication ecology allowed staff to put forth a narrative of Black Panther–oriented social justice activism to the community members of South LA, while telling a story of systematic community capacity-building through alternative food initiatives to federal funding agencies. This complex blend was fundamental to the establishment of its agenda of shifting values, reshaping institutions, and moving forward community-based social change in South LA. The journey from being founded as part of the Black Panthers to being funded by the USDA, therefore, was fraught with ambivalence and contradiction. Yet this ever-present tension was actually central to CSU's organizational identity, and it proved to be a driving force for its organizational evolution, linking it to other food justice groups in similar predicaments and continuing to push forward its strategic action in the years to come.

Competing Visions and the
Food Justice Brand

While delivering a lecture to a group of Ivy League undergraduate students, I used the opportunity to perform an unscientific experiment that investigated the role of digital storytelling in the movement for food justice. For nearly an hour I had been offering a critique of the "broken windows theory," the long-held urban policing strategy that focuses on small instances of urban disorder—graffiti on storefronts, teenagers on street corners, broken windows on cars—as precursors to more serious street crime in urban neighborhoods. Taking care of this sort of riffraff, the theory's advocates propose, is the most effective way to ensure safe, healthy, and productive communities for all.[1] I explained how, in recent decades, this philosophy had been integrated into the everyday practices of major police forces nationwide—think, for instance, of New York City's controversial "stop-and-frisk" policy. Yet, despite its cultural impact, the hypothesis had been largely debunked. As sociologists Robert Sampson and Stephen Raudenbush have aptly demonstrated, although repairing "broken windows" might, at times, provide some superficial improvements to local neighborhoods, by ignoring the enduring impacts of economic inequality and racial prejudice, the "broken windows theory" offers an insufficient quick-fix for the challenges of urban community life. Simply put, if community-based social change is to be sustained, more systemic solutions are necessary.[2]

In my lecture, I turned to examples of urban agricultural efforts that had been the focus of my research in South Los Angeles. Which of these initiatives, I asked the students, focused mostly on surface-level broken windows solutions to tackle food injustice in South LA? Which dug deeper to examine and deconstruct the impacts of long-term economic exploitation and racial bias that had characterized the area? I showed them two short videos—one produced by Community Services Unlimited (CSU) as part of a recent online fundraising drive, the other a promotional spot touting the efforts of the American Heart Association's Teaching Gardens program. The responses of the students were nearly unanimous. They found that CSU's video suffered from sound problems and a shaky camera, and the mention of the Black Panther Party—which most of them understood to be a dangerous militant organization—proved confusing and unnerving. The American Heart Association, by contrast, boasted a high-quality audio-visual production, showed support from several major Hollywood celebrities, and featured the evocative sight of children digging their hands into the dirt. If urban agriculture was to be used as a force to make real change in South LA, the students concluded, the familiar philanthropic brand of the American Heart Association was clearly better equipped to make it happen.

The results of my little experiment, I should say, supported my initial hypothesis. I expected this group of young, mostly white, mostly economically privileged students to be impressed by the storytelling prowess of the American Heart Association (AHA). It mattered less—for reasons that will be unfolded in the pages to follow—that the AHA employed what I consider a broken windows approach to addressing the challenges of urban community health, while CSU proffered a more thorough, if imperfect, agenda for community change. For an audience far removed from the places and spaces of South LA, CSU's mediated story struggled to resonate, while the AHA's hit the right notes.

Throughout this book, my analysis has been rooted in a belief that storytelling, in its varied formations, is an important driver of social life and a shaper of social change. Stories serve a vital cultural function in their ability to reveal how things work, describe what things are, and tell us what to do about them. Today, as always, diverse stories about social problems compete in an effort to shape meaning in the public mind. In order to persevere in these ongoing storytelling battles, social movements must therefore do their best to exert what Manuel Castells has termed "communication power," using influential digital media and other avenues for multiplatform expression in order to shift the cultural narratives and institutional networks that dominate society.[3]

Elsewhere in this book, I have discussed the role that communication technologies and media storytelling have played in the development of the community-based food justice movement. Through digitally linked and locally grounded actions, a host of geographically and culturally diverse residents, community organizers, movement allies, and funders have been brought together for a common cause. Yet, exemplified by CSU's challenges in connecting to Los Angeles-area media producers (chapter 3), as well as Rooted in Community's struggle to have its Day of Action garner outside attention (chapter 4), I have also pointed to the obstacles of capacity and visibility that constrain the communication power of community-based food justice activists.

This chapter provides a deeper exploration of the challenges and opportunities inherent to food justice organizing at a moment in which media storytelling and branding has become increasingly important for the work of social justice advocates and nonprofit organizers. Consistent with the working principles for sustainable change that have guided my analysis throughout this book, I contend that storytelling of, by, and for the grassroots is a necessary aspect of this process, but I also insist that this localized storytelling alone will not be sufficient to push forth an effective movement agenda in the long term. Indeed, when community-based groups lack voice in the media representations that matter to potential allies and supporters from outside of the local community—including mainstream and corporate media, as well as digital and social media—their ability to influence public opinion, set the broader policy agenda, and grow localized struggles into a broader force for change is fundamentally restricted. Just as important, when groups whose work is legitimately grounded in the needs and interests of local community members struggle to tell their own stories of injustice and resistance to others, it becomes all too easy for outside interests to tell a version of their story for them—a version that is too often disconnected from the realities of everyday life.[4]

In recent years, of course, increased media attention has successfully catapulted food system and nutrition issues into the broader public consciousness. "This issue has become very high-profile, very, in many ways, fashionable," Neelam, CSU's executive director, reflected. "You know, there's a lot of money around for it now. And we're very happy about that. And it's in part because of organizations like us who have pioneered this work. So we're happy that's the case." The increasing cultural salience of food and agricultural issues in the first decades of the twenty-first century made work like CSU's more apt to be taken seriously by funding agencies; more appealing to a host of potential volunteers, donors, institutional partners, and the general public; and, quite frankly, more likely to be approached as a topic of engaged ethnographic and collaborative research by a scholar like me. Still, the optimism that came with these novel opportunities was equally matched by a new and ambivalent reality. "The more money, the bigger the players," Heather, CSU's associate director, remarked. "That becomes more of an issue."

Often inspired by major media figures, a host of new gardening, agriculture, and nutrition programs were being developed and deployed, many by middle-class, white practitioners and philanthropic groups that had little historical connection to the communities in which their work was situated. The stories told and the strategies employed by these outsiders were playing an increasingly influential role in defining how diverse groups of Americans came to understand issues of food inequity. Over the course of several years, I saw a number of new groups come to South LA, bringing gardens, nutrition education, and other food-related projects to a community that had become almost synonymous with the dreaded "food desert" label. Were these new entrants digging deep into the issues of the community, I wondered, or were they simply offering a broken windows approach to change, presented through the lens of expertly branded digital media productions?

In the pages to follow, I highlight the networked action and narrative practices of several newer players on the increasingly competitive South LA food justice scene—including one entity that entered the "food desert" of South LA from the outside and another initiative with roots in the neighborhood itself. The outsider is the Teaching Gardens program of the AHA, which, in 2010, began to develop a school-based garden education initiative with a stated aim to "teach children how to plant seeds, nurture growing plants, harvest produce and ultimately understand the value of good eating habits."[5] The insider is the Ron Finley Project, founded by the self-proclaimed "gangsta gardener" of South LA, whose viral video manifesto on urban gardening propelled him into a position of international prominence.

The analysis to follow is deeply critical of the Teaching Gardens program, specifically. My exploration of the networks and narratives of that organization led me to a conclusion that, since its inception, the program has lacked both the social justice vision and the grassroots engagement to make community-based food justice a reality. Yet, thanks to a sophisticated communication ecology devoted to media relations, the program has been adept at bringing public attention to its cause and quite successful in acquiring major funding to support its activities. I argue that it is through storytelling and communication power, and not necessarily through the material impacts of garden-based educational work, that a group like the Teaching Gardens— bolstered by a set of high-profile media industry, corporate, and philanthropic brand connections—can emerge as a relevant player in contemporary food politics and popular culture. With respect to the Ron Finley Project, my conclusions are not quite as firm. Finley himself offers a powerful voice to tell the story of food injustice from the perspective of a long-time South LA resident. Indeed, he offers groups like CSU a model for how they might better leverage digital media to build support among diverse audiences. At the same time, however, Finley's newfound celebrity status brings with it a unique set of concerns—his food justice message is in great danger of co-optation and dilution, and the actual level of grassroots accountability and connection to a broader social justice agenda in his work remains an open question. These critiques, it must be noted, are not intended as personal attacks against specific individuals or institutions involved in these or other projects. Rather, my aim in this chapter is to evaluate these programs on their own merits, and in their own words, with an eye toward the long-term implications of these circumstances for the food justice movement.

THE TEACHING GARDENS COME TO SOUTH LA

The Teaching Gardens program was created in 2010 by environmental activist and philanthropist Kelly Meyer. Concerned about the poor quality of school lunches and rising statistics related to childhood obesity, Meyer and her friends decided to take action on these issues: "Inspired by Michelle Obama's 'Let's Move' campaign and *Jamie Oliver's Food Revolution,* we came together to create an initiative to bring real, live garden laboratories to schools across the country." Initially launched on TakePart.com—the interactive publishing and digital action arm of Participant Media, the company that produced such socially conscious films as *An Inconvenient Truth; Food, Inc.;* and *The Help*—the project focused on building gardens in elementary and middle schools, starting in Southern California, with the plan and expectation to expand to over one thousand sites across the nation. "By introducing organic gardening along with a nutritional curriculum and technology that allows schools to communicate with other participants, the hope is to reestablish what it means to be healthy for the next generation."[6]

The Teaching Gardens project was hardly the first effort undertaken by Meyer and her colleagues to focus on environmental and health-related philanthropy. A mother of two, Meyer was president of the Parent Teacher Association at Point Dume Marine Science School in her home of Malibu,

California, where she was part of an effort to install solar power to support the science lab. She also collaborated with builder and developer Tom Schey to complete the first Leadership in Energy and Environmental Design (LEED) Platinum building in California in 2008, a project bolstered by donations and support from dozens of sponsors.[7] She also served as a trustee with the National Resources Defense Council, was a board member of Heal the Bay in Southern California, and worked as the cofounder of the Women's Cancer Research Fund, which emerged as a program of the Entertainment Industry Foundation, perhaps the largest Hollywood-based charitable organization. In that role, Meyer worked with her cofounders—as well as with honorary chairs that included celebrities such as Tom Hanks, Rita Wilson, and Steven Spielberg—to raise over $40 million for women's cancer research. For these efforts, the founders of the organization received a number of public accolades, including *Glamour Magazine*'s Women of the Year award in 2004. Although Meyer was undoubtedly accomplished in her own right, the fact that she was married to Ron Meyer, the COO of Universal/NBC and the longest tenured studio chief in all of Hollywood, is likely to have also played some role in helping to forge her projects' high-profile celebrity alliances.[8]

The first Teaching Garden was established at Malibu's Point Dume Marine Science School. Situated in one of the wealthiest communities in Southern California, Malibu is not an area known for food injustice. However, the program quickly expanded to other schools, including Kelso Elementary School in Inglewood, California, and Will Rogers Elementary School in Santa Monica, California, both of which were designated as Title I schools and received federal funding on account of their economically disadvantaged student bodies.[9] Parents, teachers, and volunteers worked together at the Teaching Gardens, which, Meyer articulated, were conceptualized as a "place where community partners come together to teach. A place where students, through the simple process of putting a seed into the earth, nurturing it and ultimately harvesting the food, will learn about efforts and results, delayed gratification, and cause and effect. The ultimate goal: hands-on exploration of the life sciences that lead to positive choices for health and fitness."[10] Right from the start, Meyer brought along star power to bolster the appeal and brand image of the initiative. Women's volleyball player and fitness guru Gabrielle Reece joined the Teaching Gardens as an "ambassador," as did Cat Cora of television's *Iron Chef,* actor Tobey Maguire (the husband of Jennifer Meyer, who was the daughter of Kelly's husband Ron), and longtime professional basketball player Derrick Fisher. Michael O'Gorman of the

Farmer-Veteran Coalition and Peggy Curry of the nonprofit garden and nutrition education program GrowingGreat also came on board to help launch the early projects.[11]

It did not take long for the Teaching Gardens program to catch the eye of the American Heart Association, one of the nation's oldest and largest voluntary nonprofit organizations. With a mission to "build healthier lives, free of cardiovascular disease and stroke," the AHA is headquartered in Dallas, Texas, boasting 144 local offices, nearly 2,700 employees, 22.5 million volunteers, more than $60 million in annual revenues and expenses, and over $1 trillion in total assets.[12] By September of 2010, the AHA announced it would adopt the Teaching Gardens program, touting the partnership as a "groundbreaking" approach in the promotion of childhood nutrition and science education, part of the organization's "healthy behavior change revolution." Their plan was to roll out a revamped effort for a dozen or so elementary schools in 2011, complete with associated nutrition education curriculum, in cities that cut across the nation—such as New York, Los Angeles, Scottsdale, Houston, and Fairfax.[13] As displayed on an interactive map on the Teaching Gardens' website, over the following years, some two hundred more gardens would be planted in cities and towns across the nation.

As the Teaching Gardens program expanded across the nation, a $650,000 grant from a lead sponsor, The California Endowment, meant that the AHA would continue to focus a good deal of its efforts within the greater Los Angeles area.[14] In the early years of the program, the broadly defined South Los Angeles region become home to dozens of Teaching Gardens, established in both Los Angeles and Long Beach Counties.[15] Administrators put an emphasis on placing Teaching Gardens in what they continually referred to as "vulnerable communities." An official with the AHA explained the organization's approach to site selection in an interview:

> It's all based on health statistics. It's based on the propensity for cardiovascular disease, the rates of mortality and premature mortality. Unfortunately those coincide with low-income areas, communities of color, and communities that tend to have a lower education rate. But our gardening factor truly is where more people are dying disproportionately from cardiovascular disease. And those do tend to be, in Los Angeles anyway, areas that are predominantly African American and Latino. So it's become a health equity issue for us.

In practice, each Teaching Garden consisted primarily of a few raised garden beds filled with organic soil, seedlings, and plants. Two garden coordinators were charged with overseeing all of the Los Angeles-area sites—specifically, they visited each garden two to four times per month—but the day-to-day management of the garden beds was left up to local teachers and administrators. The schools in which Teaching Gardens were installed signed an agreement to maintain the garden and to incorporate a special curriculum provided by the AHA into the school culture—this could be done through after-school or in-school programming in a manner that fit the unique needs and capabilities of each school.[16]

The launches of most of the local Teaching Gardens were highlighted by a Garden Build and Plant Day. At this event, students would be joined by AHA and Teaching Gardens staff, local volunteer organizations, corporate partners, and, at times, celebrities and athletes—like the CBS Network's *Hawaii Five-o* cast and professional surfer Laird Hamilton. Over time, the Teaching Gardens' website became awash with professionally produced photos and videos that documented these activities. More celebrity partners continued to come on board as supporters, Meyer discussed her work on national television programs, and local Teaching Gardens planting days were frequently covered in local and regional media outlets. In 2011, Meyer was named a Huffington Post Game Changer for her work. She articulated her vision and approach in her acceptance speech:

> I didn't want to come into schools and preach to kids about eating peas and carrots, because most of them don't even have access to healthy food, nor do their parents. I wanted to come into schools and meet them on their turf, and bring a little box of green that hopefully was a metaphor for the amount of time and energy and love and nutrition and water it takes, not just to grow a healthy tomato plant, but to grow a healthy child and a healthy community.[17]

As attention to the program increased, The California Endowment was joined by an ever-growing list of other financial supporters from across the foundation landscape, the corporate world, the entertainment industry, and the health care sector. In mid-2012, that list included around three dozen groups, but within a year there were nearly one hundred sponsors listed on the Teaching Gardens' website. Notable national institutions that supported the project included Bank of America, Capital One, Chevron, Dole Nutrition Institute, FedEx, MetLife, Natural Resources Defense Council, NBA Cares, NBC/Universal, Save A Lot Foods, the Scotts Miracle-Gro Company, and the Yahoo Employee Foundation. A number of sponsors and supporters had long-standing ties to the AHA, others to work in which Kelly Meyer had been engaged previously, and others to the local contexts in which the Teaching Gardens were sited. Indeed, as the Teaching Gardens program expanded into additional cities and towns, it added a variety of local and regional supporters—from Duke Energy's sponsorship of Brentwood Elementary School in Plainfield, Indiana, to Our Lady of the Lake Regional Medical Center's support of Wildwood Elementary in Baton Rouge, Louisiana.

With strong institutional and financial backing combined with the resources of the AHA, the longstanding connections of founder Kelly Meyer, and a well-established media presence, it was no surprise that the Teaching Gardens program was able to garner significant attention and quickly expand. The question remained, however, as to just how successful the project would be in its efforts to "re-establish what it means to be healthy for the next generation." Partners and advocates in the Teaching Gardens' network continued to attest that the project's strategy could fulfill such lofty goals, but did the evidence support the narrative they pushed?

ASSESSING COMMUNITY IMPACT

In the first few months that the Teaching Gardens program began to make its way into South Los Angeles, I heard grumblings from friends and colleagues engaged in food activism in the area. The reactions were mixed. Some saw the entrance of the AHA into urban gardening as a productive sign that investment in community-based responses to the problems of the food system was going mainstream. Others were less optimistic, concerned that the initiative was conceptualized by outsiders, ignored the already-existing food and agricultural work that was underway in the area, and could ultimately prove detrimental to the broader cause of community-based food justice. Staff members of CSU usually approached new entrants into South LA's food justice scene—especially outside groups that were not led by people from the neighborhood—with a healthy dose of skepticism. "You can either move forward in a way that honors the work that folks have been doing, those who have created the space for this work to be fashionable and so well-funded," Neelam explained, "or you can try and basically elbow us out and just ignore the fact that it's partly because [of] people like us that groups know the importance of this work and there's money out there for it."

Teaching Gardens, it seems, went with the latter approach. Indeed, the first time the program intersected with the organizational network of CSU was when an administrator associated with a private educational management organization that had recently taken over a school in which CSU had built and maintained a garden for nearly a decade delivered some unexpected news. The AHA had selected the school to launch one of its Teaching Gardens, he told them, so CSU's garden would soon be removed. Hardly averse to standing up for their rights within their own community, CSU staff demanded this plan be aborted and prepared a letter to that effect signed by dozens of community supporters. Thanks to this response, CSU's gardens were spared, and its involvement in the school programming was maintained, for that moment at least.

Upon hearing about this conflict, I delved into the online materials published by Teaching Gardens, had a chance to speak with staff members, and attended public events at which Kelly Meyer and other affiliated partners spoke. In my efforts to evaluate the program's efficacy in advancing community-based social change, I first tried to identify the underlying theory of change that guided the initiative's approach.[18] By building school gardens in selected at-risk communities, their theory seemed to follow, child and family eating habits could be transformed, community health could be improved, and these successes could be replicated in communities across the nation. It was a linear perspective that came through clearly in statements like this one from Ralph Sacco, MD, the AHA's president, quoted in a press release: "Our hope is that by teaching kids where vegetables come from and the benefits of healthy eating we can inspire change and reverse the epidemic of childhood obesity in this country. . . . Besides changing their own eating habits, children may also motivate other family members to modify their diets and improve cardiovascular health."[19]

When discussing the Teaching Gardens program, AHA and Teaching Gardens staff pointed to a set of pre- and post-intervention evaluation procedures—conducted in collaboration with researchers from the University of Vermont—that would help assess the effectiveness of the organization's theory. As part of this process, elementary student participants were asked to respond to a set of questions that measured their knowledge, attitudes, and behaviors related to gardening, nutrition, and fruit and vegetable consumption. "This work advances our understanding of childhood habit formation with regards to healthy eating habits and tests the impact of a top-down, nation-level initiative on the health of local communities," a research summary poster from a graduate student involved in the project explained. Key points of emphasis in the evaluation surveys were students' level of enjoyment while working in the garden, their interest in cooking and eating fruits and vegetables, and the social norms around healthy eating that existed among their friends and caretakers.

Upon examination, it was clear that these measures hardly assessed the type of large-scale community transformation goals that were consistently trumpeted in Teaching Gardens' promotional materials. This shortfall was not simply a result of the difficulty of measuring these types of large-scale outcomes. Instead, the evaluation procedures were derived from and served to reinforce the top-down initiative's commitment to a narrowly conceptualized and individualized theory of change. It was a perspective that was made concrete across the nutritional and gardening curriculum of the program itself, grounded as it was in a public health outlook that seemed to imbue children's interactions with fresh fruits and vegetables with almost supernatural powers. This "magic carrot" approach to community health promotion was fundamentally ill-equipped to engage with the broader economic, environmental, and sociostructural barriers that have proven to actually be at the root of systemic food injustice and the health problems related to it.

To be fair, there seemed to be some recognition among certain program participants that these structural limitations did stand as a barrier to long-term success. The researchers involved in the evaluation process, for instance, noted that more explicit integration of gardens into the broader school environment, as well as a greater understanding of the challenges faced by staff and administrators in these contexts, would be a necessary component for future research and action.[20] Similarly, in discussions with AHA staff members, I was consistently told that the Teaching Gardens program was part of a broader strategy of systemic built environment change that both the AHA and The California Endowment were committed to advancing in communities like South LA. Even if this premise is accepted, however, advocates and evaluators of the project fell short of providing any clear articulation of how its school gardens actively fed into these longer-view visions of change.

As I have argued from the outset of this work, if community-based initiatives are to effectively advance social justice in the age of neoliberalism, several principled and movement-oriented foundations are necessary. Such projects must actively nourish community participation, conceptualize localized work as part of a broader push to remedy structural inequality, be fiscally and programmatically sound, and be devoted to shifting broader social norms and institutions through a long-term dedication to expansive activism.[21] Across the board, structural deficiencies in the Teaching Gardens program prevented these criteria from being met. Individual gains in student achievement that could be attributed to the program, therefore, would be fragile at best.

The initiative's most glaring problem could be seen in the leadership that characterized the organizational network of Teaching Gardens. It was clear that the organization believed that grassroots knowledge and skills related to gardening, cooking, food, and physical activity were not present within "vulnerable communities" like South LA. Instead, this expertise needed to be provided to local youth by outsiders—mostly white philanthropists and celebrities—in acts of urban agricultural charity. The initiative did little to tailor its one-size-fits-all nutritional education curriculum to the specific geographic or historical contexts in which its work was situated, and there was no mention of the cultural value that members of communities of color themselves could bring to the study and practice of health and nutrition. Furthermore, despite advocates' insistence that Teaching Gardens was committed to systemic "built environment change," neither the theory of change nor the everyday practices at the heart of the program supported this contention. As an AHA staffer told me, participating schools were supported by a three-year funding cycle, with the hope that the schools would thereafter be able to take full control of the operations. There was little assurance, however, that the initiative would be sustained unless a particularly active teacher or administrator made it his or her task to maintain the programming. And, unfortunately, despite placing Teaching Gardens in communities across the country, the program did little to conceptualize how these disparate local actions might be united as an oppositional force to counterbalance inequities in the contemporary political and economic structures of the food system. With the program offering food and food alone as an antidote to enduring health disparities, it is no surprise that Teaching Gardens staffers never explicitly stated that their actions were in any way part of a *food justice movement* for change.[22]

At this point, my intensive criticism of the Teaching Gardens program mirrors a good deal of the already existing critical scholarship on alternative food movement efforts. On account of its context-free problem definition, its individualized solutions, and its often unbearable whiteness, Teaching Gardens should not be seen as an effective means to promote systemic social justice in the food system.[23] Yet, despite these criticisms, at the time of this writing, the Teaching Gardens program seemed to be gaining some momentum. The impressive amount of money—from major foundations, corporate sponsors, and health institutions—pulled in by the organization in just a few years to support its efforts allowed it to build gardens in Los Angeles and across the nation at a rapid pace. The media coverage it received raised its profile in ways that most garden-based education projects could never dream of. But was the program ever fully committed to developing a sustainable model for community change, or was the praise and investment it received actually the outcome it desired above all else?

BRANDING FOOD JUSTICE

If you navigate to the Teaching Gardens page on the American Heart Association's website you are immediately greeted by a pop-up donation screen with a photo of a young girl forming the shape of a heart with her hands, set alongside text that reads, "Who will you give for?" Make it past the pop-up screen and another pitch appears—this time you are encouraged to purchase a Teaching Gardens Starter Kit, produced by Burpee Seeds and Plants, which has pledged to donate $1.50 to the AHA for each $9.95 kit sold. You can click on the "About Teaching Gardens" link to read about the project's mission and preview samples from Teaching Gardens' elementary school curriculum, which is matched to meet the AHA's dietary recommendations for children and adolescents to promote cardiovascular health. Visit the photos and blog sections to view pictures of smiling schoolchildren digging into the dirt and tasting fresh-picked vegetables.

Buttons for Twitter and Facebook are portals to more pictures, as well as tips and links to studies about school gardening, childhood nutrition, and physical activity. The Teaching Gardens' YouTube link opens up to dozens of professionally produced videos of garden planting and harvesting days from locations across the country. In one of the featured promotional videos, a narrator opens with a question: "Have you ever asked yourself what it would take to have our children choose garden vegetables over fast foods?" A group of mostly African American and Latin@ children are depicted in a school garden, being taught how to plant a seedling in a raised garden bed. A tight shot of the program's founder, Kelly Meyer, follows: "Feeding our kids in our lunchroom every day high-fat, high-sugar, high-sodium food and then cutting the funding for physical education—those two things together equals one third of our children suffering from childhood obesity." Her remarks are immediately juxtaposed with a young African American boy and girl, who, when asked to talk about their favorite food to eat for lunch, both emphatically reply that they like hot dogs. The remainder of the video shows Meyer, along with staff from the Teaching Gardens and a bevy of celebrity partners, giving lessons on healthy food, gardening, and cooking to smiling groups of children. "Dig in, and let's get growing," the narrator closes before the logos for Teaching Gardens and the American Heart Association are displayed.[24]

From the time of its launch, the Teaching Gardens program has been consistently lauded in the press and featured in a variety of public relations campaigns.[25] In May of 2012, for instance, founder Kelly Meyer appeared on NBC's nationally broadcast *Today* show, where she was glowingly introduced as a philanthropist developing a school-wide initiative that could make a difference in fighting childhood obesity. Also in 2012, with support from The California Endowment and *Parenting* magazine, Meyer set up a demonstration Teaching Garden during the film premiere of Universal Pictures' *The Lorax*. As described in a press release, "Student leaders from Teaching Gardens across Los Angeles enjoyed cotton candy, face paint, and even walked the 'The Lorax orange carpet' aside Taylor Swift, Zac Efron, Danny Devito and other stars in the film." Meyer was given a platform to espouse the benefits of the program's approach on the pages of *Parenting,* where she declared, "This exposure is helping us get the word out about the value of healthy eating to lots of kids and their families."[26] The Plant and Build days that were a hallmark of the Teaching Gardens strategy were often covered in local and regional media and bolstered by professional social cause marketing groups, like the Griffin Schein firm.[27] Corporate sponsors, such as Scotts Miracle-Gro, consistently took the opportunity to tout their partnership in corporate social responsibility reports, and they were given favorable press in articles like one from the *Columbus Dispatch,* headlined, "Elementary Students Plant 'Dream Garden.'"[28] The program got yet another media boost in 2013, when *Variety* named Quvenzhane Wallis—the star of *Beasts of the Southern Wild,* who became the youngest performer ever to be nominated for an Academy Award—as one of the honorees for its Power of Youth awards after she became a Teaching Gardens ambassador.[29] In January of 2014, a Teaching Gardens Plant and Build Day was even broadcast to millions of households when it was featured on NBC's popular weight-loss television show, *The Biggest Loser.*[30] A year later, a set of Teaching Gardens commercials was featured on several primetime FOX television programs, with Meyer highlighted as part of the Ford Motor Company's Go Further Everyday Heroes video series.[31]

Teaching Gardens' heavy emphasis on public relations as a central aspect of its organizational operations should come as no surprise. As cultural theorist Sarah Banet-Weiser has described, in our contemporary "brand culture," the dynamics of mediated branding have become central not only to for-profit corporations and their bottom lines but also to nonprofit organizations in their attempts to raise the profile of social advocacy issues.[32] In order to increase their visibility, social advocacy groups often become partners in corporate social responsibility campaigns—hybrid forms of advertising, public relations, and philanthropy. For nonprofit groups engaged in these activities, increased visibility can build public support, shape funding opportunities, and provide some traction in public policy and business arenas. From the corporate partners' perspective, in the words of Banet-Weiser and her colleague Rupali Mukherjee, "social justice transforms into yet another strategic venture to secure the corporate bottom line" (10).[33]

The Teaching Gardens program was quite successful in gaining media attention by billing the program as a pioneer in garden-based education, even though such programs had long been in existence. Advocates also championed the program as a particularly effective way to combat child obesity and promote children's health, even though they offered little to no empirical evidence to support these claims. Ultimately, it became clear that the program's varied activities in media production, press coverage, celebrity advocacy, and corporate sponsorship were not merely ways to promote its garden-based work in order to build capacity. Rather, garnering publicity for the sake of publicity appeared to be a driving force of the entire program's mission. Through a sophisticated communication ecology for branding and media relations, the Teaching Gardens program brought together connections from across the domains of philanthropy, entertainment media, public health, and the corporate world, using its communication power to connect with the hearts and minds of the American viewing and eating public.

Now, an argument can certainly be made that such philanthropic marketing initiatives, while hardly a large-scale remedy for social injustice, at least do *some* good. Who can argue with a program that provides access to gardening and nutrition education for historically underserved children? What's wrong with using branding and media relations to raise awareness about issues of obesity in low-income communities? This may be true in the short-term, perhaps, but ultimately, by focusing on simple problem framings and superficial solutions to issues of systemic food injustice, initiatives like the Teaching Gardens program actually limit the discourse and strategic action of food justice activism. The public relations push spearheaded by the AHA and its corporate partners offered a sanitized narrative of food system inequity, proffered individual consumer solutions to food injustice's detrimental impacts, and advanced their collective bottom lines through the process. Its conflict-averse narrative communicated to a compassionate public that all it takes to help the oppressed, marginalized, and unhealthy is a quick fix.[34] Build them gardens, the story goes, and they will learn to thrive, as images of smiling black and brown children tell us that, together, we are making a difference. This broken windows approach leaves little room for any analysis of the underlying components of structural racial and economic inequality, serving only to constrain the types of solutions that might emerge from such efforts. As The California Endowment itself described in a how-to guide for media advocates, an overemphasis on this type of "awareness-raising" storytelling consistently overshadows the need for policy and systems changes that more effectively promote healthy communities.[35]

These dynamics are all representative of what the scholar Samantha King has deemed *philanthrocapitalism,* a "corporatized public sphere in which political sentiments and critical energies are increasingly expressed through the purchase of products, the donation of money to 'good' causes or participation in volunteer activities" (490).[36] What we find, then, is that corporate social responsibility campaigns and philanthrocapitalist initiatives attach themselves to organizations that promote safe political postures that would never challenge or complicate the positive resonance of a brand. As Sarah Banet-Weiser has described, "the public visibility of urban farming in the contemporary moment makes some urban farms far more brandable than others" (161).[37] Teaching Gardens' work was based on a theory of change that would prove politically safe for corporate and philanthropic partners, and its networked connections in media relations meant it could provide consistent positive press for all involved. Perhaps more than anything else, then, what defined the Teaching Gardens program was its inherent *brandability.*

How, then, have community-based food justice groups—those that are grounded in the experiences of local community members and offer nuanced stories of historical injustice and resistance—responded to the increasingly mediated, brand-conscious landscape of nonprofit activism? While it was a question that food justice groups were certainly pondering during my years of collaborative research, most activists still lacked a fully formed strategic platform to tackle these issues, a reality that led to uneven and often ineffective apparatuses for media relations. "We are very aware that we have not been good at harnessing media, and in the past even social media, to kind of leverage what we do," Neelam explained. "Initially, it was an almost intentional thing. I would say that more recently it's been more about capacity."

For evidence of this, direct your web browser to CSU's website.[38] There, you are first greeted by the sight of a produce bag full of cabbage, chard, oranges, and lemons. The landing page touts the freshness of the local, beyond organic produce being sold through the Village Market Place, and it offers several avenues to subscribe or donate to the organization. The About Us pages introduce the group's staff, board, funders, and supporters and give a brief history of the organization's decades of work in South Central Los Angeles. Descriptions of CSU's various community-based programs are matched with a handful of still photos of children, youth interns, and community volunteers. A recent redesign improved the general appearance of the site, but several months later, a number of key links—to the events calendar, the media page, and Twitter—either lead to error pages or are entirely empty. If you manage to find your way to CSU's Facebook or Twitter pages, you find a smattering of sporadic announcements of workshop events, produce markets, and the like, as well as photos, mostly depicting the fruits and vegetables for sale or freshly made catered meals. A search on YouTube for Community Services Unlimited brings up just a few hits, mostly user-uploaded or student-produced videos that feature interviews with staff, volunteers, and local community members, as well as shots of CSU's urban farms and produce stands.

CSU's online presence is evidence of the struggles the organization faces when it works to tell its story to audiences beyond the local community. Indeed, as I described in chapter 3, staffers had a hard enough time getting traction in the local and ethnic media of South Los Angeles, let alone in the types of major media flows that shape public opinion across the nation and globe. Over the course of time, CSU had been unable—and, in some ways, unwilling—to expand its communication ecology for media relations, and the result of this was that its narrative of community-based food justice had not become a major part of a larger cultural conversation. CSU staffers did intimate that it might be nice to have greater attention granted to their work in mainstream news and entertainment outlets, since this level of exposure could help them compete with the high-profile voices in media that, for many Americans, had come to define the problems and solutions of the contemporary food system. "The truth is, there's so much work to be done right where we are," Heather explained. "And there is a lot of benefit and opportunity to create something that benefits local people and inspires people. So that has to remain our focus." Lacking confidence in mainstream media to grant them any legitimate attention, and with their limited staff already overworked, CSU consistently brushed aside topics like internal media production and media outreach to focus on the more pressing demands of their everyday community-based operations. What took shape was a media relations apparatus that had some potential for impact but ultimately lacked expertise, suffered from problems of follow-through in distribution, and did not include support from networked connections that could help staff spread their story through major media institutions and platforms.

In 2012, for instance, CSU partnered with two Los Angeles-based undergraduate students to develop a project that would share the stories of local residents who took part in its community workshops. Adam—an undergraduate film production student—and Mindy—a returning student who had spent twenty-five years in direct mail advertising—led the production of a sixteen-minute documentary film, *The Garden Gateway Project*. It set the context for the food injustice faced by South LA residents, featured interviews with local residents and CSU staff, and included shots of the mini urban farms and home gardens that they had collectively created. "I've traditionally had to drive out pretty far to get any organic produce, and this is just amazing to me that, in my community, I can just go and get organic produce," Cynthia, a South LA resident, sitting with her young son on her lap, said in the film. "It's been having a ripple effect, even in our—even in my little world. And that's why I think this program is so important and has been so effective, even just in my life."[39]

In terms of production value, the short film was undoubtedly the highest quality product that had documented CSU's work to date. In the months that followed the completion of the film, it was shared through several means. First, it was shown at a gathering of over fifty of CSU's friends and supporters at a South LA community center. Then, several screenings were set up at local universities for audiences of students and staff. It was also informally distributed through word of mouth recommendations and digital sharing. Adam and Mindy were both personally and professionally moved by the collaboration with CSU and excited that they could help the organization tell its story of community-based activism. "I think it's very important for groups like CSU to have ownership of their programs and make sure they stay well versed in how the generations of today communicate," Adam explained. "Visual storytelling through film and video is very crucial."

At the same time, however, the filmmakers recognized that the film had done little to significantly shift the tenor of public discussion related to food injustice. Ultimately, a systematic strategy for distributing the film, including thinking through ways to leverage the high-quality production to tell CSU's story to bigger and broader audiences, was not granted a priority status within the organization. For her part, Mindy understood why a grander media relations and branding push did not take shape. "The thing is, public relations doesn't put food in people's mouth. And what Neelam and CSU care about is putting food in people's mouths." CSU's primary strategy remained grounded in engaging the people and places of South LA. Investing resources and cultivating relationships with media producers and external public relations professionals who were not committed to that community-based goal was neither a priority of the organization nor something that its staff was particularly well equipped to handle. Still, Mindy argued, more work needed to be done to figure out how to raise the profile of CSU—and of other groups engaged in food justice work—while still maintaining a fundamental commitment to localized storytelling and community-based activism. "There needs to be some experimenting. There is a big disconnect between grassroots, hands-on community activism and the outside world," she explained. "We need to experiment with some new ways to get the message out. But we need more awareness *and* more actual hands-on support."

Similar challenges beset other community-based food justice groups I encountered, including several involved in the Rooted in Community (RIC) network. As I discussed in chapter 4, Gera, RIC's codirector, was excited by the power of youth-led "artivism" to spread the food justice message to groups of young people from across the country and to the broader culture at large. "We want to host a beautiful summit and have it well documented, with daily blogs and tweets and videos, and have media here to show and demonstrate this youthful creative organizing," he told me. To achieve this goal, organizational staff were depending in large part on the technological savvy of the youth food justice activists themselves. Rather than having adult mentors who were not always so fluent in new media platforms lead the charge, they assumed that the young people would be best equipped to communicate their own messages through the social media platforms that mattered to them. What emerged in practice, however, was a media strategy that lacked consistent capacity—in terms of both production quality and effective distribution—and RIC's online presence remained limited to a handful of photos, videos, and social media updates with little demonstrated impact beyond influencing those immediately involved. Just because the young people were familiar with the tools of the digital age did not mean that they were inherently trained or ready to produce and distribute media that could effectively capture the public imagination.[40] This is especially true, of course, when youth activists offer a less-than-sanitized narrative of food injustice and lack the networked media connections to have their stories more widely broadcast. Grassroots narratives of community-based food justice, it seems, face an uphill battle when trying to gain traction in the contemporary media landscape. These struggles in effectively branding food justice, however, need not be the end of the story.

THE RON FINLEY PROJECT GOES VIRAL

In a video filmed at the 2013 TED (Technology, Entertainment, Design) conference in Long Beach, California, Ron Finley stood confidently on stage, the bright-red TED logo featured prominently behind him. "Just like 26.5 million other Americans, I live in a food desert," he explained. "South Central Los Angeles. Home of the drive-thru and the drive-by. Funny thing is, the drive-thrus are killing more people than the drive-bys." By early 2015, Finley's ten-minute talk had been viewed over two million times online, and the viral video star's life had, not surprisingly, been fundamentally transformed.[41] When I spoke with him over the telephone, Finley had just returned from an appearance at the EAT Forum in Stockholm, Sweden, a two-day conference on food and sustainability that brought together global leaders from business, science, and politics. "Bill Clinton opened it and I closed it," he told me. "So Bill Clinton basically opened for me." It had been a whirlwind year of speeches and events for the "gangsta gardener" of South Central Los Angeles, a charismatic African American man whose background as a fashion designer prepared him to approach the enterprise with style and flair. Still, the energetic Finley showed no signs of slowing down his pace. "I didn't ask for this, this was not my goal. I didn't plan on becoming Godzilla," he quipped. "[But] when I'm into something, I put my foot in it. I want people to go, 'damn!' My vision is world domination."

Finley's unlikely story was one that could only have taken shape in an age of omnipresent digital technology and shareable online media. His success not only sheds light on the interactions between brand culture and the food justice movement but also underscores a key and ongoing debate regarding the role of digital media in twenty-first century social justice activism. In recent years, of course, countless scholars and practitioners have championed the capacity of new media to serve as a force for the promotion of democratic activism. Digital media platforms alone may not fully liberate contemporary society from historical imbalances of power, these advocates suggest, but the tools of digital technology *do* provide everyday citizens with a revolutionary ability to bring their cultural and political ideas into the mainstream.

With this in mind, media scholar Henry Jenkins and his colleagues have urged producers and social activists alike to pay close attention to the "spread-ability" of media content—that is, the technical, economic, and content-based attributes of digital media products that spark some to spread through digital social networks while others wallow in obscurity. Understanding the dynamics of spreadability, they argue, can be a powerful strategy for grassroots groups to leverage the potentials of digital media in order to shape public perceptions and advance their social justice aims.[42] On the other side of the spectrum, skeptical scholars such as Jodi Dean have argued that the "proliferation, distribution, acceleration, and intensification of communicative access and opportunity result in a deadlocked democracy incapable of serving as a form for political change." (22) When going viral becomes the aim of social change advocates, she suggests, what they ultimately encourage is more talk and more digital storytelling but little structural transformation.[43]

Finley's journey offers a valuable case study to explore these dynamics. Here is a long-time resident of South Los Angeles speaking candidly about issues of food injustice and sharing the challenges and solutions of his own community with interested audiences from around the world. Advocates of spreadable media might consider his success to be evidence of digital technology's power to invert traditional power dynamics, since he wrested control of the food justice narrative from celebrity philanthropists and rooted it back in the voices and experiences of the grassroots. More skeptical observers, by contrast, would recommend caution, waiting to see whether his spreadable storytelling actually empowers on-the-ground networks of activists to advance their food justice goals, or whether all of the publicity actually serves only to reinforce a brand of food activism that lacks the necessary community-based connections to sustain social change.

To tell the story of Finley's rise to prominence, however, one should not overlook the influence of another devoted urban gardener, a South Los Angeles native named Florence Nishida. Of Japanese heritage, Florence remembers returning to live in South LA after her family was released from a World War II-era internment camp in the mid-1940s. Her father was a professional gardener, and, at the time, the Los Angeles area was one of the most productive agricultural regions in the state of California. "That was what growing up in Los Angeles was like. Food was just not an issue, just not a problem," Florence explained. "We had everything we needed. It was not a food desert. In the community I grew up in, which is South LA, we had an abundance of choices of food. But it wasn't supermarket choices, it wasn't a lot of processed food. It was fresh food that you had easy access to." Florence, a former school teacher, earned a master's degree in science and biology later in life, and, although she eventually moved to Los Angeles County's Topanga Canyon, she maintained a connection to her old neighborhood through a research association with the Natural History Museum in South Los Angeles. After retiring from her day job, Florence trained at the University of California's Cooperative Extension to become a master gardener. She gave a gardening workshop to local residents in South LA, and it was there that she first met Finley, who was in attendance to sharpen the agricultural skills he had been dabbling in for some time.

The Cooperative Extension had been encouraging its master gardeners to do more to engage directly in community-based work, and as Florence surveyed her first place of residence, she began to form a vision. "The neighborhood, it just was so grim. There was no green anywhere," she explained. "I thought—there are all these yards. People can grow food in their yards!" Finley was on the ground floor of envisioning the approach as well, and, along with a third cofounder adept at organizational skills, they formed a group they called LA Green Grounds in 2010. The stated mission of the collaborative was to "bring groups of diverse people together to replace residential front lawns into edible gardens to be shared with the neighborhood." Nearly four years later, Florence estimated that LA Green Grounds, drawing from mostly volunteer power and some in-kind donations, had installed about thirty gardens in the city—although, she lamented, some had flourished more than others. Consistent with the group's initial mission of working in areas of higher need, nearly all of these gardens were set up at the homes of lower-income community residents in the South Los Angeles area.

Finley's own home was the site of LA Green Grounds' second residential "dig-in." They decided to turn the parkway in front of his house—the little strip of grass between the street and the sidewalk—into an "urban food forest." His green thumb soon helped him to cultivate a bountiful garden on the tiny plot, and the site became both a conversation starter in the neighborhood and a source of fresh food for some of Finley's neighbors who were in the most need. We can assume, however, that at least one local resident did not appreciate all of the attention. Likely prompted by a neighbor's complaint, local authorities soon rebuffed Finley's efforts by issuing him a ticket for a zoning infraction. This apparent setback, however, proved to be the launching point for Finley's new life and career. A profile in the *Los Angeles Times* soon followed, and public pressure mounted in support of the man unfairly persecuted for growing food on his own property. Eventually, the city rescinded Finley's ticket.

The biggest boost for LA Green Grounds, however, came when Finley was tapped to tell his story at a TED gathering. With style, humor, and passion, Finley recounted his own underdog story of fighting the powers that be and introduced LA Green Grounds as a "pay-it-forward kind of group" working to beautify an often-neglected neighborhood. Championing the empowering capacity of urban agriculture, he delivered one catchphrase after another, such as, "Growing your own food is like printing your own money." Speaking from his own experience of living in a neighborhood known for a history of gang violence, he argued that it was time to change the way young people think about growing up in communities like South LA: "We gotta flip the script on what a gangsta is—if you ain't a gardener, you ain't gangsta." Gardening, he argued, offered a pathway to health and happiness for children and families stuck in food deserts across the country: "If kids grow kale, kids eat kale. If they grow tomatoes, they eat tomatoes."[44]

Soon after the TED Talk was posted, Finley's story spread. It was shared on Facebook and Twitter, and Finley was profiled online and in print both locally and internationally. He was quickly catapulted into the position of being one of the nation's most recognizable voices for food justice, and he secured a spot as the most prominent food justice advocate from the community of South LA. He traveled across the United States, Europe, and the Middle East delivering his gospel that it was time to "plant some shit." A profile in the *New York Times* detailed his appeal: "The talk show host Carson Daly, the actress Rashida Jones and the celebrated Danish chef René Redzepi were among hundreds of new admirers issuing shout-outs on

Twitter. Alice Waters stopped by Mr. Finley's house, Russell Brand put him on his late-night talk show, and corporations like Reebok, Disney, Stihl and Toms Shoes had collaboration ideas."[45] Finley's message of "guerilla gardening" led to him being granted the first Natural American Heroes award by the Natural News website. He was dubbed an "Eco-lutionary Game Changer Provocateur" by Beck's Beer, and the brewing company featured a sunflower rendering designed by Finley on a specialty bottle label.[46] The California Endowment and Teaching Gardens' founder Kelly Meyer also took note of his work, filming their own video profile of Finley's efforts and plugging his story in an article in the *Huffington Post*. On any given night in 2014, Finley might be found standing alongside Sacramento mayor Kevin Johnson and celebrity chef Jamie Oliver at an event to highlight Oliver's new cooking education program or taking photos with actress Bette Midler at the New York Restoration Project's Annual Spring Picnic.[47] He also emerged as the public face of a local movement to legalize the planting of edible parkways, an ordinance that was officially passed by the City of Los Angeles in early 2015.[48] All the while, Finley received a constant stream of e-mails and Facebook and Twitter messages from fans the globe over. "I got kids in India calling themselves gangsta gardeners. I got kids in Baltimore talking about planting green roofs," he told me. "I'm a mouthpiece for this process, not just in my little piece of the world, but for the whole world."

But a funny thing happened on the way to global recognition. As Finley tells it, even though he mentioned his work with LA Green Grounds in his TED Talk, by the time the video premiered, he had cut ties with the group. "With Green Grounds, they didn't understand that my vision was world domination. You know what I'm saying? It wasn't about South Central. Yeah, it's about South Central because that's where I'm repping, that's where I'm from. Once that kitchen is clean, you know, go clean somebody else's kitchen," he explained. "They wanted to do one [garden] a month, they wanted to take off in the summer. I'm like, fuck that. I want to do a thousand a month." As a vehicle for his expanding vision, he founded the Ron Finley Project, and he began to develop a plan whose details were, at the time of this writing, still being worked out. "I don't grow food, I grow people. You know what I'm saying? Food is a byproduct. All this is about is growing people and giving them opportunity." By mid-2014, Finley was in talks to transform the grounds of South LA's Vermont Square Public Library into a major garden site, and he also had plans to turn his own residence into "Ron Finley HQ," complete with a public garden and café that would one day feature cooking education programs and create jobs for local residents. An online fundraiser, launched in November of 2014, stated that the project would require $1.5 million in "public and private funding to cover planning, architectural, marketing, and operating expenses."[49]

In a conversation with Finley, I confronted him with several underlying concerns. With all of the publicity surrounding him, was there a danger that his food justice message could be co-opted by his various new corporate and foundation partners? "We've got to change the mentality to Robin Hood shit," he replied. He insisted that he followed a personal code that prevented co-option, that he had walked away from potential partnerships that did not feel right, and that some potential partners had even walked away from him, nervous that he would not toe their company line. Ultimately, it made sense to him to take money from major corporations and philanthropic organizations—as long as he was still calling the shots. "That's not selling out. That's moving the needle forward because now you got paper. Free is not sustainable." As for the celebrity advocates with whom he had partnered—such as Jamie Oliver, Bette Midler, and Alice Waters—he insisted that they were all game-changers themselves with a demonstrated ability to make an impact. "You have a group of people who understand that this shit has to change," he said. "The bottom line is we all breathe the same air. We all drink the same water."

I pressed him to tell me more about his connections to South Los Angeles as a site of action. Now that he was no longer working with LA Green Grounds, were there other groups that were helping him engage in his local community? He mentioned InsideOutWriters, a nonprofit that uses writing to help reduce juvenile recidivism in the criminal justice system; the LA Conservation Corps, a nonprofit that provides employment for at-risk youth in conservation and service projects; and the aforementioned California Endowment. He did not give much explicit information, however, to specific efforts that might incorporate the voices of everyday people from the South LA area into the design and implementation of his initiative. Perhaps this was a fundamental oversight in his project, or perhaps it was just due to the fact that he was not particularly willing to provide much detail about his plans at this stage. "I'm not one to tell you everything. I say I'll tell you what I'm doing after it's done—after the ribbon's cut," he explained. "That little shit I gave you—that was just an apple. I got a whole fucking tree behind my back."

At this early stage, then, it would be premature to levy a verdict on the viability of Finley's approach or on his prospects for motivating sustainable community change. His passionate advocacy for urban agriculture has undoubtedly raised the profile of food justice issues among the broader public. Thanks to the spreadable nature of digital media, he has emerged as a new bottom-up voice for food justice advocacy, one whose perspective is undoubtedly more grounded in lived experience than many other food system reformers, particularly those who blindly enter marginalized communities with already-established external agendas for change. By shifting the public narrative and opening up more opportunities for food justice action, his success could go a long way toward encouraging community-based groups—who have often overlooked the importance of media storytelling—to place an increased emphasis on these dynamics. And, thanks to its influence in popular culture, the Ron Finley Project may develop the networked partnerships that are necessary for fiscal and programmatic longevity, serving as a catalyst that will usher community-based food justice activism into a new era of large-scale cultural and structural transformation.

However, Finley's rapid rise to fame should raise some red flags for food justice organizers who operate "in the shadow of the shadow state." The narrative Finley has tended to put forth in his public appearances is at least as similar to the theory of change championed by the likes of the Teaching Gardens program as it is to the food justice philosophy espoused by groups like CSU. His consistent public assertions that *gardening itself* can serve as the path toward health and well-being—"if kids grow kale, kids eat kale"— are in many ways more in line with a simplified broken windows approach to community change than a more historically grounded vision of overcoming racial discrimination through social justice organizing. When you combine Finley's familiar and conflict-averse narrative with his built-in credibility as an African American resident of South LA and his background as an artist keenly attuned to the stylistic elements of production, he emerges as a highly brandable commodity. It seems that Finley might be considered just "safe enough" as a partner for the major corporations and philanthropic organizations that have sought to bring him into their fold.

This is not to say that Finley himself does not harbor more radical leanings and a deep commitment to combatting food injustice through systemic means. In private conversation, he is more apt to enter into this discussion. "See, people think it's all about food, but it ain't about food. It's about keeping these kids out of prison," he told me. "I don't go out there necessarily all the time and spit game like that." The question, then, is whether Finley *will* push forth this more systematic narrative in the months and years to come.

Will he also work to construct a set of community-based networks that will leverage his spreadable media success into enduring social justice action? Or will the temptations of celebrity and the priorities of corporate brands prevent him from advancing a just and sustainable agenda? "Again, I didn't ask for this," Finley insisted, "but now that I'm here I'm gonna wreck some shit."

. . .

A key argument of this book has been that, in order for community-based food justice organizing to be successful, activists must work collaboratively with local residents to develop critical consciousness and cultivate actionable skills for the betterment of their communities. As this chapter has demonstrated, however, there are multiple and often competing visions of what that community-based capacity-building might look like. At a moment when digital media storytelling and the dynamics of brand culture have become central aspects of our society, our economy, and of social activism itself, advocates for food justice must be cognizant of how these processes influence their ability to motivate sustainable change.

While Community Services Unlimited has never directly collaborated with either the Teaching Gardens program or the Ron Finley Project, the presence of these newer organizations is undoubtedly reshaping the networked environment in which CSU's food justice activism takes place. There is little reason to believe that CSU's on-the-ground urban gardening efforts would need to be significantly reformulated. Ultimately, South LA has plenty of space for a variety of groups to engage in parallel or intersecting agricultural projects. In the domain of storytelling, however, it appears that CSU's operations require substantive rethinking. The case of the Teaching Gardens program demonstrates that, with strong backing from philanthropic and corporate partners, an organization with little grounding in the local community can tell a convincing, if incomplete, story about food inequity. The success of the Ron Finley Project shows that digital media offers an opportunity for voices to emerge from the ground up but also that publicity comes with its own set of challenges and the danger of co-optation. It is incumbent upon community-based food justice advocates to investigate the increasingly crowded landscape of nonprofit organizing and figure out ways to effectively tell a story that brands food justice as a long-term project of social transformation.

There is always a legitimate concern, from the perspective of many community-based organizers, that an increased focus on media relations will ultimately distract from pressing community needs, forcing groups to target their efforts on the demands of the "nonprofit industrial complex." "It takes a lot of soul searching to figure this stuff out," CSU staffer Dyane told me in a conversation. His colleague Heather agreed, adding that the organization was still in the process of trying to articulate its message for broader audiences—including audiences with deep pockets—but it was an ongoing challenge to do so while staying true to CSU's mission and ethos. Staff members remained deeply skeptical of organizations that seemed to be guided by public relations and driven by the charisma of a media personality rather than by the voices of community members. Reflecting on projects they had seen initially pick up steam only to sputter out shortly thereafter, both Dyane and Heather offered up the central question: what happens in three or four years? That is, once the media fervor settles down, will anything of appreciable change have been built? Still, they recognized that doing a better job of articulating CSU's story to those outside of the community—and understanding the role of digital media in this process—was worth significant consideration. Indeed, a few months after this conversation, when CSU launched an online fundraiser to support the purchase of a new building for its headquarters in South LA, the organization released an online video that featured the well-known musician and philanthropist Aloe Blacc.

"We have for some years, as you've seen, been building a brand slowly," Neelam explained in an interview. "Those things, as you know, they take time, they take money. We're committed to doing it. When we do that in a big way, like everything else we do, we want it to be very deliberate and very intentional and very thought out. But we're getting to that point of being able to do that." Looking forward, if they are unable to tell a convincing story of food injustice's causes and solutions to the wider world, someone else will surely step in to try and tell it for them.

It is safe to assume that navigating these dynamics will continue to characterize the hybrid praxis of community-based food justice activism in the years to come. Simply ceding the digital media space to the Teaching Gardens of the world will ultimately detract from food justice's viability as a cohesive movement for change, since the minds and monies of the public will remain focused on overly simplified and sanitized solutions. The viral spread of Ron Finley's "gangsta gardening" message demonstrates that there are new machinations of media power in the digital age, but it is also clear that storytelling alone will not sustain a movement. The key task, then, is to make sure that the spreadability of digital media content does not merely reify the broken windows ethos that has come to characterize mainstream discussions of tackling food inequity. For those serious about sustaining community change, effective storytelling must always refer back to networked efforts that actively transform the cultures and structures of a broken and unjust food system.

Conclusion

Predictions of impending social and ecological collapse have been gathering steam for decades, considered by many to be a natural outgrowth of the excesses and policy failures of modern industrial society. In the twenty-first century, scholarly research and global media coverage of economic decline, civil unrest, and environmental strain have made it difficult to ignore the bleak possibilities that our common future might hold.[1] In a well-circulated study published in 2014—conducted by an interdisciplinary team of applied mathematicians and natural and social scientists and partially funded by NASA—researchers developed a model to explain the underpinnings of societal downfalls in the past, with an eye toward predicting what our own society's fate might be. They found that "advanced, sophisticated, complex, and creative civilizations can be both fragile and impermanent" (3). Societal collapses take shape, they argued, when two intersecting dynamics occur simultaneously: when the use of natural resources outweighs the ecological carrying capacity of natural systems and when social structures are inequitably divided into distinct classes of rich and poor. Current ecological strain and economic stratification, the study's authors insisted, represent clear and present dangers for society today. Only swift and effective actions, they continued, which will transform "business as usual" through structural, cultural, and policy-oriented solutions, can help prevent a trajectory of irreversible decline.[2]

The modern industrial food system represents a vital social and ecological infrastructure in which these paradoxical dynamics of abundance and injustice are brought into full relief. And, on account of food's central role in the lives of everyone across the globe, diverse stakeholder groups—ranging from geopolitical power players to grassroots organizers—have come to see the food system as a potentially powerful site through which the fight against unsustainability and inequality might be effectively waged. "I don't think we have put a huge focus on food and it's time we did," Rachel Kyte, the World Bank's vice president for climate change, was quoted as saying shortly before the Intergovernmental Panel on Climate Change released a report highlighting the connections between global climate and food insecurity. "The public connects with these issues through food better than through any other issue," she added.[3] It was a sentiment that a number community-based food justice groups had been advocating for some time. "Using food as an access point to engage community, we raise critical awareness of the issues that impact us the most in our neighborhood and, more importantly, build responses," Neelam Sharma, the executive director of Community Services Unlimited (CSU), explained.

Everywhere in our social worlds, of course, we are surrounded by food. We structure our days around meals, which are occasions that bring us together for shared conversation and enjoyment with family, friends, and coworkers. Varied cuisines have come to characterize central aspects of our collective personal, regional, and cultural identities. Food serves as a major force for global and local market exchange, and it is also a source of employment and economic development. Our mediated environment is inundated with messages about food, as we are constantly implored by celebrity advocates, industry marketers, medical experts, agricultural producers, and elected officials to follow certain ways of eating that will supposedly lead to optimal health and happiness.

Yet even with this vast preponderance of food-focused discussion, and alongside the countless calls to shift the status quo of how we eat and grow food, the voices of those most marginalized within the contemporary food system are rarely given a platform to speak. It should come as no surprise, then, that as I write this, food injustice remains a fact of life. While the contexts vary significantly both across and within the developed and developing worlds, it is undeniable that nutrition-related health disparities continue to persist; wealth and power in the food system continues to funnel into the hands of a few corporate players; and dominant agrifood practices continue to perpetuate the abuse of workers and animals while rapidly depleting environmental resources across the globe. More and more of us have come to recognize that by actively grappling with the challenges of the food system, we have the opportunity to confront some of the twenty-first century's most pressing social, environmental, and economic crises. But where will the momentum for a long-term movement for food justice begin?

Based on years of ethnographic research and scholar-activism, *More Than Just Food* has joined a growing chorus of scholarly and practitioner voices that highlight the potential of culturally driven grassroots and people-powered activism to lead the charge toward food system transformation. The analysis in this book has emphasized how, even as community-based activists make food a centerpiece of their organizing work, they also insist that an isolated focus on food and food alone will not lead them to their ultimate goals. Instead, guided by a broader social justice vision, food justice organizations offer up food as a uniquely engaging tool that helps build critical consciousness, develop alternative institutions, promote economic development, and cultivate skills for health and well-being among those who have long been subject to injustice in the food system and beyond. Only with this expansive mission in mind, the strategy's proponents argue, will food ever offer an effective platform through which leaders of the past, present, and future can collectively advance a just, equitable, and sustainable society.

As this book detailed, food justice efforts have unfolded from within a broader social and economic context, one that has necessarily shaped the political possibilities available to activists. Notably, the age of neoliberalism has encouraged the growth of a "shadow state" of voluntary service and non-profit organizations that have been designed to meet the needs of the public at a time when the power of the centralized government has waned. Subsequently, groups from diverse political perspectives have turned their attention to *the local community* as an operative site to advance social change. Not all of this community-based action, however, has been created equal. The varied forms of alternative food activism that have emerged in recent years offer a prime example of this.

In cities and towns across the United States, locally focused alternative food movement efforts have certainly made some positive strides in promoting health and sustainability. Yet, in confronting the challenges of the food system, many community-focused initiatives have ultimately taken a surface-level broken windows approach to tackle food-related disparities, particularly when working in low-income communities and communities of color. Projects that have promoted community health in food desert neighborhoods by establishing urban gardens, farmers' markets, grocery stores, and nutrition education programs have often been established with the best of intentions. Too frequently, however, these initiatives have lacked the political consciousness that would allow their organizers to address the histories of discrimination that are at the root of systemic economic and environmental inequity, and they have consistently treated local residents as "targets" of intervention rather than included them as leaders in the community development process itself. The result is that the mainstream of the American alternative food movement has generally benefitted already-privileged white communities, while those programs that are centered in historically marginalized neighborhoods have tended to produce as much in the way of positive public relations for their sponsors as enduring food justice for local residents.

In response to the ineffectiveness of such programs, some advocates for a more just food system have insisted that food and agricultural *policy* solutions offer a more substantive vision for transforming "business as usual." Even these policy-oriented strategies, however, have not proven themselves to be a cure-all to remedy our current predicament. Policy initiatives have come up against opposition in a political system that has proven itself to be beholden to vested and well-capitalized interests, have faced the exceedingly slow pace of moving through multiple levels of gridlocked governmental bureaucracy, and have confronted the inconvenient reality that the populous is neither particularly organized nor particularly motivated to express food justice demands with the type of force that policymakers will be unable to ignore. One need not look further than the most recent federal Farm Bill as a prime example of this. The bill's passage through Congress was stalled a full two years due to partisan bickering, its champions celebrated deep cuts to the Supplemental Nutrition Assistance Program (SNAP), and it preserved major subsidies to corporate agribusiness while slashing funding for sustainable agriculture and conservation programs. Ultimately, as long as the political lobbying capacity of the alternative food movements is so dramatically overshadowed by the power of those who support the status quo, it seems that systemic policy change is likely to remain an elusive goal.[4]

Organizations engaged in community-based food justice activism offer another way forward. Operating "in the shadow of the shadow state," these groups maintain both a commitment to localized activism and a politically conscious vision for long-term societal transformation. Community-based food justice activists assert that the programmatic focus of the alternative food movement has too often failed to address the food injustice faced by everyday people. At the same time, however, they contend that food system policy initiatives, while a valuable piece of an agenda for food system transformation, have been largely disconnected from the grassroots and have proven too slow to enact. What is needed, they insist, is a commitment to on-the-ground community action that reflects the needs, interests, and visions of local residents today. How else will the people victimized most by food injustice be rallied together into a force for change?

One key contribution of this book, then, has been to simply provide a platform for the voices of these community-based food justice practition-ers—those citizens, activists, youth leaders, and community organizers who, while cognizant that social, environmental, and food injustice stretches well beyond their own zip codes, remain determined to develop localized solu-tions to combat persistent social and structural dilemmas. Guided by a set of working principles for sustainable community change, I have used ethno-graphic research as a means of evaluating the effectiveness, limitations, and potential futures of this approach. My analysis has pointed to several of the fundamental strengths of community-based food justice organizing. The movement's foundation in the realities of residents' lived experience, its dedi-cation to grassroots collaboration, and its theory-driven and historically rooted commitment to social justice transformation represent necessary building blocks for change. Through local storytelling, the transformation of public space, and the development of alternative institutions, community-based food justice organizing has allowed for the cultivation of diverse civic epistemologies, helped youth and adults build vital personal and professional skills, and created economic opportunity and encouraged long-term com-munity empowerment in historically oppressed neighborhoods.

I have also highlighted those areas in which the movement clearly requires additional capacity-building in the years to come. Most substantively, at this moment, the strategy still lacks a coherent ability to reshape cultural and political norms through media storytelling and engagement in the policy domain. In addition, I have analyzed aspects of the movement that are in the midst of ongoing evolution, experimentation, and accommodation. Organizers have made significant strides, for instance, in constructing net-worked partnerships that help them achieve programmatic and fiscal sustain-ability, but unassailable stability and outright self-determination remain future goals rather than present-day truths.

Notwithstanding these issues, it is my hope that this work may convince readers that food justice organizations, by making cultural empowerment and people-of-color-led organizing a foundation of their approach, have found a productive way to pursue their social justice goals. Community-based food justice activists provide a counterbalance not only to the networks and narratives of the dominant food system but also to mainstream elements of the American alternative food movement itself. They recognize that local community organizing alone will not wholly resolve the fundamental economic and environmental justice challenges of the twenty-first century. Still, food justice activists insist that their locally driven approach provides a necessary foundation upon which a growing movement for long-term health, equity, and sustainability can be built.

Of course, a movement that is driven by the interests and actions of local community members does not necessarily rely on the power of the community alone. On the contrary, I have demonstrated in this book that community-based food justice activism has never—and likely will never—move forward in a completely autonomous or independent fashion. Like other social justice initiatives in the age of neoliberalism, food justice activism has become integrated into networked relationships of diverse knowledge practices, storytelling strategies, funding streams, and economic imperatives. On account of these networked dynamics, community-based food justice organizing is best characterized as a hybrid praxis, an evolving mix of philosophy and action in which grassroots organizing incorporates perspectives and tools from both within and outside its own communities of practice. What results is a reflexive process of navigation through the landscape of nonprofit activism, an ambivalent negotiation of opportunity and constraint that is a defining trait of community-based organizations working "in the shadow of the shadow state."

From the perspective of those who consistently ignore the legacies of systemic racial and economic inequity in our society, fretting over these cultural and racialized dynamics would likely be deemed overly sensitive or "politically correct." Let the market do its work, they might suggest, and let people of all ethnic and economic backgrounds take personal responsibility by learning to choose the "right foods" that will improve their own health and the health of their community. As long as this ahistorical worldview remains in place, there will always be groups that promote shallow broken windows approaches to food system change, which garner plenty of glowing media coverage but produce little actual social change. On the opposite side of the political continuum, some dedicated social justice activists would likely find any recognition of their own hybrid interactions with the institutions and logics of neoliberalism to be dissatisfying and unnerving. What is needed, they might suggest, are truly anticapitalist and culturally driven forms of food justice activism that deconstruct neoliberalism at its core, destroy the "nonprofit industrial complex," and usher in an era of pure egalitarianism. In response to this, I once again echo scholar Ruth Wilson Gilmore's assertion that, "If contemporary grassroots activists are looking for a pure form of doing things, they should stop."[5] For food justice activists, faced with the persistent challenges of everyday inequity in the communities in which they live and work, purity has proven less useful than value-driven pragmatism. In my estimation, this hybrid praxis of community-based food justice organizing should be recognized for what it is—a valuable, albeit limited and evolving, avenue for advancing social, environmental, and food justice into the future. Understanding the potentials, constraints, and tensions of this approach, I contend, has both practical and conceptual benefits, and can provide insights for both activists and scholars who hope to improve the scale, reach, and impact of social justice initiatives—throughout the food system and beyond.

SERVING THE PEOPLE, BODY AND SOUL

I first met the staff, volunteers, and friends of Community Services Unlimited when a colleague of mine suggested I attend one of the organization's Food Party fundraisers in South LA. My $20 donation that evening provided me not only with a great meal but also with my first insight into the strategic action of CSU specifically and the broader movement for community-based food justice at large. It was there that I first learned about CSU's roots as the nonprofit arm of the Southern California chapter of the Black Panther Party; heard about the set of community programs that had been developed in recent years to promote youth leadership, economic development, healthy lifestyles, and urban sustainability; and met the diverse group of local residents, community-based activists, and partners from outside of the South LA area who collectively pushed forward their agenda for food justice.

The grassroots vision of food justice that I began to learn about that evening differed fundamentally from much of the rhetoric of the alternative food movement that I had previously encountered. I was struck by the movement's historically rooted mission, its systems-based approach, and its networked capacity for impact. Cognizant of my own positionality as a white, male, middle-class professional ally, I recognized that my outsider status meant there would always be aspects of food injustice I could never fully understand and subsequently roles within the food justice landscape that would never be appropriate for me to occupy. There were ways, however, that I could contribute my skills of research, analysis, and evaluation to the cause.

By describing food justice action, reflecting upon food justice philosophy, and offering evidence-based recommendations for food justice organizing, I could help activists sustain, refine, and communicate their own visions and values, and we could work together to build capacity as part of a long-term movement for food justice and community change.

Starting with an overview of the political and economic foundations of contemporary community organizing practice and the problems and solutions of global and local food systems, this book has outlined my process and described my insights in great detail. Blending networked concepts with theories of storytelling and an ethnographic research approach, I analyzed the communication ecologies that food justice groups constructed and activated to achieve their goals. Through a networked case study of the South LA–based CSU, I demonstrated how neighborhood storytelling—about intersecting issues related to food systems, environmental sustainability, community empowerment, and economic opportunity—served as a foundation to encourage youth and adults to embrace their cultural histories, stand up for their rights, transform local institutions, and advance community health. From there, I showed how engagement in Rooted in Community, a network of youth-focused food justice organizations, helped community-based activists from across the country situate their localized struggles within broader histories and visions of social movement activism. That analysis also shed light on the inherent obstacles faced by social justice groups operating in the era of the "nonprofit industrial complex."

Next, I looked at the history of CSU to offer an in-depth perspective on how that organization, in particular, developed its strategic model for food justice organizing while evolving within the very system it opposed. "You can't very well drop out of the system without dropping out of the universe," Huey Newton, founder of the Black Panther Party, once declared. "You contradict the system while you are in it until it's transformed into a new system."[6] CSU found itself following the lead of the community service arm of the Black Panther Party, deploying an entrepreneurial model of health promotion through the development of community programs. In order to advance its goals, CSU constructed diverse networks of partnerships and integrated sometimes divergent cultural narratives into its efforts. The organization blended radical liberation political philosophy with capitalistic entrepreneurship; it depended on grant funds in addition to community support and formed relationships with local social justice organizations as well as national environmental groups. Moving through this complicated progression—from being founded by the Black Panther Party to getting funded by the USDA and developing an entrepreneurial social enterprise—was both a source of significant tension and a space of foundational opportunity for CSU, as it is for other groups in similar predicaments.

The entrance of new players into the food justice scene was the subject of the book's final chapter. As the research demonstrated, outside groups often brought substantial levels of funding and impressive star-power into communities of need, but these media-friendly overtures were not always matched by substantive levels of community-based participation. In this context, community-based food justice groups found that they were often not "safe" or "brandable" enough for potential partners and sponsors in corporate, government, or foundation worlds. Groups like CSU and its partners in Rooted in Community faced the very real threat of being overshadowed by sanitized versions of food system improvement—but hope remained that digital media might help them spread their own stories. All in all, this struggle was another example of the ongoing evolution of community-based food justice organizing, a space of action in which competing notions of autonomy and dependence, revolution and reform, and resistance and collaboration are put into consistent and complex interaction.

ADVANCING FOOD JUSTICE: THOUGHTS FOR FUNDERS, PRACTITIONERS, AND ALLIES

These reflections point to the undeniable potential of community-based food justice activism, even as they push back, in part, against scholarly and activist narratives that lean toward an unquestioning celebration of wholly autonomous, anticapitalist, grassroots initiatives for community change. In my food justice research and activist efforts, I saw not outright autonomy, but rather pragmatic collaboration, guided by deeply held principles and value systems that were committed to racial, social, and economic justice. Indeed, while my project has remained optimistic about the cultural and structural benefits of community-based food justice organizing—responding to critiques that have underplayed its transformative capacity—my analysis has also maintained a critical stance about the strategy's limits and its room for growth. As my research has asserted, community-based food justice activism is at a moment of great opportunity, although significant work will be required if its scale and scope is to be expanded in the future. I will take the liberty in these final pages to offer a set of recommendations—targeted toward the diverse and intersecting communities of funders, practitioners, and allies—that I hope will contribute to the broader movement ahead.

To begin, it is vital to recognize that effective activism has always and will always require a sound economic base. Today, the many foundations, government agencies, and corporate and institutional partners with an interest in funding community-based action have the potential to either constrain or catalyze justice-driven action. I have been dismayed in recent years by the significant investment placed in a variety of food-related interventions— many situated within low-income communities and communities of color— that have proven more adept at philanthrocapitalist branding than actually improving health, equity, or sustainability. Yet I know there are actors within this landscape that have an interest in charting a better way forward. These potential fiscal partners could channel their efforts more effectively with the incorporation of several key concepts. First, they must recognize that sustainable program development takes place when it is based in the needs and interests of community members themselves, meaning that funded projects should always be grounded in high levels of legitimately participatory and collaborative methods. Second, they must be cognizant of the fact that systemic food injustice has emerged over decades and centuries, meaning that funded projects should always be considered long-term investments rather than short-term fixes. Third, they must consider the social and political capital that funders bring to partnerships with community organizations, meaning that funded projects should always be understood as opportunities to build capacity within organizations, to construct networked relationships between peers in the movement, and to evaluate and publicize the successes of these collective efforts.[7] The so-called failure of programs that aim to reduce obesity in food desert neighborhoods by adding grocery stores and limiting fast food restaurants should serve as a cautionary tale for funders and policymakers.[8] Programs that improve food access matter, but their transformative potential will only be unlocked when such initiatives are connected to systemic networks and narratives for change. By offering cultural, institutional, and economic support, external allies can play a productive role in helping community-based groups build sustainable initiatives, protecting programs from shortsighted funding whims, ensuring that activists are legitimately included in the political process, and helping groups build equity by supporting community control of land and real estate.

With respect to community-based activists themselves, it is worth re-emphasizing something that they already know but can certainly always use more confirmation about—that is, their food justice work does matter, and it does make a difference in the everyday lives of those with whom they collaborate and serve. In the face of often daunting inequities in power, these organizers have the enviable tenacity to push forward an enduring agenda for change. It is an agenda that is made possible by practitioners' deeply held convictions, their ongoing participatory collaborations, and their historically rooted visions for social transformation. This process, however, will not be one that goes smoothly at all times, will not be able to accomplish all things at once, and will not be without its share of internal contradictions and challenges that force activists to question the viability and authenticity of their work. This is to be expected and embraced. As Dr. Martin Luther King Jr. once said, "A strong man must be militant as well as moderate. He must be a realist as well as an idealist."[9] Having reflexivity and compassion about the hybrid praxis of nonprofit organizing is essential to maintaining focus and building capacity in the long run.

On a more concrete level, in their efforts to shift the networks and narratives of the food system toward greater justice, community-based practitioners should continue to expand what they do best. On-the-ground consciousness-raising and alternative institution-building should be supported by the creation and refinement of community-driven models of popular education, economic development, and sustainable agriculture. At the same time, if food justice activism remains centered solely at the level of the local community in the years to come, the long-term influence of the movement will be severely hamstrung. There is therefore a need and an opportunity to work diligently and strategically to lift the voices of food justice activists beyond the local area, transforming the cultural and structural norms of society through sustained storytelling and political engagement.

What can be done to deepen the impact of food justice activism? Direct coalition-building across the unprecedented levels of twenty-first century cultural pluralism offers one valuable point of emphasis. Indeed, understanding ways of promoting storytelling across cultural and linguistic differences while simultaneously championing the unique contributions and histories of distinct ethnic groups is a necessary aspect of a long-term social justice agenda. The preceding chapters have highlighted some of these dynamics in action—food justice organizers already navigate ethnolinguistic barriers, integrate youth leadership with adult advocacy, link local groups into common regional and national causes, and bridge gaps between funding agencies and grassroots activists. Food justice groups must continue to construct networked partnerships that allow them to tell their stories to varied audiences, create collaborative agendas, and promote projects that meet the needs and interests of unique but complementary constituent groups. In this landscape, it is important to recognize that different models for activism will take shape—direct action, community organizing, social enterprises, and policy advocacy among them. What the food justice movement requires is increased capacity and collaboration across all of these domains, a development that can only emerge through multicultural, intergenerational, international, and economically diverse interactions over time.

An important part of this process will be continuing to develop and sustain multiple sites of relationship-building—including, but not limited to, municipal and regional food policy councils; grassroots networks, like Rooted in Community; funder-initiated collectives, like the Kellogg Foundation's Food and Community Gathering; and global platforms for knowledge-sharing, like La Vía Campesina. It will also be incumbent upon these networking initiatives to be clear about the added value that engagement brings to community-based groups, with an eye toward using this collective capacity to enact long-term and expansive social, economic, and policy changes.

As part of this collaborative agenda, the food justice movement must also do more to cultivate the digital media affordances of the information and communication revolution. Indeed, in order to harness the collective capacity of collaborative movement-building, networked technologies must continue to play a role in linking activist groups into common cause. Just as vital, activists must do more to create and disseminate compelling narratives through effective, emotive, spreadable, and action-oriented media storytelling. As previous chapters of this work have discussed, in a crowded landscape of food-related media coverage, food justice groups have struggled mightily to get their story told. They are unfortunately faced with a media environment that is not always responsive to their justice-driven messages and internal organizational dynamics that make developing an infrastructure for media relations an ongoing challenge. Still, stronger engagement in this environment and more sophisticated digital media storytelling practices are necessary if the food justice movement is to be optimally effective at the community level, in the policy arena, or in the market. Without a stronger storytelling presence, food justice will continually be overshadowed by sanitized and simplified versions of food system change, and activists will miss out on an opportunity to build support among the historically marginalized and to recruit allies from privileged communities across the nation. Enhancing cultural and media brandability, of course, must always be weighed against the dangers of co-option, tokenism, and distraction. Still, cultivating a digital media strategy that productively reflects this balancing act represents an essential project that will allow the movement to scale up its scope and impact in the years ahead.

These recommendations for food justice activists should not and must not be carried out by community-based practitioners alone. Rather, these reflections make it clear that there are opportunities for a host of engaged researchers, civic advocates, policy specialists, students, media-makers, and other allies to actively contribute to the broader cause. Importantly, if the driving ethos of this engagement is grounded in a philosophy of charity and sporadic volunteerism, it will prove more detrimental than productive. For years now, potential allies of the food justice movement have been bombarded by cultural narratives that encourage them to *get involved*—we are told to buy from farmers' markets, contribute to community garden projects, or donate to philanthropic organizations. These actions are certainly worthwhile places to start, but in too many instances the commitment they encourage remains at the surface-level, with these actions themselves sometimes co-opted by actors who do not have true community interests in mind. Instead, driven by shared visions of social justice transformation, outside partners should collaborate deliberately with practitioners whose community connections are truly substantive, work to assess the needs of the movement, identify organizational capacity concerns, and then leverage their own skills and positionality to advance these collective aims.

Academic researchers, as one example, can work with practitioners and activists to develop evaluation metrics that reflect a community-driven theory of change and highlight local impacts. With data in hand, these scholars can work to influence the funding strategies and research priorities of government, foundations, and institutions of higher learning who have shown legitimate commitments to promoting health and equity. Together with legal experts, they can also help activists refine models for change that will grant them increasing autonomy and economic viability in the years to come.

Media producers also have a potentially powerful role to play, in that they can help community-based groups more effectively capture and spread their messages of resistance and perseverance to local, national, and global audiences. However, in so doing, they must be careful not to tokenize their collaborators, actively resisting journalistic and celebrity media norms that often favor simplified and overly stylized narratives of struggle and perseverance. The goal, instead, should be to create new types of narratives that effectively communicate the complexity of food injustice, its history, and its possible solutions. Such stories will only be crafted, of course, if community members themselves are treated as partners in creative production from the outset.

From the policy perspective, there are countless initiatives—some with direct connections to the food system and others with broader social justice aims—that advocates and allies could advance in participatory solidarity. The opportunities for engagement—which include preserving anti-hunger support systems, supporting affordable housing initiatives that would allow local residents to invest more of their hard-earned income on nourishing foods, providing avenues for community land ownership, and promoting investment in sustainable forms of agriculture—are wide and varied. Consider, as one example, a media system that would actively protect the public interest and ensure communication rights for all communities.[10] If strong media policies were enacted to bring about these changes, food justice activists would have a greater opportunity to produce and disseminate their stories, allowing them to connect with an informed and engaged populous. Progressive policy changes related to poverty, housing, and media would be victories for food justice because, at its roots, the food justice movement is, was, and always will be about more than just food.

This last observation should push both food justice activists and social justice allies to do more to integrate food system concerns into existing and developing social movements. Food's centrality in our social, economic, environmental, and political lives gives it a unique power to engage diverse stakeholder groups—a fact as true in the time of the Black Panther Party as it is today. Contemporary movements related to climate change, racial justice, and wealth inequality—to name just a few salient causes—would be wise to actively bring community-based food justice activists into the fold of their activities. The long-cultivated experience of many leaders in the food justice movement can contribute to the sophistication of these movements' community organizing practices, pedagogical procedures, and long-term political visions. On the flip side, there is a great deal that community-based food justice activists could learn from the leaders of other movements, particularly those who have been adept at catalyzing social action by using digital and social media to resonate in the hearts and minds of younger generations.

At this point it should be obvious that, on a personal level, food has proved quite a valuable access point for me to think critically about social justice, effective organizing, and the process of academic research itself. On that final point, as I move toward this book's ultimate conclusion, I am compelled to offer a few remarks regarding the scholarly import of my work and to recognize some of the limitations contained herein. This book has undoubtedly been limited by aspects of my methodological approach that constrain its outright generalizability, as well as by my own positionality, which limits my ability to effectively speak with and for others. Regardless, I do feel comfortable in asserting that *More Than Just Food* can offer several useful contributions to the study and practice of ethnographic research, engaged scholarship, and community activism, to name a few domains.

From the start of this project, I argued that the key to understanding a social change organization was to look at the cultural narratives that characterized its networks of communication connections—that is, the communication ecologies through which it derived its organizational identity, built partnerships with other groups, found solidarity with other social change organizations, and connected with the community in which it operated and worked to effect change. As networked logic maintains its place at the foundation of contemporary society, an in-depth, qualitative, networked understanding of community activism offers a constructive lens through which both scholars and practitioners can understand the development and evolution of social change work over the course of time. Ultimately, my ethnographic approach aimed not to give a totalizing account of community-based food justice, but rather to provide a set of networked snapshots of this activism. The insights gained by looking through this networked theoretical lens certainly have parallels in the work of social justice organizers from around the nation and around the world, both for those working on food and those focused on other complex social issues.

I have tried to use this book as a means to advance my normative commitment to social, environmental, and economic justice; it has been an effort of engaged scholarship. Guided by a set of working principles for sustainable community change, my aim has been not only to describe food justice activism but also to actively participate in a constructive analysis of its effectiveness and potential futures. The movement for engaged scholarship in American academia is growing, but it still faces strong institutional barriers that need to be worked through over time. It is my hope that this project will serve as one model among many that demonstrates a path that engaged scholars might take. Indeed, if it were not for my active engagement in food justice efforts in Los Angeles, and in particular my years of collaboration with Community Services Unlimited, I would never have been able to gain the types of insights that formed the foundation for the ethnographic project that developed. By applying scholarly theory to our activist efforts, engaged scholars can advance the interests of those practitioners with whom we act in solidarity and also promote a scholarly agenda that meets the expectations and standards of our academic profession.

Ultimately, then, my aim with this book has been to do my best to tell the story of community-based food justice—a story that was written from my own perspective, yes, but which was also grounded in countless hours of conversation with grassroots activists and incorporated the perspectives of other actors from across the food movement landscape. Indeed, whether at a local, regional, national, or international level, understanding and promoting storytelling about the issues that matter—in our media systems, in our organizations and institutions, and in our interpersonal networks—is fundamental to any networked movement for social change. In the case of our global food system, our system of storytelling has generally failed to make the case for why food justice matters, and it has certainly failed to articulate how our food system might be transformed toward greater health, equity, and sustainability. For better or for worse, it is up to us to change the way that story is told.

A Note on Theory and Method

As is the case with the first book project of many academic researchers, this work has gone through a countless number of permutations and draft versions before reaching its final form. Its foundations began in a graduate seminar on ethnographic research methods, several papers were then written and presented at professional conferences, my doctoral dissertation continued to expand the scope of the project, and a postdoctoral fellowship gave me the opportunity to refine and deepen my analysis. Over the course of nearly five years, I conducted and transcribed over thirty in-depth interviews, analyzed hundreds of primary source documents, reviewed dozens of organizational websites, and spent countless hours taking part in ethnographic participant observation. I kept consistent records—with the use of an audio recorder and handwritten field notes—from start to finish. On multiple occasions during this period, I shared my ideas with research participants through research briefs, conversations, and presentations, integrating their feedback into my analytical process moving forward. Through it all, an interdisciplinary set of theoretical considerations were woven into my thinking, helping to situate my observations within broader conceptual understandings of community-based social change and food movements in the age of neoliberalism. While previous sections of this book have outlined various aspects of my research and writing process, this brief note on theory and method is meant to serve as a supplement to those readers interested in learning more.

To begin, my general methodological approach was strongly influenced by the work of Michael Burawoy and his extended case method of ethnography. At its base, the extended case method puts empirical case study research into a dialogic relationship with preexisting theory. The ultimate aim of extended case ethnography is to build upon, elaborate, and refine theoretical considerations in light of new evidence from the social world. I analyzed my qualitative research materials through an adapted grounded theory approach, using an iterative method of constant comparison to inductively identify and synthesize emergent themes. These themes were then put back into conversation with extant theory in line with the extended case method.[1] I am indebted to the sociologist Paul Lichterman for introducing me to this perspective in a doctoral seminar, as well as for providing me with an example of the ways in which ethnographic investigations of community-based groups can serve as a valuable tool for advancing theory related to broader social movements.[2]

For further theoretical insight into the processes of social change, I turned my attention to the work of network theorists like Mario Diani. He defined a social movement as a "network of informal interactions between a plurality of individuals, groups and/or organizations, engaged in political or cultural conflict, on the basis of a shared collective identity" (13).[3] By making networks a primary analytical tool for social change analysis, Diani's concepts offered a route through which the dominant but generally discrete frameworks for social movement research—that is, structural observations of "how" and cultural investigation of "why" social movements take shape—could be blended and synthesized. In terms of parlaying this networked theoretical perspective into a methodological approach for my own work, however, two primary challenges remained. First, previous research that drew from network-oriented theories of social movements had been largely quantitative and graphical, rarely engaging with the types of qualitative methods that were fundamental to my ethnographic research approach. Second, most scholars interested in networked social change commonly explored interactions between major organizations and institutions at the macro-level of society, while my work was primarily concerned with the networked action of community-based organizations at the meso-level.

In order to bridge these theoretical and methodological gaps, I drew upon the insights of the *communication ecology perspective,* which I described in some detail in the first chapter of this book and employed throughout. To provide some additional scholarly context, the direct roots of the communication ecology perspective can be found in two theories of communication and media—media system dependency theory and communication infrastructure theory. Both of these were developed over the course of several decades by my academic advisor and mentor, Sandra Ball-Rokeach, in conjunction with a host of colleagues. Media system dependency theory (MSD) was developed in the 1970s and 1980s as a multilevel theory of media power. It explores how individuals actively construct different constellations of media connections in order to accomplish particular goals, but also details how individuals and groups remain constrained by a media system that maintains an asymmetric imbalance of power over them. Indeed, MSD research has demonstrated that the political and economic agenda of major media systems can have a strong impact on the nature of discursive interaction on the ground, as media producers often set the context for the type of storytelling that takes place between and among individuals and organizations around a variety of important social concerns.[4]

Communication infrastructure theory (CIT) was developed by Ball-Rokeach's Los Angeles-based research team, the Metamorphosis Project, beginning in the early 2000s. CIT is a framework that investigates the structures and impacts of communication processes at the level of the local urban community and within the digital, globalized age. It works from the notion that "storytelling resources" are central to the process of building and maintaining a community, and that they can effect social change at the community level. Through shared discourses *about* the community by members *of* that community, a community-level identity can be forged, and community-level action can be encouraged and realized.[5] As the theory details, the central piece of a community's communication infrastructure is its neighborhood storytelling network, a concept that describes what occurs when residents, community organizations, and local or ethnic media (referred to as "geo-ethnic" media) participate in communicative actions about the local community. This storytelling network is situated within a communication action context, considered any piece of the built and social environments that enables or constrains discursive interaction. When individuals are connected to a strong neighborhood storytelling network—in which residents, organizations, and geo-ethnic media engage in communicative action about the same community issues—this neighborhood storytelling has been shown to have significant impacts on the nature of community engagement, including facilitating high levels of neighborhood belonging, civic participation, and collective efficacy.[6]

Taken together, MSD and CIT set the foundation for the communication ecology perspective, an analytical orientation that has been employed in recent years by several researchers with connections to the Metamorphosis

Project.[7] Both of those earlier theories analyzed the dynamic networked communication practices of individuals and groups, taking storytelling seriously as central to understanding the nature of knowledge practices and action. In this sense, both theories were in line with the assertion that human beings think through the social world in narrative terms and that media systems, organizations, and institutions work in concert with interpersonal communication to shape a host of influential societal narratives. Not constrained to consider only the meaning-making function of communicative interaction, MSD and CIT also examined the role of *networked structures* in these dynamics. That is, both theories situated individual and organizational agents within broader contextual environments and communication networks from which they could connect with resources in order to construct knowledge and achieve specific goals.

As I continued to develop the communication ecology perspective for this book project, I integrated insights from both CIT and MSD with concepts from contemporary network theory. Importantly, while traditional network analysis has tended to quantitatively examine complete, large-scale networks of interacting individuals and groups, I employed an *egocentric* network approach. An egocentric network focuses on the communicative interactions of a particular social agent—in my case, specific community-based organizations—in order to understand how that agent operates in its networked social world.[8] My focus of analysis highlighted organizations' *goal-oriented communication ecologies,* the multiple networks of communication resources constructed by an agent in pursuit of various goals and in the context of that agent's broader egocentric network. With these structures as a point of departure, I was able to trace the roots and evolution of organizational narratives of meaning, culture, and history as they took shape through ongoing and dynamic networked relationships over time.

More Than Just Food used the egocentric network of Community Services Unlimited as a centering artifact of study. Fundamentally, my multimodal qualitative investigation explored the evolving networked action of CSU—as well as those of other groups connected to its broader organizational network—by using a set of goal-oriented organizational communication ecologies as analytical guides. The research process was informed by theories of networked social movements, narrative storytelling, and community-based change, while the empirical findings were situated within an ecological context of the globalized, digital age of neoliberalism. Supported by the extended case method of ethnography, I used insights from open-ended interviews, engaged methods of participant observation, critical media, and document analysis to elaborate upon the theoretical concerns that shaped the project from the outset. The final outcome is a work that aims to advance our collective understanding of the movement for community-based food justice, including its successes, challenges, and future avenues for growth.

NOTES

INTRODUCTION

Epigraph: David Hilliard, "The Black Panther Party: Food Sovereignty Awards 2011," Food First, November 17, 2011, http://vimeo.com/32274352.

1. Hollie McKay, "Los Angeles Schools Bite Back at Jamie Oliver's 'Food Revolution,'," April 12, 2011, www.foxnews.com/entertainment/2011/04/12/los-angeles-schools-bite-jamie-olivers-food-revolution/; Richard Verrier, "L.A. School District Suspends Reality TV Shoots," *Los Angeles Times*, February 4, 2011, http://articles .latimes.com/2011/feb/04/business/la-fi-ct-lausd-20110204.

2. Lori Corbin and Lisa Hernandez, "LAUSD Fires Back at 'Jamie Oliver's Food Revolution,'" April 13, 2011, http://abclocal.go.com/kabc/story?id=8070320; Philiana Ng, "ABC Pulls 'Jamie Oliver's Food Revolution,'" *Hollywood Reporter*, May 3, 2011, www.hollywoodreporter.com/live-feed/abc-pulls-jamie-olivers-food-184598.

3. Annie Park, Nancy Watson, and Lark Galloway-Gilliam, *South Los Angeles Health Equity Scorecard*, Community Health Councils (2008), http://chc-inc.org /downloads/South%20LA%20Scorecard.pdf; Janet Poppendieck, *Free for All: Fixing School Food in America* (Berkeley and Los Angeles: University of California Press, 2010). In recent years, the LAUSD has made legitimate strides in improving its overall food service operations. See LA Food Policy Council, *The Good Food Purchasing Pledge: A Case Study Evaluation & Year One Progress Update* (June 2014), http://goodfoodla.org/wp-content/uploads/2014/06/Good-Food-Purchasing-Policy_Final_0614.pdf.

4. For more on Oliver, see Garrett Broad, "Revolution on Primetime TV—Jamie Oliver Takes on the US School Food System," in *The Rhetoric of Food: Discourse, Materiality and Power*, ed. Joshua Frye and Michael Bruner (New York: Routledge, 2012), 190–205; and Kristina E. Gibson and Sarah E. Dempsey, "Make Good Choices, Kid: Biopolitics of Children's Bodies and School Lunch Reform in Jamie Oliver's *Food Revolution*," *Children's Geographies* 13, no. 1 (2015), doi: 10.1080/14733285.2013.827875.

5. Center on Budget and Policy Priorities, "SNAP Helps Struggling Families Put Food on the Table," January 8, 2015, www.cbpp.org/cms/index.cfm?fa=view&id=3744; Rakesh Kochhar and Richard Fry, "Wealth Inequality Has Widened along Racial, Ethnic Lines since End of Great Recession," Pew Research Center, December 12, 2014, www.pewresearch.org/fact-tank/2014/12/12/racial-wealth-gaps-great-recession; Stanford Center on Poverty and Inequality, *State of the Union: The Poverty and Inequality Report* (2014), http://web.stanford.edu/group/scspi/sotu/SOTU_2014_CPI.pdf.

6. Joshua Frye and Michael Bruner, eds., "Introduction," in *The Rhetoric of Food: Discourse, Materiality, and Power* (New York: Routledge, 2012), 1–6; Alison Hope Alkon and Julian Agyeman, eds., "Introduction: The Food Movement as Polyculture," in *Cultivating Food Justice: Race, Class and Sustainability* (Cambridge, MA: MIT Press, 2011), 1–20.

7. Tanya Basok, Suzan Ilcan, and Jeff Noonan, "Citizenship, Human Rights, and Social Justice," *Citizenship Studies* 10, no. 3 (2006): 267–273; David Harvey, *Social Justice and the City* (Athens: University of Georgia Press, 2009); George Lipsitz, "The Possessive Investment in Whiteness," *American Quarterly* 47, no. 3 (1995): 369–387.

8. Patricia Allen, "Mining for Justice in the Food System: Perceptions, Practices, and Possibilities," *Agriculture and Human Values* 25, no. 2 (2008): 157–161; Rachel Slocum, "Whiteness, Space and Alternative Food Practice," *Geoforum* 38, no. 3 2007: 520–533; Julie Guthman, "If They Only Knew: The Unbearable Whiteness of Alternative Food," in Alkon and Agyeman, *Cultivating Food Justice,* 263–282.

9. Robert Gottlieb and Anupama Joshi, *Food Justice* (Cambridge, MA: MIT Press, 2010); Alkon and Agyeman, *Cultivating Food Justice.*

10. Alkon and Agyeman's *Cultivating Food Justice* does a fine job of encapsulating this debate.

11. These themes of networked hybridity are explored from a macro-level in David Goodman, E. Melanie DuPuis, and Michael Goodman, *Alternative Food Networks: Knowledge, Practice and Politics* (New York: Routledge, 2012).

12. Paulo Freire, *Pedagogy of the Oppressed* (New York: Continuum, 2000).

13. Quote from "South LA to host national summit of youth food justice leaders," a press release issued by CSU for the 2013 Rooted in Community Summit. Available at www.youthfoodbillofrights.com/uploads/1/9/4/3/19436323/ricrelease2013.pdf.

14. Research in this general orientation can go by any number of names. Each has its own particularities, assumptions, and goals, but they all share a general engaged research commitment. See Michael Burawoy, "For Public Sociology," *American Sociological Review* 70, no. 1 (2005): 4–28; and Randy Stoecker, "Are Academics Irrelevant?: Roles for Scholars in Participatory Research," *The American Behavioral Scientist* 42, no. 5 (1995): 840–854.

15. Burawoy, "For Public Sociology"; Jennifer Simpson and David Seibold, "Practical Engagements and Co-Created Research," *Journal of Applied Communication Research* 36, no. 3 (2008): 266–280.

16. John L. Jackson Jr., *Thin Description: Ethnography and the African Hebrew Israelites of Jerusalem* (Cambridge, MA: Harvard University Press, 2013).

1. Manuel Castells, *Networks of Outrage and Hope* (Cambridge, UK: Polity Press, 2012).

2. Jeffrey Juris, "Reflections on #Occupy Everywhere: Social Media, Public Space, and Emerging Logics of Aggregation," *American Ethnologist* 39, no. 2 (2012): 259–279; Todd Wolfson, *Digital Rebellion: The Birth of the Cyber Left* (Chicago: University of Illinois Press, 2014).

3. Some food movement activists have pushed for greater involvement in activities like the Occupy movement. See, for instance, https://twitter.com/occupybigfood; Tom Philpott, "Foodies, Get Thee to Occupy Wall Street," *Mother Jones,* October 14, 2011, www.motherjones.com/environment/2011/10/food-industry-monopoly-occupy-wall-street; and Willie Nelson and Anne Lappé, "Why We Must Occupy Our Food Supply," *Huffington Post,* February 24, 2012, www.huffingtonpost.com /willie-nelson/occupy-food_b_1299401.html.

4. Ulrich Beck, "Critical Theory of World Risk Society: A Cosmopolitan Vision," *Constellations* 16, no. 1 (2009): 3–22.

5. Manuel Castells, *Communication Power* (Oxford, UK: Oxford University Press, 2009).

6. Robert Putnam, *Bowling Alone: The Collapse and Revival of American Community* (New York: Simon and Schuster, 2000).

7. Robert Sampson, *Great American City: Chicago and the Enduring Neighborhood Effect* (Chicago: University of Chicago Press, 2012).

8. Lewis Friedland, "Communication, Community, and Democracy: Toward a Theory of the Communicatively Integrated Community," *Communication Research* 28, no. 4 (2001): 358–391; Yong-Chan Kim and Sandra Ball-Rokeach, "Civic Engagement from a Communication Infrastructure Perspective," *Communication Theory* 16 (2006): 173–197.

9. Michel Foucault, *Society Must Be Defended: Lectures at the Collège de France, 1976–1977* (New York: Picador Press, 2003); Michel Foucault, *Security, Territory and Population: Lectures at the Collège de France, 1977–1978* (New York: Picador Press, 2007).

10. Nikolas Rose, *Powers of Freedom: Reframing Political Thought* (Cambridge, UK: Cambridge University Press, 1999).

11. This is not to say that federal programs do not exist—they do. Yet most federal food access programs are intended as safety nets and/or are administered through decentralized means. This is exemplified, for instance, by the work of Feeding America, a national organization that leverages federal funding and private donations to support state and local emergency food providers such as food banks, pantries, soup kitchens, and shelters.

12. Office of the Administration of Community Services, "CED Grantees," US Department of Health and Human Services, www.acf.hhs.gov/programs/ocs /programs/ced/ced-grantees.

13. Wendy Brown, *Edgework: Critical Essays on Knowledge and Politics* (Princeton, NJ: Princeton University Press, 2005).

14. David Harvey, *Brief History of Neoliberalism* (Oxford, UK: Oxford University Press, 2005).

15. Brown, *Edgework*.

16. Nikolas Rose referred to this broader context as *advanced liberalism*. Referring to it as the *age of neoliberalism,* I believe, leaves slightly less possibility of confusion in differentiating the terminology of these dynamics.

17. Carmen Sirianni and Lewis Friedland, *Civic Innovation in America* (Berkeley and Los Angeles: University of California Press, 2001).

18. Jennifer Wolch, *Shadow State: Government and Voluntary Sector in Transition* (New York: Foundation Center, 1990).

19. Rose, *Powers of Freedom*.

20. Raymond Williams, *Keywords: A Vocabulary of Culture and Society* (Oxford, UK: Oxford University Press, 1985).

21. William Schambra, "Place and Poverty," in *Why Place Matters: Geography, Identity, and Civic Life in Modern America,* ed. Wilfred McClay and Ted McAllister (New York: Encounter Books, 2014), 162–170.

22. Sirianni and Friedland, *Civic Innovation in America*.

23. Meredith Minkler, "Introduction to Community Organizing," in *Community Organizing and Community Building for Health and Welfare,* ed. Meredith Minkler (New Brunswick: Rutgers University Press, 2012), 5–26.

24. Andrea Smith, "Introduction," in *The Revolution Will Not Be Funded: Beyond the Non-Profit Industrial Complex,* ed. Incite! Women of Color Against Violence (Cambridge, MA: South End Press, 2007), 1–20. It is worth noting that, as this book went to press, Andrea Smith was under intense criticism for falsely claiming Native American heritage.

25. Nina Eliasoph, *Making Volunteers* (Princeton, NJ: Princeton University Press, 2011).

26. Ruth Wilson Gilmore, "In the Shadow of the Shadow State," in *The Revolution Will Not Be Funded: Beyond the Non-Profit Industrial Complex,* ed. Incite! Women of Color Against Violence (Cambridge, MA: South End Press, 2007), 41–52.

27. Sasha Costanza-Chock, *Out of the Shadows and into the Streets* (Cambridge, MA: MIT Press, 2014).

28. James DeFilippis, Robert Fisher, and Eric Shragge, *Contesting Community: The Limits and Potential of Local Organizing* (New Brunswick: Rutgers University Press, 2010).

29. Manuel Pastor and Rhonda Ortiz, *Making Change: How Social Movements Work and How to Support Them* (Los Angeles: Program for Environmental and Regional Equity, 2009).

30. Francesca Polletta, "Culture and Movements," *Annals of the American Academy of Political and Social Science* 619 no. 1 (2008): 78–96.

31. Manuel Castells, *End of Millennium,* vol. 3, *The Information Age: Economy, Society and Culture* (Cambridge, MA: Blackwell, 2000).

32. Prominent scholars Bruno Latour and Michelle Callon were at the forefront of actor-network theory, for instance, which investigates the relational interactions

between human and nonhuman actors that contribute to major technological change, and Nicholas Christakis and James Fowler were among the notable researchers who brought social network theory into the study of public health.

33. Mario Diani, "Networks and Social Movements: A Research Programme," in *Social Movements and Networks: Relational Approaches to Collective Action,* ed. Mario Diani and Doug McAdam (Oxford, UK: Oxford University Press, 2003), 299–318.

34. Mario Diani, "Network Analysis," in *Methods Of Social Movement Research,* ed. Bert Klandermans and Suzanne Staggenborg (Minneapolis: University of Minnesota Press, 2002), 173–200.

35. Raul Lejano, Mrill Ingram, and Helen Ingram, *The Power of Narrative in Environmental Networks* (Cambridge, MA: MIT Press, 2013).

36. See, for instance, Robert Benford and David Snow, "Framing Processes and Social Movements: An Overview and Assessment," *Annual Review of Sociology* 20 (2008): 611–639.

37. George Gerbner, "The Stories We Tell," *Peace Review* 11, no. 1 (1999), 9–15; see also Walter Fisher, "The Narrative Paradigm: In the Beginning," *Journal of Communication* 35 (1985), 74–89.

38. The Metamorphosis Project is based at the University of Southern California's Annenberg School for Communication and Journalism. For more information, see www.metamorph.org.

39. Communication ecology scholarship is an ongoing area of research and theory-building. Notably, while scholars who employ this perspective are influenced by previous work on "media ecology"—put forth by Neil Postman and others—we depart from this work through our increased attention to multiple forms of mediated, nonmediated, and organizational communicative activity. See Ball-Rokeach et al., "Understanding Individuals in the Context of Their Environment: Communication Ecology as a Concept and Method" (paper presented at the Annual Conference of the International Communication Association, Phoenix, AZ, May 2012); and Garrett Broad et al., "Understanding Communication Ecologies to Bridge Communication Research and Community Action," *Journal of Applied Communication Research* 41, no. 4 (2013), 325–345.

2. FOOD SYSTEMS, FOOD MOVEMENTS, FOOD JUSTICE

1. United States Department of Agriculture, "USDA Introduces Online Tool for Locating 'Food Deserts,'" May 2, 2011, www.usda.gov/wps/portal/usda /usdahome?contentid=2011/05/0191.xml.

2. Food, Conservation, and Energy Act of 2008, Pub. L. No. 110–234, H.R. 2419, 122 Stat. 923, 110th Cong. (2008).

3. "Taking on Food Deserts," *White House Blog,* February 24, 2010, www .whitehouse.gov/blog/2010/02/24/taking-food-deserts.

4. United States Department of Agriculture, "Obama Administration Details Healthy Food Financing Initiative," February 19, 2010, www.usda.gov/wps/portal /usda/usdamediafb?contentid=2010/02/0077.xml.

5. This quote is from an unpublished internal document included by CSU as part of a 2012 grant application for the Community Economic Development Program of Health and Human Services.

6. "The Future of Food: Crisis Prevention," *Economist,* February 24, 2011, www .economist.com/node/18229412; Oxfam International, "Broken Food System and Environmental Crises Spell Hunger for Millions," May 31, 2011, www.oxfam.org /en/pressroom/pressreleases/2011–05–31/broken-food-system-and-environmental-crises-spell-hunger-millions.

7. Robert Wood Johnson Foundation and Trust for America's Health, *F as in Fat: How Obesity Threatens America's Future,* July 2011, http://healthyamericans .org/reports/obesity2011/Obesity2011Report.pdf.

8. Although I point to a variety of global trends and international examples in this chapter, my analysis relies heavily on an understanding of the food system dynamics within the United States. This not only reflects my own area of expertise but also emerges from the fact that the activities of the US government and US-based corporations are, in many ways, the fundamental drivers of both the structure and culture of global industrial food. See Patricia Allen, *Together at the Table: Sustainability and Sustenance in the American Agrifood System* (University Park: Pennsylvania State University Press, 2004).

9. Hugh Campbell, "Food and the Audit Society," in *Handbook of Food Research,* ed. Anne Murcott, Warren Belasco, and Peter Jackson (New York: Bloomsbury, 2013), 177–191.

10. Anil Gupta, "Origin of Agriculture and Domestication of Plants and Animals Linked to Early Holocene Climate Amelioration," *Current Science,* 87, no. 1 (2004): 54–59.

11. Ivette Perfecto, John Vandermeer, and Angus Wright, *Nature's Matrix: Linking Agriculture, Conservation and Food Sovereignty* (London: Earthscan, 2009).

12. Sidney Mintz, *Sweetness and Power* (New York: Penguin, 1985).

13. Perfecto, Vandermeer, and Wright, *Nature's Matrix.*

14. G.J. Leigh, *The World's Greatest Fix* (Oxford, UK: Oxford University Press, 2004).

15. Eric Holt-Gimenez and Raj Patel, *Food Rebellions: The Real Story of the World Food Crisis and What We Can Do About It* (Oxford, UK: Fahumu Books, 2009).

16. Leigh, *World's Greatest Fix.*

17. The Food and Agriculture Organization of the United Nations (FAO) estimates that, since the number of people suffering from hunger in the developing world reached a peak of nearly one billion in the early 1990s, progress has been made, stating that that number has been brought down by approximately 200 million. However, nearly 70 percent of that reduction was located in China alone, which suggests that that country's national strategy has been more successful than the

global strategy. See Food and Agriculture Organization of the United Nations, *The State of Food Insecurity in the World 2014*, FAO, Rome, 2014, www.fao .org/3/a-i4030e.pdf.

18. Holt-Gimenez and Patel, *Food Rebellions;* World Hunger Education Service, *World Hunger and Poverty Facts and Statistics,* 2013, www.worldhunger.org /articles/Learn/world%20hunger%20facts%202002.htm.

19. Ulrich Beck, "Critical Theory of World Risk Society: A Cosmopolitan Vision," *Constellations* 16, no. 1 (2009): 3–22.

20. Terry Marsden, "Contemporary Food Systems," in Murcott, Belasco, and Jackson, *Handbook of Food Research,* 135–147.

21. These numbers are always rising and will surely be outdated by the time of publication. See Mary Hendrickson, *The Dynamic State of Agriculture and Food,* Farm Credit Administration, February 19, 2014, www.fca.gov/Download /Symposium14/hendrickson19feb2014.pdf; and United States Department of Agriculture, *Retailing and Wholesaling: Retail Trends,* USDA Economic Research Service, October 27, 2014, www.ers.usda.gov/topics/food-markets-prices/retailing-wholesaling/retail-trends.aspx.

22. Raj Patel, *Stuffed and Starved: The Hidden Battle for the World Food System,* (New York: Melville, 2008).

23. Seth Holmes, *Fresh Fruit, Broken Bodies: Migrant Farmworkers in the United States,* (Berkeley: University of California Press, 2013).

24. Holt-Gimenez and Patel, *Food Rebellions;* Peter Rosset, "Fixing our Global Food System: Food Sovereignty and Redistributive Land Reform," *Monthly Review* 61, no. 3 (2009): 114–128.

25. Barbara Adam, "Industrial Food for Thought: Timescapes of Risk," *Environmental Values* 8, no. 2 (1999): 219–238.

26. Tom Philpott, "A Reflection on the Lasting Legacy of 1970s USDA Secretary Earl Butz," February 8, 2008, http://grist.org/article/the-butz-stops-here/.

27. For a remarkably optimistic reading of this issue, see Steven Kotler and Peter Diamandis, *Abundance: The Future Is Better Than You Think* (New York: Free Press, 2012).

28. Doug Gurian-Sherman, *Failure to Yield: Evaluating the Performance of Genetically Engineered Crops,* Union of Concerned Scientists, Cambridge, MA, 2009; J. L. P., "Smelling a Rat: GM Maize, Health and the Séralini Affair," *Economist,* December 5, 2013, http://econ.st/1boSTHC; Fred Pearce, "Why Are Environmentalists Taking Anti-Science Positions?" *Yale Environment 360,* October 22, 2012, http://e360.yale.edu/feature/why_are_environmentalists_taking_anti-science_positions/2584/; Lauren C. Ponisio et al., "Diversification Practices Reduce Organic to Conventional Yield Gap," *Proceedings of the Royal Society of London B: Biological Sciences* 282, no. 1799 (2015): 1396.

29. Mark Gold, *The Global Benefits of Eating Less Meat,* Compassion in World Farming Trust, 2004, www.ciwf.org.uk/includes/documents/cm_docs/2008/g /global_benefits_of_eating_less_meat.pdf.

30. Julian Cribb, *"Coming Famine: The Global Food Crisis and What We Can Do to Avoid It* (Berkeley: University of California Press, 2010); David Pimentel et al., "Environmental, Energetic, and Economic Comparisons of Organic and Conventional Farming Systems," *BioScience* 55, no. 7 (2005): 573–582; Timothy Pachirat, *Every Twelve Seconds: Industrialized Slaughter and the Politics of Sight* (New Haven: Yale University Press, 2011); Perfecto, Vandermeer, and Wright, *Nature's Matrix.*

31. Alisha Coleman-Jensen, Christian Gregory, and Anita Singh, *Household Food Security in the United States in 2013*, United States Department of Agriculture, September 2014, www.ers.usda.gov/media/1565415/err173.pdf.

32. For updated statistics on SNAP and the NSLP, see Food Research and Action Center, "Data and Publications," http://frac.org/reports-and-resources/.

33. David Katz and Stephanie Meller, "Can We Say What Diet Is Best for Health?" *Annual Review of Public Health* 35 (2014): 83–103.

34. Carlos Monteiro, "Nutrition and Health: The Issue Is Not Food, Nor Nutrients, So Much as Processing," *Public Health Nutrition* 12, no. 5 (2009): 729–731.

35. Michael Moss, *Salt, Sugar, Fat* (New York: Random House, 2013).

36. Marion Nestle, *Food Politics: How the Food Industry Influences Nutrition and Health* (Berkeley: University of California Press, 2007).

37. Janet Poppendeick, *Free for All: Fixing School Food in America* (Berkeley and Los Angeles: University of California Press, 2010).

38. Tim Lang and Michael Heasman, *Food Wars: The Global Battle for Mouths, Minds, and Markets* (London: Earthscan, 2004).

39. Michael Carolan, *The Real Cost of Cheap Food* (New York: Earthscan, 2011).

40. Nicole Larson, Mary Story, and Melissa Nelson, "Neighborhood Environments: Disparities in Access to Healthy Foods in the U.S.," *American Journal of Preventive Medicine* 36, no. 1 (2009): 74–81.

41. Julie Beaulac, Elizabeth Kristjansson, and Steven Cummins, "A Systematic Review of Food Deserts, 1966–2007," *Preventing Chronic Disease* 6, no. 3 (2009): A105.

42. Julie Guthman, *Weighing In: Obesity, Food Justice, and the Limits of Capitalism* (Berkeley and Los Angeles: University of California Press, 2011).

43. Steven Cummins, Ellen Flint, and Stephen A. Matthews, "New Neighborhood Grocery Store Increased Awareness of Food Access but Did Not Alter Dietary Habits or Obesity," *Health Affairs* 33, no. 2 (2014): 283–291; Roland Sturm and Aiko Hattori, "Diet and Obesity in Los Angeles County 2007–2012: Is There a Measurable Effect of the 2008 'Fast-Food Ban'?" *Social Science & Medicine* 133 (2015): 205–211.

44. Allen, *Together at the Table;* David Goodman, Melanie DuPuis, and Michael Goodman, *Alternative Food Networks: Knowledge, Practice and Politics* (New York: Routledge, 2012).

45. Michael Pollan, "The Food Movement, Rising," *New York Review of Books,* June 10, 2010, www.nybooks.com/articles/archives/2010/jun/10/food-movement-rising.

46. Norman Borlaug, "Ending World Hunger: The Promise of Biotechnology and the Threat of Antiscience Zealotry," *Plant Physiology* 124, no. 2 (2000): 487–490; Eric Holt-Gimenez, "Food Security, Food Justice, or Food Sovereignty?" in *Cultivating Food Justice: Race, Class, and Sustainability,* ed. Alison Hope Alkon and Julian Agyeman (Cambridge, MA: MIT Press, 2011), 309–330.

47. La Vía Campesina, "The International Peasant's Voice," February 9, 2011, http://viacampesina.org/en/index.php/organisation-mainmenu-44.

48. Patel, *Stuffed and Starved.*

49. Rachel Slocum, "Whiteness, Space and Alternative Food Practice," *Geoforum* 38, no. 3 (2007): 520–533.

50. Allen, *Together at the Table;* Robert Gottlieb and Anupama Joshi, *Food Justice* (Cambridge, MA: MIT Press, 2010); Holt-Giménez, "Food Security"; Josee Johnston and Shyon Baumann, *Foodies: Democracy and Distinction in the Gourmet Foodscape* (New York: Routledge, 2010).

51. Let's Move, "Learn the Facts," www.letsmove.gov/learn-facts/epidemic-childhood-obesity.

52. Jamie Oliver Food Foundation, "Campaign Overview," November 2011, http://www.jamieoliverfoodfoundation.org/usa/pdf/JOFF-Campaign-overview.pdf.

53. I should say that, like many other Americans, my own food consumption was heavily influenced by the new voices in alternative food that I began to hear during the 2000s. Today, I abstain entirely from animal-derived products and try to support organic, fair trade, and local food producers through my own food purchases.

54. Daniel J. Flynn, "The Whole Foods Hustle," *American Spectator,* September 7, 2012, http://spectator.org/articles/34858/whole-foods-hustle.

55. Michelle Obama and Jamie Oliver, in particular, have often been critiqued for having a too-cozy relationship with the food industry. Furthermore, initiatives spearheaded by public figures like Obama and Oliver have been rightly criticized for consistently and often singularly focusing on obesity as *the* defining problem of the food system while neglecting other systemic issues. See Garrett Broad, "Revolution on Primetime TV—Jamie Oliver Takes on the US School Food System," in *The Rhetoric of Food: Discourse, Materiality & Power,* ed. Joshua Frye and Michael Bruner (New York: Routledge, 2012), 190–205; and Guthman, *Weighing In.*

56. Michael Hamm and Anne Bellows, "Community Food Security and Nutrition Educators," *Journal of Nutrition Education and Behavior* 35, no. 1 (2003): 37–43.

57. Allen, *Together at the Table.* The now-defunct Community Food Security Coalition played a major role in this advocacy process.

58. W. K. Kellogg Foundation, "Food and Community," May 2013, www.wkkf.org/what-we-do/healthy-kids/food-and-community.

59. Goodman, DuPuis, and Goodman, *Alternative food networks.*

60. Julie Guthman, "If They Only Knew: The Unbearable Whiteness of Alternative Food," in *Cultivating Food Justice: Race, Class, and Sustainability,* ed. Alison Hope Alkon and Julian Agyeman (Cambridge, MA: MIT Press, 2011), 263–282; Yuki Kato, "Not Just the Price of Food: Challenges of an Urban Agriculture Organization in Engaging Local Residents," *Sociological Inquiry* 83, no. 3 (2013):

369–391; Kristin Reynolds, "Disparity Despite Diversity: Social Injustice in New York City's Urban Agriculture System," *Antipode* 47, no.1 (2014): 240–259.

61. Patricia Allen and Julie Guthman, "From 'Old School' to 'Farm-to-School': Neoliberalization from the Ground Up," *Agriculture and Human Values* 23, no. 4 (2006): 401–415.

62. James Lester, David Allen, and Kelly Hill, *Environmental Injustice in the United States: Myths and Realities* (San Diego: Westview Press, 2001).

63. Robert Gottlieb, "Where We Live, Work, Play . . . and Eat: Expanding the Environmental Justice Agenda," *Environmental Justice* 2, no. 1 (2009): 7–8.

64. There are some food justice groups that also explicitly consider their work to provide a platform for advancing justice on issues related to gender and sexual identity, which I discuss in chapter 4. That said, the organizations highlighted in this ethnography focus primarily on racial and economic concerns.

65. Detroit Black Community Food Security Network, "About Us," http://detroitblackfoodsecurity.org/about.html.

66. Social Justice Learning Institute, "About Us: Our Mission and Vision," www.sjli.org/about-us/mission-vision.

67. Malik Yakini, "A Disturbing Trend," *Be Black and Green* (blog), May 31, 2012, https://web.archive.org/web/20130728234352/http://www.beblackandgreen.com/content/disturbing-trend.

68. Teresa Mares, "Engaging Latino Immigrants in Seattle Food Activism Through Urban Agriculture," in *Food Activism: Agency, Democracy and Economy,* ed. Carole Counihan and Valeria Siniscalchi (New York: Bloomsbury, 2014), 31–46.

69. Teresa Mares and Devon G. Peña, "Environmental and Food Justice: Toward Local, Slow, and Deep Food Systems," in *Cultivating Food Justice: Race, Class, and Sustainability,* ed. Alison Hope Alkon and Julian Agyeman (Cambridge, MA: MIT Press, 2011), 31–46.

70. Guthman, *Weighing In.*

71. Alison Hope Alkon, *Black, White, and Green* (Athens: University of Georgia Press, 2012).

72. "Detroit Black Community Food Security Network Awarded $750,000 grant," *Michigan Citizen,* August 15, 2013, https://web.archive.org/web/20130828164752/http://michigancitizen.com/detroit-black-community-food-security-network-awarded-750000-grant/.

73. Garrett Broad, "Ritual Communication and Use Value: The South Central Farm and the Political Economy of Place," *Communication, Culture and Critique* 6, no. 1 (2013): 20–40.

74. Huey P. Newton, "Black Capitalism Re-Analyzed I: June 5, 1971," in *The Huey P. Newton Reader,* ed. David Hilliard and Donald Weise (New York: Seven Stories Press, 2002), 227–233.

75. A similar stance was put forth in Nathan McClintock, "Radical, Reformist, and Garden-Variety Neoliberal: Coming to Terms with Urban Agriculture's Contradictions," *Local Environment* 19, no. 2 (2014): 147–171.

76. Los Angeles Food Policy Council, "Los Angeles Food System Snapshot 2013," www.goodfoodla.org/good-food/2013-food-system-snapshot//; Rachel A. Surls, "From Cows to Concrete: A History of Los Angeles Agriculture," *Los Angeles Agriculture,* July 16, 2010, http://ucanr.edu/blogs/blogcore/postdetail.cfm?postnum=3050

77. Linda Ashman et al., "Seeds of Change: Strategies for Food Security for the Inner City" (Master's thesis, University of University of California, Los Angeles, 1993).

3. IN A COMMUNITY LIKE THIS

1. I have always regretted that my Spanish-language proficiency never approached fluency, although after several years of living and working in Los Angeles, my vocabulary became strong enough that I could carry on basic conversations, especially when they revolved around talk of food and agriculture. As I discuss in this chapter and elsewhere, this language barrier has undoubtedly constrained my effectiveness as both a researcher and an activist, but it also highlights an enduring challenge faced by those who seek to advance culturally diverse movements for change.

2. These intersecting mini case studies represent several of the key community-based programs cultivated by CSU in their first full decade as a food-focused organization, but they are hardly exhaustive of the organization's catalog of activities.

3. Refer to the methodological appendix for a deeper discussion of the communication infrastructure concept. See also Yong-Chan Kim and Sandra Ball-Rokeach, "Civic Engagement from a Communication Infrastructure Perspective," *Communication Theory* 16 (2006): 173–197.

4. The personnel of CSU changed over the course of my research, but the number of full- and part-time staff members was generally around ten.

5. Calvin Sims, "In Los Angeles, It's South-Central No More," *New York Times,* April 10, 2003, www.nytimes.com/2003/04/10/us/in-los-angeles-it-s-south-central-no-more.html.

6. *Los Angeles Times,* "Mapping L.A.: South L.A," http://maps.latimes.com/neighborhoods/region/south-la/.

7. Sorin Matei and Sandra Ball-Rokeach, "Watts, the 1965 Los Angeles Riots and the Communicative Construction of the Fear Epicenter of Los Angeles," *Communication Monographs* 72, no. 3 (2005): 301–323.

8. Lucie Cheng and Philip Yang, "Asians: The 'Model Minority' Deconstructed," in *Ethnic Los Angeles,* ed. Roger Waldinger and Mehdi Bozorgmehr (New York: Russell Sage Foundation, 1996): 305–344.

9. Garrett Broad, Carmen Gonzalez, and Sandra Ball-Rokeach, "Intergroup Relations in South Los Angeles: Combining Communication Infrastructure and Contact Hypothesis Approaches," *International Journal of Intercultural Relations* 38 (2014): 47–59; Catherine Cloutier, "Japanese American History in South Los

Angeles," April 26, 2010, www.youtube.com/watch?v=31KcEo3jMMA; Dowell Myers, *Special Report: Demographic and Housing Transitions in South Central Los Angeles, 1990 to 2000*, Population Dynamics Research Group, School of Policy, Planning, and Development, University of Southern California, 2002; Paul Ong et al., *The State of South LA*, UCLA School of Public Affairs, 2008; Jared Sanchez and Jennifer Ito, *Changing Demographics of South LA*, USC Program for Environmental and Regional Equity, 2011; US Census Bureau, "American Fact Finder," 2012, www .factfinder.census.gov/faces/nav/jsf/pages/index.xhtml; "Watts and West Adams," South Central History, www.southcentralhistory.com/watts-and-west-adams.php.

10. Los Angeles County Department of Public Health, "Key Indicators of Health by Service Planning Area," www.publichealth.lacounty.gov/ha/docs /kir_2013_finals.pdf.

11. LaVonna Blair Lewis et al., "African Americans' Access to Healthy Food Options in South Los Angeles Restaurants," *American Journal of Public Health* 95, no. 4 (2005): 668; David Sloane et al., "Improving the Nutritional Resource Environment for Healthy Living Through Community-Based Participatory Research," *Journal of General Internal Medicine* 18, no. 7 (2003): 568–575.

12. Amanda Shaffer, *The Persistence of L.A.'s Grocery Gap: The Need for a New Food Policy and Approach to Market Development,* Center for Food and Justice, Occidental College, 2002. A number of scholars and practitioners have debated the value of the term "food desert." I use the phrase here with a recognition of its inadequacy.

13. Los Angeles County Department of Public Health, "Key Indicators of Health by Service Planning Area"; Annie Park, Nancy Watson, and Lark Galloway-Gilliam, *South Los Angeles Health Equity Scorecard* (Community Health Councils, 2008), http://chc-inc.org/downloads/South%20LA%20Scorecard.pdf.

14. Broad et al., "Understanding Communication Ecologies to Bridge Communication Research and Community Action," *Journal of Applied Communication Research* 41, no. 4 (2013): 325–345; Laura Pulido, "Multiracial Organizing Among Environmental Justice Activists in Los Angeles," in *Rethinking Los Angeles,* ed. Michael Dear, H. Eric Schockman, and Greg Hise, (Thousand Oaks: Sage, 1996), 171–89.

15. Here I draw on Benedict Anderson's notion of imagined communities. See Benedict Anderson, *Imagined Communities: Reflections on the Origin and Spread of Nationalism* (London: Verso, 1983).

16. A scholarly and activist conversation around "decolonizing your diet" has been underway for some time. See, for example, www.decolonizeyourdiet.org.

17. Sheila Jasanoff, *Designs on Nature: Science and Democracy in Europe and the United States* (Princeton, NJ: Princeton University Press, 2005).

18. Community Build, "Community Build Mission," www.communitybuild .org.

19. For a fascinating study of illness, citizenship, and state intervention, see Adriana Petryna, *Life Exposed: Biological Citizens after Chernobyl* (Princeton, NJ: Princeton University Press, 2002).

20. Vikki Katz, *Kids in the Middle: How Children of Immigrants Negotiate Community Interactions for Their Families* (New Brunswick: Rutgers University Press, 2014).

21. Sandra Ball-Rokeach, Yong-Chan Kim, and Sorin Matei, "Storytelling Neighborhood: Paths to Belonging in Diverse Urban Environments," *Communication Research* 28, no. 4 (2011): 392–428; Broad et al., "Understanding Communication Ecologies."

22. The Positive, April 19, 2010 (3:14 p.m.), comment on "Tell Us What Vermont Square Means to You," *Los Angeles Times,* http://maps.latimes.com/neighborhoods /neighborhood/vermont-square/comments/.

23. Alison Hope Alkon, *Black, White, and Green* (Athens: University of Georgia Press, 2012).

24. Carmen Sirianni and Lewis Friedland, *Civic Innovation in America* (Berkeley and Los Angeles: University of California Press, 2001).

25. James DeFilippis, Robert Fisher, and Eric Shragge, *Contesting Community: The Limits and Potential of Local Organizing* (New Brunswick: Rutgers University Press, 2010).

26. Kwaku Duren, "Community Economic Development: Its Origins and Philosophy," *Black Panther Intercommunal News Service,* Summer 1999, 18–19.

27. Eric Shragge, *Community Economic Development: In Search of Empowerment* (Montreal: Black Rose Books, 1993).

28. Community Services Unlimited, "Re-Rooted to Better Serve the People," Online Newsletter, November 7, 2013.

29. Community Services Unlimited, "Donate Today to Support South LA's 1st Organic Produce Market," Online Newsletter, May 12, 2015.

30. See www.ridesouthla.com.

31. Alkon, *Black, White, and Green;* Guthman, *Weighing In.*

32. Teresa Mares and Devon G. Peña, "Environmental and Food Justice," in *Cultivating Food Justice: Race, Class, and Sustainability,* ed. Alison Hope Alkon and Julian Agyeman (Cambridge, MA: MIT Press, 2011), 197–220.

4. THE YOUTH FOOD JUSTICE MOVEMENT

1. For another valuable discussion of this tension in community organizing, see James DeFilippis, Robert Fisher, and Eric Shragge, *Contesting Community: The Limits and Potential of Local Organizing* (New Brunswick: Rutgers University Press, 2010).

2. Raymond Williams, *Keywords: A Vocabulary of Culture and Society* (Oxford University Press, 1985); Nikolas Rose, *Powers of Freedom: Reframing Political Thought* (Cambridge, UK: Cambridge University Press, 1999).

3. Nina Eliasoph, *Making Volunteers* (Princeton, NJ: Princeton University Press, 2011).

4. Seema Shah, *Building Transformative Youth Leadership: Data on the Impacts of Youth Organizing* (Funders' Collaborative on Youth Organizing, 2011), www.fcyo.org/media/docs/2525_Paper_11_CompleteWeb.pdf.

5. Shawn Ginwright and Taj James, "From Assets to Agents of Change: Social Justice, Organizing, and Youth Development," *New Directions for Youth Development* 96 (2002): 27–46.

6. Earth Island Institute, "Rooted in Community," www.earthisland.org/index.php/projects/rooted-in-community; Rooted in Community, "What We Do," www.rootedincommunity.org/about/what-we-do/.

7. Sasha Costanza-Chock, *Youth and Social Movements: Key Lessons for Allies,* Born This Way Foundation and the Berkman Center for Internet & Society at Harvard University, December 17, 2012, http://cyber.law.harvard.edu/sites/cyber.law.harvard.edu/files/KBWYouthandSocialMovements2012_0.pdf.

8. Within the broadly defined field of youth engagement, there is a great deal of contestation regarding exactly what role youth can and should play in setting organizational agendas and developing initiatives for change. Scholars and practitioners who work in this area have placed the varied youth engagement strategies on a wide spectrum of philosophy and action. This continuum includes interventionist approaches that emphasize treatment and prevention, strategies that provide youth with opportunities for growth and capacity-building, initiatives aimed at collective empowerment through leadership and civic engagement training, and agendas for systemic change that feature youth as core leaders involved in direct action and advocacy. See Melvin Delgado and Lee Staples, *Youth-Led Community Organizing: Theory and Action* (Oxford, UK: Oxford University Press, 2008).

9. Sheila Jasanoff, *Designs on Nature: Science and Democracy in Europe and the United States* (Princeton, NJ: Princeton University Press, 2005).

10. This point was included in the Black Panther Party's original Ten-Point Platform, a set of principles discussed in detail in chapter 5.

11. Each of these examples of land grabbing, it must be noted, is highly contested and interpreted in widely divergent ways.

12. Robert Gottlieb and Anupama Joshi, *Food Justice* (Cambridge, MA: MIT Press, 2010).

13. Anim Steel, "Youth and Food Justice: Lessons from the Civil Rights Movement," in *Food Movements Unite! Strategies to Transform Our Food System,* ed. Eric Holt-Gimenez (Oakland: Food First Books, 2011), 120–139.

14. Doron credited Anim Steel, his friend and food justice colleague, with coining the term "move-entity."

15. Nina Eliasoph's *Making Volunteers* provides insight into the drawbacks of mainstream youth empowerment programs.

16. Steel, "Youth and Food Justice."

17. Patricia Allen and Julie Guthman, "From 'Old School' to 'Farm-to-School': Neoliberalization from the Ground Up," *Agriculture and Human Values* 23, no. 4

(2006): 401–415; Branden Born and Mark Purcell, "Avoiding the Local Trap: Scale and Food Systems in Planning Research," *Journal of Planning Education and Research* 26, no. 2 (2006): 195–207.

18. Gerda R. Wekerle, "Food Justice Movements Policy, Planning, and Networks,"*Journal of Planning Education and Research* 23, no. 4 (2004): 378–386.

19. Alison Hope Alkon and Teresa Mares, "Food Sovereignty in US Food Movements: Radical Visions and Neoliberal Constraints," *Agriculture and Human Values* 29, no. 3 (2012): 347–359.

20. "Youth Food Bill of Rights," July 2011, www.youthfoodbillofrights.com.

21. Mark S. Pancer, Linda Rose-Krasnor, and Lisa D. Loiselle. "Youth Conferences as a Context for Engagement," *New Directions for Youth Development* 96 (2002): 47–64.

22. See, for instance, Sunshine Superboy, "Youth Food Bill of Rights," *Food Justice & Anti-Racism* (Mariposa Food Co-Op blog), June 26, 2011, http://mariposafood-justice.wordpress.com/2011/06/26/youth-food-bill-of-rights/; Brett Ramey, "'Youth Food Bill of Rights' on Board the Food and Freedom Ride," WellCommons, August 10, 2011, http://wellcommons.com/groups/locavores/2011/aug/10/youth-food-bill-of-rights-on-board-the-f/; and Glynnis Wadsworth, "Youth Food Bill of Rights," Beyond the Farm, October 10, 2011, https://web.archive.org/web/20140114130404/http://beyondthefarm.org/growing/youth-food-bill-of-rights/.

23. Lauren Ladov, "CFET Eco Interns @ RIC Conference," January 31, 2014, https://www.youtube.com/watch?v=9mFa7rjIiLg.

24. For more information about the Coalition of Immokalee Workers, see http://ciw-online.org/about/.

25. Sahra Sulaiman, "Got Justice?: Observations on a Food Justice Youth Summit and Food as a Means to Youth and Community Empowerment," *Streetsblog LA,* July 31, 2013, http://la.streetsblog.org/2013/07/31/got-justice-observations-on-a-food-justice-youth-summit-and-food-as-a-means-to-youth-and-community-empowerment/.

26. Eric Braxton, Will Buford, and Lorraine Marasigan, *2013 National Field Scan,* Funders' Collaborative on Youth Organizing, 2013, www.fcyo.org/media/docs/7343_FCYO-11–01.pdf; Gottlieb and Joshi, *Food Justice.*

27. Alkon and Mares, "Food Sovereignty"; Alethea Harper et al., *Food Policy Councils: Lessons Learned,* Food First, 2009, http://foodfirst.org/wp-content/uploads/2014/01/DR21-Food-Policy-Councils-Lessons-Learned-.pdf.

28. Guthman, *Weighing In.*

29. David Goodman, Melanie DuPuis, and Michael Goodman, "Engaging Alternative Food Networks: Commentaries and Research Agendas," *International Journal of Sociology of Agriculture & Food* 20, no. 3 (2013): 425–431.

30. Timothy A. Gibson, "The Limits of Media Advocacy." *Communication, Culture & Critique* 3, no. 1 (2010): 44–65.

1. Multiple scholarly reviews outline the diverse and at times conflicting historiographies that have been written about the Black Panthers. See, for instance, David J. Garrow, "Picking Up the Books: The New Historiography of the Black Panther Party," *Reviews in American History* 35, no. 4 (2007): 650–670; and Joe Street, "The Historiography of the Black Panther Party," *Journal of American Studies* 44, no. 2 (2010): 351–375. The footnotes in this chapter, of course, serve as a guide to several of the extensive histories and primary source materials that I have found particularly useful.

2. Paul Alkebulan, *Survival Pending Revolution: The History of the Black Panther Party* (Tuscaloosa: University of Alabama Press, 2007); Joshua Bloom and Waldo E. Martin Jr., *Black against Empire* (Berkeley and Los Angeles: University of California Press, 2013).

3. Bloom and Martin, *Black against Empire;* Christopher Murray, "Black Panther Party for Self-Defense," in *Encyclopedia of Black Studies,* ed. Molefi Kete Asante and Ama Mazama (Thousand Oaks: Sage Publications, 2005), 136–138.

4. Michael Clemons and Charles E. Jones, "Global Solidarity: The Black Panther Party in the International Arena," *New Political Science* 21, no. 2 (1999): 177–203; Floyd Hayes and Francis Kiene, "All Power to the People: The Political Thought of Huey P. Newton and the Black Panther Party," in *The Black Panther Party Reconsidered,* ed. Charles E. Jones (Baltimore: Black Classic Press, 1998), 157–176.

5. Clemons and Jones, "Global Solidarity," 187.

6. Alkebulan, *Survival Pending Revolution.*

7. Clemons and Jones, "Global Solidarity," 187; Charles Jones and Judson Jeffries, "Don't Believe the Hype: Debunking the Panther Mythology," in *The Black Panther Party reconsidered,* ed. Charles E. Jones (Baltimore: Black Classic Press, 1998), 25–56.

8. Bloom and Martin, *Black against Empire,* 160.

9. For an in-depth overview of this internal struggle, see Bloom and Martin, *Black against Empire,* 352–371.

10. Garrow, "Picking Up the Books."

11. Donald Cox, "The Split in the Party," *New Political Science* 21, no. 2 (1999): 171–176.

12. Ollie A. Johnson, "Explaining the Demise of the Black Panther Party: The Role of Internal Factors," in *The Black Panther Party Reconsidered,* ed. Charles E. Jones (Baltimore: Black Classic Press, 1998), 391–416.

13. Jones and Jeffries, "Don't Believe the Hype."

14. Johnson, "Explaining the Demise of the Black Panther Party."

15. Charles E. Jones, "Reconsidering Panther History: The Untold Story," in *The Black Panther Party reconsidered,* ed. Charles E. Jones (Baltimore: Black Classic Press, 1998), 1–24; Jones and Jeffries, "Don't Believe the Hype."

16. David Hilliard, ed., Huey P. Newton Foundation, *The Black Panther Party: Service to the People Programs* (Albuquerque: University of New Mexico Press, 2008).

17. Hilliard, *Black Panther Party.*

18. JoNina Abron, "Serving the People: The Survival Programs of the Black Panther Party," in *The Black Panther Party Reconsidered,* ed. Charles E. Jones. (Baltimore: Black Classic Press, 1998), 177–192.

19. Alondra Nelson, *Body and Soul: The Black Panther Party and the Fight against Medical Discrimination* (Minneapolis: University of Minnesota Press, 2011).

20. Bloom and Martin, *Black against Empire,* 184.

21. Nelson, *Body and Soul.*

22. Curtis Austin, *Up against the Wall: Violence in the Making and Unmaking of the Black Panther Party* (Fayetteville: University of Arkansas Press, 2008).

23. Quoted in Jones and Jeffries, "Don't Believe the Hype."

24. Quoted in Abron, "Serving the People."

25. Austin, *Up against the Wall;* Bloom and Martin, *Black against Empire.*

26. Huey P. Newton, "Black Capitalism Re-Analyzed I: June 5, 1971," in *The Huey P. Newton Reader,* ed. David Hilliard and Donald Weise (New York: Seven Stories Press, 2002), 227–233.

27. Nelson, *Body and Soul.*

28. Bloom and Martin's *Black against Empire* leans toward an interpretation that the revolutionary capacity of the Black Panther Party was lost when violence as a tactic was minimized. Austin's *Up against the Wall* takes the opposite perspective, arguing that the community programs were a high note for the organization.

29. Nelson, *Body and Soul.*

30. Akinyele Umoja, "Repression Breeds Resistance: The Black Liberation Army and the Radical Legacy of the Black Panther Party," *New Political Science* 21, no. 2 (1999): 131–155.

31. Alkebulan, *Survival Pending Revolution.*

32. Nelson, *Body and Soul.*

33. Judson Jeffries and Malcolm Foley, "To Live and Die in L.A.," in *Comrades: A Local History of the Black Panther Party,* ed. Judson Jeffries (Bloomington: Indiana University Press, 2007), 255–289.

34. Nelson, *Body and Soul.*

35. Kwaku Duren, "The Demise of the Black Panther Party and the Rise of a Black Independent Political Movement," *Black Panther International News Service,* Autumn 2000, 18–19.

36. J. Vern Cromartie, "B. Kwaku Duren and the Black Panther Party: A Case Study of Black Leadership in a Social Movement, 1976–1981," *NAAAS & Affiliates Conference Monographs* (January 2010): 1618.

37. Duren, "Demise of the Black Panther Party."

38. Frank Williams, "Reinventing the Black Panthers," *Los Angeles Times,* October 14, 1994, http://articles.latimes.com/1994–10–14/local/me-50178_ 1_black-panther-party.

39. New Panther Vanguard Movement, "The Struggle Continues: The Origins, Platform and Program of the New Panther Vanguard Movement," unpublished document, November 2002, www.itsabouttimebpp.com/Chapter_History/pdf /Los_Angeles/NVPM.pdf.

40. New Panther Vanguard Movement, "Ten Point Platform and Program," *Black Panther International News Service,* Autumn 2000, 2.

41. New Panther Vanguard and Mexica Movements, "Education in Our Interests," *Black Panther International News Service,* Summer 1999, 11–13.

42. Kwaku Duren, "Community Economic Development: Its Origins and Philosophy," New Panther Vanguard Movement, *Black Panther Intercommunal News Service,* Summer 1999, 18–19.

43. Alkebulan, *Survival Pending Revolution.*

44. Charles E. Jones, "Talkin' the Talk and Walkin' the Walk: An Interview with Panther Jimmy Slater," in *The Black Panther Party Reconsidered,* ed. Charles E. Jones (Baltimore: Black Classic Press, 1998), 147–155.

45. Duren, "Community Economic Development."

46. The issue of gender in food justice activism is a topic that is underexplored in this work and others. Its absence as an explicit area of inquiry here can be attributed to the fact that my own research was not guided by feminist theory, that my research collaborators did not actively name gender as a central aspect of their work (particularly when compared to the importance they paid to the issue of race), and that space limitations in this book simply prevent a full analysis of the many relevant areas of interrogation that could be explored. It is an admitted limitation of this project and deserves further attention. For a closer look at gender issues in food movements, see Josee Johnston and Kate Cairns, "Searching for the 'Alternative,' Caring, Reflexive Consumer," *International Journal of Sociology of Agriculture and Food,* 20, no. 3 (2013): 403–408.

47. Kameshwari Pothukuchi, "Community Food Assessment," *Journal of Planning Education and Research* 23, no. 4 (2004), 356–377; David Sawicki and Patrice Flynn, "Neighborhood Indicators: A Review of the Literature and an Assessment of Conceptual and Methodological Issues," *Journal of the American Planning Association* 62, no. 2 (1996): 165–183.

48. John Kretzmann and John McKnight, *Building Communities from the Inside Out* (Chicago: ACTA Publications, 1993).

49. Kami Pothukuchi et al., *What's Cooking in Your Food System?: A Guide to Community Food Assessment,* Community Food Security Coalition, 2002, www.foodsecurity.org/CFAguide-whatscookin.pdf. See also Barbara Cohen, *Community Food Security Assessment Toolkit,* USDA Economic Research Service, 2002, www.ers.usda.gov/media/327699/efan02013_1_.pdf.

50. Pothukuchi, "Community Food Assessment."

51. Julie Beaulac, Elizabeth Kristjansson, and Steven Cummins, "A Systematic Review of Food Deserts, 1966–2007," *Preventing Chronic Disease* 6, no. 3 (2009): A105.

52. Not to be overlooked, the entire endeavor was bound by a collective commitment to audit-oriented evaluation techniques, which are central to neoliberal governmentality. See Michael Power, *The Audit Society: Rituals of Verification* (Oxford, UK: Oxford University Press, 1997); and Nikolas Rose, *Powers of Freedom: Reframing Political Thought* (Cambridge, UK: Cambridge University Press, 1999).

53. Manuel Castells, *Communication Power* (Oxford, UK: Oxford University Press, 2009). For more on "hybrid coalitions" see Steven Epstein, *Inclusion: The Politics of Difference in Medical Research* (Chicago: University of Chicago Press, 2007).

54. Saskia Sassen, "Informal Knowledge and Its Enablements: The Role of the New Technologies," in *The Politics of Knowledge,* ed. Fernando Domínguez Rubio and Patrick Baert (New York: Routledge, 2012), 96–117.

55. Several parallel projects launched by other organizations were also kicking off around this time that set out to systematically document some of the same issues related to the area's status as a food desert. It was in the interest of government agencies and grant-making institutions, however, to incubate multiple projects in this realm, pushing a variety of connected but distinct community-based groups to build capacity and become integrated into the assessment-oriented mindset of contemporary nonprofit organizing. See, for instance, David Sloane et al., "Improving the Nutritional Resource Environment for Healthy Living Through Community-Based Participatory Research," *Journal of General Internal Medicine* 18, no. 7 (2003): 568–575.

56. Active Community to Improve Our Nutrition, *ACTION Food Assessment Report,* Community Services Unlimited, November 2004, csuinc.org/csuinc/wp-content/uploads/2013/11/Report.pdf.

57. Ibid.

58. Ibid.

59. Tom Philpott, "Walmart Drops $1 Million on Urban-Ag Pioneer Growing Power," *Mother Jones,* September 20, 2011, www.motherjones.com/tom-philpott/2011/09/walmart-drops-1-million-urban-ag-pioneer.

60. Duren, "Community Economic Development."

61. Neelam pointed to a report by the Greenlining Institute that explored inequality in grant funding of minority-led organizations. See Christian Gonzalez-Riverz et al., *Funding the New Majority: Philanthropic Investment in Minority-Led Nonprofits* (Greenlining Institute, Spring 2008), http://greenlining.org/wp-content/uploads/2013/02/FundingtheNewMajority.pdf.

62. See, for instance, Teresa Mares and Devon G. Peña, "Environmental and Food Justice: Toward Local, Slow, and Deep Food Systems," in *Cultivating Food Justice: Race, Class, and Sustainability,* ed. Alison Hope Alkon and Julian Agyeman (Cambridge, MA: MIT Press, 2011), 197–220.

63. A perspective that I am critiquing in this argument is presented in Alison Hope Alkon, *Black, White and Green* (Athens: University of Georgia Press, 2012).

64. Alkebulan, *Survival Pending Revolution.*

65. Quoted in Abron, "Serving the People."

66. Leaders of the Detroit Black Food Security Network, Social Justice Learning Institute, and People's Grocery discuss these very issues in Nikki Silvestri, Malik Yakini, and D'Artagnan Scorza, *Chant Down Babylon: Building Relationship, Leadership, and Power in the Food Justice Movement,* WhyHunger, 2014, www.whyhunger.org/uploads/fileAssets/1d6191_6fc3bb.pdf.

67. In discussing the generative power of ambivalence, I am influenced by the work of Sarah Banet-Weiser. See Sarah Banet-Weiser, *Authentic™: The Politics of Ambivalence in a Brand Culture* (New York: New York University, 2012).

6. COMPETING VISIONS AND THE FOOD JUSTICE BRAND

1. George Kelling and James Wilson, "Broken Windows: The Police and Neighborhood Safety," *Atlantic,* March 1982, www.theatlantic.com/magazine /archive/1982/03/broken-windows/304465/.

2. Robert Sampson and Stephen Raudenbush, "Seeing Disorder: Neighborhood Stigma and the Social Construction of "Broken Windows," *Social Psychology Quarterly* 67, no. 4 (2004): 319–342.

3. Manuel Castells, *Networks of Outrage and Hope* (Cambridge, UK: Polity Press, 2012); George Gerbner, "The Stories We Tell," *Peace Review* 11, no. 1 (1999): 9–15

4. Here I build from the work of several scholars of communication and social change, including Sandra Ball-Rokeach, Yong-Chan Kim, and Sorin Matei, "Storytelling Neighborhood: Paths to Belonging in Diverse Urban Environments," *Communication Research* 28, no. 4 (2001): 392–428; and Sasha Costanza-Chock, *Out of the Shadows and into the Streets* (Cambridge, MA: MIT Press, 2014).

5. More material about the Teaching Gardens Program of the American Heart Association can be found at www.heart.org/teachinggardens.

6. Kelly Meyer, "National Launch of the First Teaching Garden," *Huffington Post,* April 5, 2010, www.huffingtonpost.com/kelly-meyer/national-launch-of-the-fi_b_522498.html; "People: Kelly Meyer," UCLA Institute of the Environment and Sustainability, www.environment.ucla.edu/people/kelly-meyer.

7. These sponsors included General Electric and Kohler, to name a few. See Project7Ten, "About," https://web.archive.org/web/20120118071840/http://www .project7ten.com/site/index.htm.

8. The Deadline Team, "Ron Meyer Set As UCLA Commencement Speaker," *Deadline Hollywood,* June 6, 2012, www.deadline.com/2012/06/ron-meyer-set-as-ucla-commencement-speaker-gil-cates-to-be-honored/; "Kelly Meyer: Co-Founder, American Heart Association Teaching Gardens," Grades of Green, www .gradesofgreen.org/biographies/kelly-meyer.

9. Santa Monica-Malibu Unified School District, "Will Rogers Elementary School Hosts a Nationwide Kickoff of the Teaching Garden," press release, April 22, 2010, www.smmusd.org/press/press0910/WillRogersTeachingGard.htm.

10. Meyer, "National Launch."

11. "About Teaching Gardens," American Heart Association, www.heart.org /teachinggardens.

12. American Heart Association, *Annual Report 2011–2012*, 2013, www.heart .org/idc/groups/heart-public/@wcm/@adt/documents/downloadable/ucm_

449081.pdf; American Heart Association, "About the American Heart Association," www.heart.org/HEARTORG/General/About-Us———American-Heart-Association_UCM_305422_SubHomePage.jsp.

13. PR Newswire, "American Heart Association and Activist Kelly Meyer Team Up to Plant 'Teaching Gardens' Nationwide," American Heart Association, September 27, 2010, http://newsroom.heart.org/news/1126.

14. The California Endowment, it should be noted, is a private, statewide health foundation that was formed in 1996 when Blue Cross of California created its for-profit subsidiary, WellPoint Health Networks. In recent years, the organization has shifted its focus toward a "place-based" health promotion framework, exemplified in the launch of their Health Happens Here campaign and their ten-year, $1 billion Building Healthy Communities project. For Building Healthy Communities, the California Endowment selected fourteen broadly defined neighborhoods across the state of California to serve as community-level incubators in which significant grant funding would be allocated to a variety of community-based and advocacy organizations. Teaching Gardens were installed in at least three of those selected regions in Southern California: Boyle Heights, Central Long Beach, and South Los Angeles.

15. The California Endowment, "Grantfinder Details: American Heart Association, Los Angeles, Teaching Gardens for Community Health," http://grantfinder.calendow.org/gf/getindividual.aspx?id=20112345.

16. In South Los Angeles, specifically, AHA worked directly with individual elementary schools, as well as with some of the education management groups that oversee them—notably, the Partnership for Los Angeles Schools and LA's Promise—to institute the program over time.

17. Kelly Meyer, "Game Changers 2011: Kelly Meyer Talks Healthy Food," *Huffington Post,* October 27, 2011, www. huffingtonpost.com/2011/10/27/game-changers-2011-kelly-_n_1035082.html.

18. "Theory of change" is a popular term in nonprofit circles that refers to the vision of how an organization's goals will be achieved on a step-by-step basis.

19. PR Newswire, "American Heart Association."

20. In conversations with Teaching Gardens staff, I was told that the organization was in the process of collecting evaluation data but that they were unable to share it with me at that time. Through online research, I was able to find research presentations and posters that outlined the research project's methodology, initial findings, and areas for future research. See Jenna Banning, "Environmental Influences on the Effectiveness of School Garden Programs," August 4, 2014, https://prezi.com/iuy91ywmfndq/environmental-influences-on-the-effectiveness-of-school-gard/; and Meagan Pharis, "Evaluation of a School-Based Garden Education Program," October 2012, Student Scholars Poster Competition, University of Vermont.

21. James DeFilippis, Robert Fisher, and Eric Shragge, *Contesting community: The Limits and Potential of Local Organizing* (New Brunswick: Rutgers University Press, 2010); Eliasoph, *Making Volunteers* (Princeton, NJ: Princeton University Press, 2011); Ruth Wilson Gilmore, "In the Shadow of the Shadow State," in *The*

Revolution Will Not Be Funded: Beyond the Non-Profit Industrial Complex, ed. Incite! Women of Color Against Violence (Cambridge, MA: South End Press, 2007), 41–52.

22. It was no surprise either that obesity played a central role in the presentation of the Teaching Gardens' approach. As a number of scholars have convincingly argued, the popular framing of obesity is that of an out-of-control epidemic, a crisis defined in the quantified language of risk analysis, with the popular proffered "solutions" found by encouraging changes in the individualized and food-oriented decision making practices of neoliberal subjects. See Julie Guthman, "Neoliberalism and the Constitution of Contemporary Bodies," in *The Fat Studies Reader,* ed. Esther Rothblum and Sandra Solovay (New York: New York University Press, 2009), 187–196.

23. See, for instance, Julie Guthman, *Weighing In: Obesity, Food Justice, and the Limits of Capitalism* (Berkeley and Los Angeles: University of California Press, 2011); and Rachel Slocum, "Whiteness, Space and Alternative Food Practice," *Geoforum* 38, no. 3 (2007): 520–533.

24. American Heart Association, "American Heart Association Teaching Gardens," May 10, 2011, www.youtube.com/watch?v=hHJi8vlslTE.

25. Of course, the Teaching Gardens were hardly the most powerful or high-profile social actor engaged in work around nutrition education and gardening. Their work is only a small part of a much larger operation at the American Heart Association, and a host of other prominent figures—Michelle Obama and Jamie Oliver included, not to mention a wide array of other policy-makers, philanthropists, and businesspersons—have demonstrated an ability to shape public dialogue with much greater force.

26. The California Endowment, "The California Endowment and American Heart Association Celebrate Home-Grown Success of Teaching Gardens Partnership and Reward VIP Students With World Premiere Screening of Dr. Seuss' The Lorax," press release, January 21, 2012, http://tcenews.calendow.org/releases/california-endowment-and-american-229484; Kelly Meyer, "The Teaching Garden," *Parenting* (blog), April 25, 2012, www.parenting.com/blogs/mom-congress/kelly-meyer/teaching-garden.

27. Rally, "The California Endowment Celebrates Teaching Gardens Budding in Long Beach," March 27, 2013, http://wearerally.com/the-california-endowment-celebrates-teaching-gardens-budding-in-long-beach/.

28. Allison Ward, "Elementary Students Plant 'Dream Garden,'" *Columbus Dispatch,* May 22, 2013, www.dispatch.com/content/stories/life_and_entertainment/2013/05/22/elementary-students-plant-dream-garden.html.

29. Iain Blair, "Quvenzhane Wallis for Teaching Gardens: Variety Power of Youth Honoree," *Variety,* July 24, 2013, http://variety.com/2013/biz/news/quvenzhane-wallis-variety-power-of-youth-honoree-1200566669/.

30. Becky Coment, "Becky Comet from the Biggest Loser: This Is My Story," *American Heart Association Blog,* January 15, 2014, http://blog.heart.org/becky-comet-from-the-biggest-loser-this-is-my-story/.

31. American Heart Association News, "Fox Features Teaching Gardens during 'Brooklyn Nine-Nine,' other hit shows," *American Heart Association Blog,* May 1, 2015, http://blog.heart.org/fox-features-teaching-gardens-during-brooklyn-nine-nine-other-hit-shows/.

32. Sarah Banet-Weiser, *Authentic™: The Politics of Ambivalence in a Brand Culture* (New York: New York University Press, 2012).

33. Roopali Mukherjee and Sarah Banet-Weiser, "Introduction: Commodity Activism in Neoliberal Times," in *Commodity Activism: Cultural Resistance in Neoliberal Times,* ed. Mukherjee and Banet-Weiser (New York: New York University Press, 2012), 1–22.

34. See Eliasoph, *Making Volunteers,* for a relevant discussion of these types of "empowerment projects."

35. Center for Healthy Communities and Health ExChange Academy, *Communicating for Change,* California Endowment, 2006, http://archive.calendow.org/uploadedFiles/about/HEA_CFC_Man01_iPDF_R2.pdf.

36. Samantha King, "Pink Ribbons Inc: Breast Cancer Activism and the Politics of Philanthropy," *International Journal of Qualitative Studies in Education,* 17, 4 (2004), 473–492.

37. Banet-Weiser, *Authentic™.*

38. This description is based on an analysis of CSU's website, www.csuinc.org, conducted in March of 2014.

39. *The Garden Gateway Project* film can be viewed at http://vimeo.com/43322522.

40. See Costanza-Chock, *Out of the Shadows,* for a discussion on how these dynamics played out in youth immigrant rights organizing.

41. Ron Finley, "Ron Finley: A Guerilla Gardener in South Central LA," *TED Talk,* March, 2013, www.ted.com/talks/ron_finley_a_guerilla_gardener_in_south_central_la.html.

42. Henry Jenkins, Sam Ford, and Joshua Green, *Spreadable Media: Creating Value and Meaning in a Networked Culture,* (New York: New York University Press, 2013).

43. Jodi Dean, *Democracy and Other Neoliberal Fantasies: Communicative Capitalism and Left Politics,* (Durham: Duke University Press, 2009).

44. Finley, "Guerilla Gardener."

45. Mike Adams, "Ron Finley, Guerilla Gardener of South Central LA, Awarded 'Natural American Heroes' Award from Natural News," *Natural News,* August 20, 2013, http://www.naturalnews.com/041688_Ron_Finley_guerilla_gardener_Natural_American_Heroes_award.html; David Hochman, "Urban Gardening: An Appleseed With Attitude," *New York Times,* May 3, 2013, www.nytimes.com/2013/05/05/fashion/urban-gardening-an-appleseed-with-attitude.html.

46. Beck's Beer, "Beck's 2014 Artist Labels—Ron Finley," June 24, 2014, www.youtube.com/watch?v=uC8SLonFy-M

47. Kelly Meyer, "Video: Gardens that Teach," *Huffington Post,* March 28, 2012, www.huffingtonpost.com/kelly-meyer/urban-gardening-_b_1383665.html; Getty

Images, "Bette Midler's NYRP 13th Annual Spring Picnic," May 29, 2014, www
.gettyimages.com/detail/news-photo/ron-finley-attends-bette-midlers-nyrp-13th-
annual-spring-news-photo/494515289; Rally, "Jamie Oliver Continues the Food
Revolution with Sacramento Visit," January 10, 2014, http://wearerally.com
/jamie-oliver-continues-the-food-revolution-in-sacramento/.

48. City of Los Angeles, "Council File: 13–0478, Edible Landscapes," March 10,
2015, http://cityclerk.lacity.org/lacityclerkconnect/index.cfm?fa=vcfi.dsp_CFMS_
Report&rptid=99&cfnumber=13–0478.

49. See RonFinley.com and www.crowdrise.com/ronfinleyHQ.

CONCLUSION

1. Notable examples of this literature include Rachel Carson, *Silent Spring* (Boston: Houghton Mifflin Harcourt, 2002); Jared Diamond, *Collapse: How Societies
Choose to Fall or Survive* (London: Penguin, 2005); Donella H. Meadows et al., *The
Limits to Growth: A Report for the Club of Rome's Project on the Predicament
of Mankind,* (London: Earth Island Ltd., 1972). Other scholars have offered
decidedly more optimistic projections. See, for instance, Steven Kotler and Peter
Diamandis, *Abundance: The Future Is Better Than You Think* (New York: Free Press,
2012).

2. Safa Motesharrei, Jorge Rivas, and Eugenia Kalnay, "Human and Nature
Dynamics (HANDY): Modeling Inequality and Use of Resources in the Collapse
or Sustainability of Societies," *Ecological Economics* 101 (2014): 90–102. See also
Nafeez Ahmed, "Nasa-Funded Study: Industrial Civilisation Headed for 'Irreversible Collapse'?" *Guardian,* March 14, 2014, www.theguardian.com/environment
/earth-insight/2014/mar/14/nasa-civilisation-irreversible-collapse-study-scientists.

3. Suzanne Goldenberg, "Frame Climate Change as a Food Issue, Experts Say,"
Guardian, April 1, 2014, www.theguardian.com/environment/2014/apr/01
/climate-change-food-issue-ipcc-report.

4. Food and Water Watch, *Cultivating influence: The 2008 Farm Bill Lobbying
Frenzy,* July 2012, http://documents.foodandwaterwatch.org/doc/FarmBillLobby
.pdf; Tom Philpott, "The New Farm Bill: Yet Again, Not Ready for Climate
Change," *Mother Jones,* January 31, 2014, www.motherjones.com/tom-
philpott/2014/01/farm-bill-food-stamps-climate-change.

5. Ruth Wilson Gilmore, "In the Shadow of the Shadow State," in *The Revolution
Will Not Be Funded: Beyond the Non-Profit Industrial Complex,* ed. Incite! Women
of Color Against Violence (Cambridge, MA: South End Press, 2007), 41–52.

6. Quoted in Alondra Nelson, *Body and Soul: The Black Panther Party and the
Fight against Medical Discrimination* (Minneapolis: University of Minnesota Press,
2011), 63.

7. This argument is particularly influenced by Manuel Pastor and Rhonda Ortiz,
Making Change: How Social Movements Work and How to Support Them (Los Angeles: Program for Environmental and Regional Equity, 2009).

8. Roland Sturm and Aiko Hattori, "Diet and Obesity in Los Angeles County 2007–2012: Is There a Measurable Effect of the 2008 'Fast-Food Ban'?" *Social Science & Medicine* 133 (2015): 205–211.

9. Alex Haley, "1965 Playboy Interview with Rev. Martin Luther King Jr.," *Daily Beast,* January 19, 2014, www.thedailybeast.com/articles/2014/01/19/alex-haley-s-1965-playboy-interview-with-rev-martin-luther-king-jr.html.

10. See Andrew Calabrese, "The Promise of Civil Society: A Global Movement for Communication Rights," *Continuum: Journal of Media & Cultural Studies* 18, no. 3 (2004): 317–329.

APPENDIX

1. Michael Burawoy, "The Extended Case Method," *Sociological Theory* 16, no. 1 (1998): 4–33; Kathy Charmaz, "Grounded Theory in the 21st Century: Applications for Advancing Social Justice Studies," in *Handbook of qualitative research,* ed. N. K. Denzin and Y. S. Lincoln, 509–537 (Thousand Oaks: Sage Publications, 2000).

2. Paul Lichterman, "Seeing Structure Happen: Theory-Driven Participant Observation," in *Methods of Social Movement Research,* ed. Bert Klandermans and Suzanne Staggenborg (Minneapolis: University of Minnesota Press, 2002), 118–145.

3. Mario Diani, "The Concept of Social Movement," *Sociological Review* 40, no. 1 (1992): 1–25.

4. Sandra Ball-Rokeach, "A Theory of Media Power and a Theory of Media Use: Different Stories, Questions, and Ways of Thinking," *Mass Communication & Society,* 1 (1998), 5–40.

5. Sandra Ball-Rokeach, Yong-Chan Kim, and Sorin Matei, "Storytelling Neighborhood: Paths to Belonging in Diverse Urban Environments," *Communication Research* 28, no. 4 (2001): 392–428.

6. Yong-Chan Kim and Sandra Ball-Rokeach, "Civic Engagement from a Communication Infrastructure Perspective," *Communication Theory* 16 (2006): 173–197.

7. For an early exploration of the communication ecology concept, see Holly Wilkin et al., "Comparing the Communication Ecologies of Geo-Ethnic Communities: How People Stay on Top of Their Community," *Journal of Electronic Communication* 17, no. 2 (2007): 1–2.

8. Danyel Fisher, "Using Egocentric Networks to Understand Communication," *Internet Computing IEEE* 9, no. 5 (September–October 2005): 20–28; John Scott, *Social Network Analysis: A Handbook* (Thousand Oaks: Sage Publications, 2000).

REFERENCES

Abron, JoNina. "Serving the People: The Survival Programs of the Black Panther Party." In *The Black Panther Party Reconsidered,* edited by Charles E. Jones, 177–192. Baltimore: Black Classic Press, 1998.

Adam, Barbara. "Industrial Food for Thought: Timescapes of Risk." *Environmental Values* 8, no. 2 (1999): 219–238.

Alkebulan, Paul. *Survival Pending Revolution: The History of the Black Panther Party.* Tuscaloosa: University of Alabama Press, 2007.

Alkon, Alison Hope. *Black, White, and Green.* Athens: University of Georgia Press, 2012.

Alkon, Alison Hope, and Julian Agyeman. "Introduction: The Food Movement as Polyculture." In *Cultivating Food Justice: Race, Class, and Sustainability,* edited by Alison Hope Alkon and Julian Agyeman, 1–20. Cambridge, MA: MIT Press, 2011.

Alkon, Alison Hope, and Teresa Mares. "Food Sovereignty in US Food Movements: Radical Visions and Neoliberal Constraints." *Agriculture and Human Values* 29, no. 3 (2012): 347–359.

Allen, Patricia. *Together at the Table: Sustainability and Sustenance in the American Agrifood System.* University Park: Pennsylvania State University Press, 2004.

———. "Mining for Justice in the Food System: Perceptions, Practices, and Possibilities." *Agriculture and Human Values* 25, no. 2 (2008): 157–161.

Allen, Patricia, and Julie Guthman. "From 'Old School' to 'Farm-to-School': Neoliberalization from the Ground Up." *Agriculture and Human Values* 23, no. 4 (2006): 401–415.

Anderson, Benedict. *Imagined Communities: Reflections on the Origin and Spread of Nationalism.* London: Verso, 1983.

Ashman, Linda, Jaime de la Vega, Marc Dohan, Andy Fisher, Rosa Hippler, Billi Romain et al. "Seeds of Change: Strategies for Food Security for the Inner City." Master's thesis, University of California, Los Angeles, 1993.

Austin, Curtis. *Up against the Wall: Violence in the Making and Unmaking of the Black Panther Party.* Fayetteville: University of Arkansas Press, 2008.

Ball-Rokeach, Sandra. "A Theory of Media Power and a Theory of Media Use: Different Stories, Questions, and Ways of Thinking." *Mass Communication & Society* 1, no. 1–2 (1998): 5–40.

Ball-Rokeach, Sandra, Carmen Gonzalez, Minhee Son, and Neta Kligler-Vilenchik. "Understanding Individuals in the Context of Their Environment: Communication Ecology as a Concept and Method." Paper presented at the Annual Conference of the International Communication Association, Phoenix, AZ, May 2012.

Ball-Rokeach, Sandra, Yong-Chan Kim and Sorin Matei. "Storytelling Neighborhood: Paths to Belonging in Diverse Urban Environments." *Communication Research* 28, no. 4 (2001): 392–428.

Banet-Weiser, Sarah. *Authentic™: The Politics of Ambivalence in a Brand Culture.* New York: New York University Press, 2012.

Basok, Tanya, Suzan Ilcan, and Jeff Noonan. "Citizenship, Human Rights, and Social Justice." *Citizenship Studies* 10, no. 3 (2006): 267–273.

Beaulac, Julie, Elizabeth Kristjansson, and Steven Cummins. "A Systematic Review of Food Deserts, 1966–2007." *Preventing Chronic Disease* 6, no. 3 (2009): A105.

Beck, Ulrich. "Critical Theory of World Risk Society: A Cosmopolitan Vision." *Constellations* 16, no. 1 (2009): 3–22.

Benford, Robert, and David Snow. "Framing Processes and Social Movements: An Overview and Assessment." *Annual Review of Sociology* 26 (2000): 611–639.

Bloom, Joshua, and Waldo E. Martin Jr. *Black Against Empire.* Berkeley and Los Angeles: University of California Press, 2013.

Borlaug, Norman. "Ending World Hunger: The Promise of Biotechnology and the Threat of Antiscience Zealotry." *Plant Physiology* 124, no. 2 (2000): 487–490

Born, Branden, and Mark Purcell. "Avoiding the Local Trap: Scale and Food Systems in Planning Research." *Journal of Planning Education and Research* 26, no. 2 (2006): 195–207.

Braxton, Eric, Will Buford, and Lorraine Marasigan. *2013 National Field Scan.* Funders' Collaborative on Youth Organizing, 2013, www.fcyo.org/media/docs/7343_FCYO-11-01.pdf.

Broad, Garrett. "Revolution on Primetime TV—Jamie Oliver Takes on the US School Food System." In *The Rhetoric of Food: Discourse, Materiality & Power,* edited by Joshua Frye and Michael Bruner, 190–205. New York: Routledge, 2012.

———. "Ritual Communication and Use Value: The South Central Farm and the Political Economy of Place." *Communication, Culture and Critique* 6, no. 1 (2013): 20–40.

Broad, Garrett, Carmen Gonzalez, and Sandra Ball-Rokeach. "Intergroup Relations in South Los Angeles: Combining Communication Infrastructure and Contact Hypothesis Approaches." *International Journal of Intercultural Relations* 38 (2014): 47–59.

Broad, Garrett, Sandra J. Ball-Rokeach, Katherine Ognyanova, Benjamin Stokes, Tania Picasso, and George Villanueva. "Understanding Communication Ecologies to Bridge Communication Research and Community Action." *Journal of Applied Communication Research* 41, no. 4 (2013): 325–345.

Brown, Wendy. *Edgework: Critical Essays on Knowledge and Politics.* Princeton, NJ: Princeton University Press, 2005.

Burawoy, Michael. "The Extended Case Method." *Sociological Theory* 16, no. 1 (1998): 4–33.

———. "For Public Sociology," *American Sociological Review* 70, no. 1 (2005): 4–28.

Burrell, J. "The Field Site as a Network: A Strategy for Locating Ethnographic Research." *Field Methods* 21, no. 2 (2009): 181–199

Calabrese, Andrew. "The Promise of Civil Society: A Global Movement for Communication Rights." *Continuum: Journal of Media & Cultural Studies* 18, no. 3 (2004): 317–329.

Callon, Michel, Pierre Lascoumes, and Yannick Barthe. *Acting in an Uncertain World.* Cambridge, MA: MIT Press, 2009.

Campbell, Hugh. "Food and the Audit Society." In *Handbook of Food Research,* edited by Anne Murcott, Warren Belasco, and Peter Jackson, 177–191. New York: Bloomsbury, 2013.

Carolan, Michael. *The Real Cost of Cheap Food.* New York: Earthscan, 2011.

Carson, Rachel. *Silent Spring.* Boston: Houghton Mifflin Harcourt, 2002.

Castells, Manuel. *End of Millennium.* Vol. 3, *The Information Age: Economy, Society and Culture.* Cambridge, MA: Blackwell, 2000.

———. *Communication Power.* Oxford, UK: Oxford University Press, 2009.

———. *Networks of Outrage and Hope.* Cambridge, UK: Polity Press, 2012.

Charmaz, Kathy. "Grounded Theory in the 21st Century: Applications for Advancing Social Justice Studies." In *Handbook of Qualitative Research,* edited by N. K. Denzin and Y. S. Lincoln, 509–537. Thousand Oaks: Sage, 2000.

Cheng, Lucie, and Philip Yang. "Asians: The 'Model Minority' Deconstructed." In *Ethnic Los Angeles,* edited by Roger Waldinger and Mehdi Bozorgmehr, 305–344. New York: Russell Sage Foundation, 1996.

Christakis, Nicholas, and James Fowler. *Connected: The Surprising Power of Our Social Networks and How They Shape Our Lives.* New York: Little, Brown and Company, 2009.

Clemons, Michael, and Charles E. Jones. "Global Solidarity: The Black Panther Party in the International Arena." *New Political Science* 21, no. 2 (1999): 177–203.

Cohen, Barbara. *Community Food Security Assessment Toolkit.* Washington, DC: USDA Economic Research Service, 2002.

Costanza-Chock, Sasha. *Youth and Social Movements: Key Lessons for Allies.* Born This Way Foundation and the Berkman Center for Internet & Society at Harvard University, December 17, 2012, http://cyber.law.harvard.edu/sites/cyber.law .harvard.edu/files/KBWYouthandSocialMovements2012_0.pdf.

———. *Out of the Shadows and into the Streets.* Cambridge, MA: MIT Press, 2014.

Cox, Donald. "The Split in the Party." *New Political Science* 21, no. 2 (1999): 171–176.

Cribb, Julian. *The Coming Famine: The Global Food Crisis and What We Can Do to Avoid It.* Berkeley and Los Angeles: University of California Press, 2010.

Cromartie, J. Vern. "B. Kwaku Duren and the Black Panther Party: A Case Study of Black Leadership in a Social Movement, 1976–1981." *NAAAS & Affiliates Conference Monographs* (January 2010): 1618.

Cummins, Steven, Ellen Flint, and Stephen Matthews. "New Neighborhood Grocery Store Increased Awareness of Food Access but Did Not Alter Dietary Habits or Obesity." *Health Affairs* 33, no. 2 (2014): 283–291.

Dean, Jodi. *Democracy and Other Neoliberal Fantasies: Communicative Capitalism and Left Politics.* Durham: Duke University Press, 2009.

DeFilippis, James, Robert Fisher, and Eric Shragge. *Contesting Community: The Limits and Potential of Local Organizing.* New Brunswick: Rutgers University Press, 2010.

Delgado, Melvin, and Lee Staples. *Youth-Led Community Organizing: Theory and Action.* Oxford, UK: Oxford University Press, 2008.

Diamond, Jared. *Collapse: How Societies Choose to Fall or Survive.* London: Penguin, 2005.

Diani, Mario. "The Concept of Social Movement." *Sociological Review* 40, no. 1 (1992): 1–25.

———. "Network Analysis." In *Methods Of Social Movement Research,* edited by Bert Klandermans and Suzanne Staggenborg, 173–200. Minneapolis: University of Minnesota Press, 2002.

———. "Networks and Social Movements: A Research Programme." In *Social Movements and Networks: Relational Approaches to Collective Action,* edited by Mario Diani and Doug McAdam, 299–318. Oxford, UK: Oxford University Press, 2003.

Duren, Kwaku. "Community Economic Development: Its Origins and Philosophy." *Black Panther Intercommunal News Service,* Summer 1999: 18–19.

———. "The Demise of the Black Panther Party and the Rise of a Black Independent Political Movement." *Black Panther International News Service,* Autumn 2000: 18–19.

Eliasoph, Nina. *Making Volunteers.* Princeton, NJ: Princeton University Press, 2011.

Epstein, Steven. *Inclusion: The Politics of Difference in Medical Research.* Chicago: University of Chicago Press, 2007.

Fisher, Danyel. "Using Egocentric Networks to Understand Communication." *Internet Computing IEEE* 9, no. 5 (September–October 2005): 20–28.

Fisher, Walter. "The Narrative Paradigm: In the Beginning." *Journal of Communication* 35 (1985): 74–89.

Foucault, Michel. *Society Must Be Defended: Lectures at the Collège de France, 1976–1977.* New York: Picador Press, 2003.

———. *Security, Territory and Population: Lectures at the Collège de France, 1977–1978.* New York: Picador Press, 2007.

Freire, Paulo. *Pedagogy of the Oppressed.* New York: Continuum, 2000.

Friedland, Lewis. "Communication, Community, and Democracy: Toward a Theory of the Communicatively Integrated Community." *Communication Research* 28, no. 4 (2001): 358–391.

Frye, Joshua, and Michael Bruner, eds. *The Rhetoric of Food: Discourse, Materiality, and Power.* New York: Routledge, 2012.

Garrow, David. "Picking Up the Books: The New Historiography of the Black Panther Party." *Reviews in American History* 35, no. 4 (2007): 650–670.

Gerbner, George. "The Stories We Tell." *Peace Review* 11, no. 1 (1999): 9–15.

Gibson, Kristina, and Sarah Dempsey. "Make Good Choices, Kid: Biopolitics of Children's Bodies and School Lunch Reform in Jamie Oliver's *Food Revolution.*" *Children's Geographies* 13, no. 1 (2015): 44–58, doi:10.1080/14733285.2013.827875.

Gibson, Timothy A. "The Limits of Media Advocacy." *Communication, Culture & Critique* 3, no. 1 (2010): 44–65.

Gilmore, Ruth Wilson. "In the Shadow of the Shadow State." In *The Revolution Will Not Be Funded: Beyond the Non-Profit Industrial Complex,* edited by Incite! Women of Color Against Violence, 41–52. Cambridge, MA: South End Press, 2007.

Ginwright, Shawn, and Taj James. "From Assets to Agents of Change: Social justice, Organizing, and Youth Development." *New Directions for Youth Development* 96 (2002): 27–46.

Gold, Mark. *The Global Benefits of Eating Less Meat.* Compassion in World Farming Trust, 2004, www.ciwf.org.uk/includes/documents/cm_docs/2008/g/global_benefits_of_eating_less_meat.pdf.

Gonzalez-Rivera, Christian, Courtney Donnell, Adam Briones, and Sasha Werblin. *Funding the New Majority: Philanthropic Investment in Minority-Led Nonprofits.* Greenlining Institute, 2008, http://greenlining.org/wp-content/uploads/2013/02/FundingtheNewMajority.pdf.

Goodman, David, Melanie DuPuis, and Michael Goodman. *Alternative Food Networks: Knowledge, Practice and Politics.* New York: Routledge, 2012.

———. "Engaging Alternative Food Networks: Commentaries and Research Agendas." *International Journal of Sociology of Agriculture & Food* 20, no. 3 (2013): 425–431.

Gottlieb, Robert. "Where We Live, Work, Play . . . and Eat: Expanding the Environmental Justice Agenda." *Environmental Justice* 2, no. 1 (2009): 7–8.

Gottlieb, Robert, and Anupama Joshi. *Food Justice.* Cambridge, MA: MIT Press, 2010.

Gupta, Anil. "Origin of Agriculture and Domestication of Plants and Animals Linked to Early Holocene Climate Amelioration." *Current Science* 87, no. 1 (2004): 54–59.

Gurian-Sherman, Doug. *Failure to Yield: Evaluating the Performance of Genetically Engineered Crops.* Union of Concerned Scientists, 2009.

Guthman, Julie. "Neoliberalism and the Constitution of Contemporary Bodies." In *The Fat Studies Reader,* edited by Esther Rothblum and Sandra Solovay, 187–196. New York: New York University Press, 2009.

———. *Weighing In: Obesity, Food Justice, and the Limits of Capitalism.* Berkeley and Los Angeles: University of California Press, 2011.

————. "If They Only Knew: The Unbearable Whiteness of Alternative Food." In *Cultivating Food Justice: Race, Class, and Sustainability,* edited by Alison Hope Alkon and Julian Agyeman, 263–282. Cambridge, MA: MIT Press, 2011.

Hamm, Michael, and Anne Bellows. "Community Food Security and Nutrition Educators." *Journal of Nutrition Education and Behavior* 35, no. 1 (2003): 37–43.

Harper, Alethea, Alison Alkon, Annie Shattuck, Eric Holt-Giménez and Frances Lambrick. *Food Policy Councils: Lessons Learned.* Food First, 2009, http://foodfirst.org/wp-content/uploads/2014/01/DR21-Food-Policy-Councils-Lessons-Learned-.pdf.

Harvey, David. *A Brief History of Neoliberalism.* Oxford, UK: Oxford University Press, 2005.

————. *Social Justice and the City.* Athens: University of Georgia Press, 2009.

Hayes, Floyd, and Francis Kiene. "All Power to the People: The Political Thought of Huey P. Newton and the Black Panther Party." In *The Black Panther Party Reconsidered,* edited by Charles E. Jones, 157–176. Baltimore: Black Classic Press, 1998.

Hilliard, David, ed. *The Black Panther Party: Service to the People Programs.* Huey P. Newton Foundation. Albuquerque: University of New Mexico Press, 2008.

Holmes, Seth. *Fresh Fruit, Broken Bodies: Migrant Farmworkers in the United States.* Berkeley and Los Angeles: University of California Press, 2013.

Holt-Gimenez, Eric. "Food Security, Food Justice, or Food Sovereignty?" In *Cultivating Food Justice: Race, Class, and Sustainability,* edited by Alison Hope Alkon and Julian Agyeman, 309–330. Cambridge, MA: MIT Press, 2011.

Holt-Gimenez, Eric, and Raj Patel. *Food Rebellions: The Real Story of the World Food Crisis and What We Can Do About It.* Oxford, UK: Fahamu Books, 2009.

Jackson, John L. Jr. *Thin Description: Ethnography and the African Hebrew Israelites of Jerusalem.* Cambridge, MA: Harvard University Press, 2013.

Jasanoff, Sheila. *Designs on Nature: Science and Democracy in Europe and the United States.* Princeton, NJ: Princeton University Press, 2005.

Jeffries, Judson, and Malcolm Foley. "To Live and Die in L.A." In *Comrades: A Local History of the Black Panther Party,* edited by Judson Jeffries, 255–289. Bloomington: Indiana University Press, 2007.

Jenkins, Henry, Sam Ford, and Joshua Green. *Spreadable Media: Creating Value and Meaning in a Networked Culture.* New York: New York University Press, 2013.

Johnson, Ollie. "Explaining the Demise of the Black Panther Party: The Role of Internal Factors." In *The Black Panther Party Reconsidered,* edited by Charles E. Jones, 391–416. Baltimore: Black Classic Press, 1998.

Johnston, Josee, and Shyon Baumann. *Foodies: Democracy and Distinction in the Gourmet Foodscape.* New York: Routledge, 2010.

Johnston, Josee, and Kate Cairns. "Searching for the 'Alternative', Caring, Reflexive Consumer." *International Journal of Sociology of Agriculture and Food* 20, no. 3 (2013): 403–408.

Jones, Charles. "Reconsidering Panther History: The Untold Story." In *The Black Panther Party Reconsidered,* edited by Charles E. Jones, 1–24. Baltimore: Black Classic Press, 1998.

———. "Talkin' the Talk and Walkin' the Walk: An Interview with Panther Jimmy Slater." In *The Black Panther Party Reconsidered,* edited by Charles E. Jones, 147–155. Baltimore: Black Classic Press, 1998.

Jones, Charles, and Judson Jeffries. "Don't Believe the Hype: Debunking the Panther Mythology." In *The Black Panther Party Reconsidered,* edited by Charles E. Jones, 25–56. Baltimore: Black Classic Press, 1998.

Juris, Jeffrey. "Reflections on #Occupy Everywhere: Social Media, Public Space, and Emerging Logics of Aggregation." *American Ethnologist* 39, no. 2 (2012): 259–279.

Kato, Yuki. "Not Just the Price of Food: Challenges of an Urban Agriculture Organization in Engaging Local Residents." *Sociological Inquiry* 83, no. 3 (2013): 369–391.

Katz, David, and Stephanie Meller. "Can We Say What Diet Is Best for Health?" *Annual Review of Public Health* 35 (2014): 83–103.

Katz, Vikki. *Kids in the Middle: How Children of Immigrants Negotiate Community Interactions for Their Families.* New Brunswick: Rutgers University Press, 2014.

Kelling, George, and James Wilson. "Broken Windows: The Police and Neighborhood Safety." *Atlantic,* March 1982, www.theatlantic.com/magazine /archive/1982/03/broken-windows/304465/.

Kim, Yong-Chan, and Sandra Ball-Rokeach. "Civic Engagement from a Communication Infrastructure Perspective." *Communication Theory* 16 (2006): 173–197.

King, Samantha. "Pink Ribbons Inc: Breast Cancer Activism and the Politics of Philanthropy." *International Journal of Qualitative Studies in Education* 17, no. 4 (2004): 473–492.

Kotler, Steven, and Peter Diamandis. *Abundance: The Future Is Better Than You Think.* New York: Free Press, 2012.

Kretzmann, John, and John McKnight. *Building Communities from the Inside Out.* Chicago: ACTA Publications, 1993.

Lang, Tim, and Michael Heasman. *Food Wars: The Global Battle for Mouths, Minds and Markets.* London: Earthscan, 2004.

Larson, Nicole, Mary Story, and Melissa Nelson. "Neighborhood Environments: Disparities in Access to Healthy Foods in the U.S." *American Journal of Preventive Medicine* 36, no. 1 (2009): 74–81.

Latour, Bruno. *Reassembling the Social: An Introduction to Actor–Network Theory,* Oxford, UK: Oxford University Press, 2005.

Leigh, G. J. *The World's Greatest Fix.* Oxford, UK: Oxford University Press, 2004.

Lejano, Raul, Mrill Ingram, and Helen Ingram. *The Power of Narrative in Environmental Networks.* Cambridge, MA: MIT Press, 2013.

Lester, James, David Allen, and Kelly Hill. *Environmental Injustice in the United States: Myths and Realities.* San Diego: Westview Press, 2001.

Lewis, LaVonna Blair, David C. Sloane, Lori Miller Nascimento, Allison L. Diamant, Joyce Jones Guinyard, et al. "African Americans' Access to Healthy Food Options in South Los Angeles Restaurants." *American Journal of Public Health* 95, no. 4 (2005): 668.

Lichterman, Paul. "Seeing Structure Happen: Theory-driven Participant Observation," in *Methods of Social Movement Research,* edited by Bert Klandermans and Suzanne Staggenborg, 118–145. Minneapolis: University of Minnesota Press, 2002.

Lipsitz, George. "The Possessive Investment in Whiteness." *American Quarterly* 47, no. 3 (1995): 369–387.

Mares, Teresa. "Engaging Latino Immigrants in Seattle Food Activism through Urban Agriculture." In *Food Activism: Agency, Democracy and Economy,* edited by Carole Counihan and Valeria Siniscalchi, 31–46. New York: Bloomsbury, 2014.

Mares, Teresa, and Devon G. Peña. "Environmental and Food Justice: Toward Local, Slow, and Deep Food Systems." In *Cultivating Food Justice: Race, Class, and Sustainability,* edited by Alison Hope Alkon and Julian Agyeman, 197–220. Cambridge, MA: MIT Press, 2011.

Marsden, Terry. "Contemporary Food Systems: Managing the Capitalist Conundrum of Food Security and Sustainability." In *Handbook of Food Research,* edited by Anne Murcott, Warren Belasco, and Peter Jackson, 135–147. New York: Bloomsbury, 2013.

Matei, Sorin, and Sandra Ball-Rokeach. "Watts, the 1965 Los Angeles Riots and the Communicative Construction of the Fear Epicenter of Los Angeles." *Communication Monographs* 72, no. 3 (2005): 301–323.

McClintock, Nathan. "Radical, Reformist, and Garden-Variety Neoliberal: Coming to Terms with Urban Agriculture's Contradictions." *Local Environment* 19, no. 2 (2014): 147–171.

Meadows, Donella, Dennis L. Meadows, Jorgen Randers, and William W. Behrens. *The Limits to Growth: A Report for the Club of Rome's Project on the Predicament of Mankind.* London: Earth Island Ltd., 1972.

Minkler, Meredith. "Introduction to Community Organizing and Community Building." In *Community Organizing and Community Building for Health and Welfare,* edited by Meredith Minkler, 5–26. New Brunswick: Rutgers University Press, 2012.

Mintz, Sidney. *Sweetness and Power.* New York: Penguin Books, 1985.

Monteiro, Carlos. "Nutrition and Health: The Issue Is Not Food, Nor Nutrients, So Much as Processing." *Public Health Nutrition* 12, no. 5 (2009): 729–731.

Moss, Michael. *Salt, Sugar, Fat.* New York: Random House, 2013.

Motesharrei, Safa, Jorge Rivas, and Eugenia Kalnay. "Human and Nature Dynamics (HANDY): Modeling Inequality and Use of Resources in the Collapse or Sustainability of Societies." *Ecological Economics* 101 (2014): 90–102.

Mukherjee, Roopali, and Sarah Banet-Weiser. "Introduction: Commodity Activism in Neoliberal Times." In *Commodity Activism: Cultural Resistance in Neoliberal*

Times, edited by Roopali Mukherjee and Sarah Banet-Weiser, 1–22. New York: New York University Press, 2012.

Murray, Christopher. "Black Panther Party for Self-Defense." In *Encyclopedia of Black Studies,* edited by Molefi Kete Asante and Ama Mazam, 136–138. Thousand Oaks: Sage, 2005.

Myers, Dowell. *Special Report: Demographic and Housing Transitions in South Central Los Angeles, 1990 to 2000.* Population Dynamics Research Group, School of Policy, Planning, and Development, University of Southern California, 2002.

Nelson, Alondra. *Body and Soul: The Black Panther Party and the Fight against Medical Discrimination.* Minneapolis: University of Minnesota Press, 2011.

Nestle, Marion. *Food Politics: How the Food Industry Influences Nutrition and Health.* Berkeley and Los Angeles: University of California Press, 2007.

Newton, Huey P. "Black Capitalism Re-Analyzed I: June 5, 1971." In *The Huey P. Newton Reader,* edited by David Hilliard and Donald Weise, 227–233. New York: Seven Stories Press, 2002.

Ong, Paul, Theresa Firestine, Deirdre Pfeiffer, Oiyan Poon, and Linda Tran. *The State of South LA.* UCLA School of Public Affairs, 2008.

Pachirat, Timothy. *Every Twelve Seconds: Industrialized Slaughter and the Politics of Sight.* New Haven: Yale University Press, 2011.

Pancer, Mark S., Linda Rose-Krasnor, and Lisa D. Loiselle. "Youth Conferences as a Context for Engagement." *New Directions for Youth Development* 96 (2002): 47–64.

Park, Annie, Nancy Watson, and Lark Galloway-Gilliam. *South Los Angeles Health Equity Scorecard.* Community Health Councils, 2008. http://chc-inc.org /downloads/South%20LA%20Scorecard.pdf.

Pastor, Manuel, and Rhonda Ortiz. *Making Change: How Social Movements Work and How to Support Them.* Los Angeles: Program for Environmental and Regional Equity, 2009.

Patel, Raj. *Stuffed and Starved: The Hidden Battle for the World Food System.* New York: Melville House, 2008.

Pearce, Fred. "Why Are Environmentalists Taking Anti-Science Positions?" *Yale Environment 360,* October 22, 2012, http://e360.yale.edu/feature/why_are_ environmentalists_taking_anti-science_positions/2584/.

Perfecto, Ivette, John Vandermeer, and Angus Wright. *Nature's Matrix: Linking Agriculture, Conservation and Food Sovereignty.* London: Earthscan, 2009.

Petryna, Adriana. *Life Exposed: Biological Citizens after Chernobyl.* Princeton, NJ: Princeton University Press, 2002.

Pimentel, David, Paul Hepperly, James Hanson, David Douds, and Rita Seidel. "Environmental, Energetic, and Economic Comparisons of Organic and Conventional Farming Systems." *BioScience* 55, no. 7 (2005): 573–582.

Pollan, Michael. "The Food Movement, Rising." *New York Review of Books,* June 10, 2010, www.nybooks.com/articles/archives/2010/jun/10/food-movement-rising.

Polletta, Francesca. "Culture and Movements." *The Annals of the American Academy of Political and Social Science* 619, no. 1 (2008): 78–96.

Ponisio, Lauren C., Leithen K. M'Gonigle, Kevi C. Mace, Jenny Palomino , Perry de Valpine, and Claire Kremen. "Diversification Practices Reduce Organic to Conventional Yield Gap." *Proceedings of the Royal Society of London B: Biological Sciences* 282, no. 1799 (2015): 1–7.

Poppendieck, Janet. *Free for All: Fixing School Food in America.* Berkeley and Los Angeles: University of California Press, 2010.

Pothukuchi, Kameshwari. "Community Food Assessment." *Journal of Planning Education and Research* 23, no. 4 (2004): 356–377.

Pothukuchi, Kami, Hugh Joseph, Hannah Burton, and Andy Fisher. *What's Cooking in Your Food System?: A Guide to Community Food Assessment.* Community Food Security Coalition, 2002, www.foodsecurity.org/CFAguide-whatscookin.pdf.

Power, Michael. *The Audit Society: Rituals of Verification.* Oxford, UK: Oxford University Press, 1997.

Pulido, Laura. "Multiracial Organizing Among Environmental Justice Activists in Los Angeles." In *Rethinking Los Angeles,* edited by Michael Dear, H. Eric Schockman, and Greg Hise, 171–189. Thousand Oaks: Sage, 1996.

Putnam, Robert. *Bowling Alone: The Collapse and Revival of American Community.* New York: Simon and Schuster, 2000.

Reynolds, Kristin. "Disparity Despite Diversity: Social Injustice in New York City's Urban Agriculture System." *Antipode* 47, no. 1 (2015): 240–259.

Rose, Nikolas. *Powers of Freedom: Reframing Political Thought.* Cambridge, UK: Cambridge University Press, 1999.

Rosset, Peter. "Fixing our Global Food System: Food Sovereignty and Redistributive Land Reform." *Monthly Review* 61, no. 3 (2009): 114–128.

Sampson, Robert. *Great American City: Chicago and the Enduring Neighborhood Effect.* Chicago: University of Chicago Press, 2012.

Sampson, Robert, and Stephen Raudenbush. "Seeing Disorder: Neighborhood Stigma and the Social Construction of Broken Windows." *Social Psychology Quarterly* 67, no. 4 (2004): 319–342.

Sanchez, Jared, and Jennifer Ito. *Changing Demographics of South LA.* USC Program for Environmental and Regional Equity, 2011.

Sassen, Saskia. "Informal Knowledge and Its Enablements: The Role of the New Technologies." In *The Politics of Knowledge,* edited by Fernando Domínguez Rubio and Patrick Baert, 96–117. New York: Routledge, 2012.

Sawicki, David, and Patrice Flynn. "Neighborhood Indicators: A Review of the Literature and an Assessment of Conceptual and Methodological Issues." *Journal of the American Planning Association* 62, no. 2 (1996): 165–183.

Schambra, William. "Place and Poverty." In *Why Place Matters: Geography, Identity, and Civic Life in Modern America,* edited by Wilfred McClay and Ted McCallister, 162–170. New York: Encounter Books, 2014.

Scott, John. *Social Network Analysis: A Handbook.* Thousand Oaks: Sage, 2000.

Shaffer, Amanda. *The Persistence of LA's Grocery Gap: The Need for a New Food Policy and Approach to Market Development.* Center for Food and Justice, Occidental College, 2002.

Shah, Seema. *Building Transformative Youth Leadership: Data on the Impacts of Youth Organizing.* Funders' Collaborative on Youth Organizing, 2011, www.fcyo .org/media/docs/2525_Paper_11_CompleteWeb.pdf.

Shragge, Eric. *Community Economic Development: In Search of Empowerment.* Montreal: Black Rose Books, 1993.

Silvestri, Nikki, Malik Yakini, and D'Artagnan Scorza. *Chant Down Babylon: Building Relationship, Leadership, and Power in the Food Justice Movement.* Why-Hunger, 2014, www.whyhunger.org/uploads/fileAssets/1d6191_6fc3bb.pdf.

Simpson, Jennifer, and David Seibold. "Practical Engagements and Co-Created Research." *Journal of Applied Communication Research* 36, no. 3 (2008): 266–280.

Sirianni, Carmen, and Lewis Friedland. *Civic Innovation in America.* Berkeley and Los Angeles: University of California Press, 2001.

Sloane, David, Allison L Diamant, LaVonna B Lewis, Antronette K Yancey, Gwendolyn Flynn, Lori Miller Nascimento et al. "Improving the Nutritional Resource Environment for Healthy Living Through Community-Based Participatory Research." *Journal of General Internal Medicine* 18, no. 7 (2003): 568–575.

Slocum, Rachel. "Whiteness, Space and Alternative Food Practice." *Geoforum* 38, no. 3 (2007): 520–533.

Smith, Andrea ."Introduction: The Revolution Will Not Be Funded." In *The Revolution Will Not Be Funded: Beyond the Non-Profit Industrial Complex,* edited by Incite! Women of Color Against Violence, 1–20. Cambridge, MA: South End Press, 2007.

Steel, Anim. "Youth and Food Justice: Lessons from the Civil Rights Movement." In *Food Movements Unite! Strategies to Transform Our Food System,* edited by Eric Holt-Gimenez, 120–139. Oakland: Food First Books, 2011.

Stoecker, Randy. "Are Academics Irrelevant?: Roles for Scholars in Participatory Research." *The American Behavioral Scientist* 42, no. 5 (1995): 840–854.

Strate, Lance. "A Media Ecology." *Communication Research Trends* 23, no. 2 (2004): 1–48.

Street, Joe. "The Historiography of the Black Panther Party." *Journal of American Studies* 44, no. 2 (2010): 351–375.

Sturm, Roland, and Aiko Hattori. "Diet and Obesity in Los Angeles County 2007–2012: Is There a Measurable Effect of the 2008 'Fast-Food Ban'?" *Social Science & Medicine* 133 (2015): 205–211.

Umoja, Akinyele. "Repression Breeds Resistance: The Black Liberation Army and the Radical Legacy of the Black Panther Party." *New Political Science* 21, no. 2 (1999): 131–155.

Wekerle, Gerda R. "Food Justice Movements: Policy, Planning, and Networks." *Journal of Planning Education and Research* 23, no. 4 (2004): 378–386.

Wilkin, Holly, Sandra Ball-Rokeach, Matthew Matsaganis, and Pauline Cheong. "Comparing the Communication Ecologies of Geo-Ethnic Communities: How People Stay on Top of Their Community." *Journal of Electronic Communication* 17, no. 2 (2007): 1–2.

Williams, Raymond. *Keywords: A Vocabulary of Culture and Society.* Oxford, UK: Oxford University Press, 1985.

Wolch, Jennifer. *The Shadow State: Government and Voluntary Sector in Transition.* New York: Foundation Center, 1990.

Wolfson, Todd. *Digital Rebellion: The Birth of the Cyber Left.* Chicago: University of Illinois Press, 2014.

INDEX

Page numbers in italics indicate illustrations.

48; and "Friends of the Panthers,"
139–140; history of, 138–141; and
NPVM, 141–46; and Oakland
Community School, 140; and
PANTHER (London, Eng.), 142–43;
and Scott-Smith Justice Committee,
140–41; and Seniors Against a Fearful
Environment, 141

Brand, Russell, 188

branding, 10, 166–68, 179–180, 184; and
brandability, 180, 190–91; and "brand
culture," 179, 185, 191; and CSU, *32*, 183,
192; recommendations for, 202–3, 206;
and Ron Finley Project, 185, 190–91;
and Teaching Gardens Program
(AHA), 166, 169–170, 179–180

Brentwood Elementary School (Plainfield,
Ind.), 173

broken windows approaches, 165–66, 168,
180, 190, 193, 196, 199

Brower, David, 105

Brown, Elaine, 134, 139–141

Brown, Kizzy, 142

Brown, Wendy, 21

Brown Berets (S. Calif.), 133

Bunchy Carter People's Free Medical
Clinic (BPP), 140

Burawoy, Michael, 211

Burpee Seeds and Plants, 177

Butz, Earl, 42

Cabell County School District (W.V.), 1–2

California: Department of Public Health,
32, 156; Highway Police Officers, 140;
state legislature, 152

The California Endowment: and Building
Healthy Communities project, 237n14;
and Health Happens Here campaign,
237n14; and Ron Finley Project, 188–
89; and Teaching Gardens Program
(AHA), 171–72, 175, 178, 180, 188,
237n14

Callon, Michelle, 220n32

Camden (N.J.), 121

capitalism, 7; Black capitalism, 137; and
BPP, 56, 133, 136–37, 145, 161–62;
capitalist agro-industrialism, 37–38, 41;
capitalistic entrepreneurship, 201–2;

and CSU, 96–97, 100, 201; and food
justice movement, 55–56, 96–97, 120,
199; and neoliberalism, 21, 23, 55; and
NPVM, 145; and philanthrocapitalism,
180, 203; reluctant capitalists, 97, 100

Capital One, 172

cardiovascular health, 44, 65, 171, 174, 177

Cargill, 41

Carolan, Michael, 45

Carter, Alprentice "Bunchy," 139

Casale, Kate, 107

Castells, Manuel, 16, 28, 166

CCEDA (California Community
Economic Development Corporation),
93

CDCs (Community Development
Corporations), 91

CED (community economic
development), *32*, 91–92, 144–46

celebrity advocates, 2, 195, 207; and BPP,
140; and CSU, *32*, 192; and RIC, 122;
and Ron Finley Project, 168–69, 185,
187–89, 191; and Teaching Gardens
Program (AHA), 166, 170–72, 176,
178–79; and Women's Cancer
Research Fund, 170. *See also names of
celebrity advocates*

Center South LA arts program, 85, 88

Central America, 94; and ancestral foods,
77; and crop pairings, 80; immigrants
from, 64, 97–98

CFAs (Community Food Assessments),
32, 129–131, 148–154; and audit-
oriented evaluation techniques, 149,
154, 163, 234n52, 235n55

charity, 55, 170, 176, 206. *See also
philanthropy*

Chevron, 172

Chez Panisse restaurant, 49

Chicago School of sociology, 29

Chicanos, 133, 141

childhood obesity. *See* obesity

Christakis, Nicholas, 220n32

CIT (communication infrastructure
theory), 61, 212–14, 227n3

civic epistemologies, 71–72; and CSU, 72,
74, 83–85, 98, 100, 126; and RIC, 110,
113, 126

Civil Rights movement, 22, 132, 144; and nonviolent civil disobedience, 132

class, social, 58, 168, 194; and alternative food movements, 45, 50, 55; class consciousness, 55; and class struggle, 133; middle class, 13, 168, 200

Cleaver, Eldridge, 133–34, 139

climate change, 34, 195, 207; and greenhouse gases, 43; and land use changes, 43

Clinton, Bill, 184

Coalition Against Police Abuse (BPP), 141

Coalition of Immokalee Workers (Fla.), 123

coalitions, 20, 204; and alternative food movements, 51; and CFAs (Community Food Assessments), 148, 151–52; and RIC, 127. *See also names of coalitions*

collaboration, 10–11, 13–14, 54, 167, 202–7; and alternative food movements, 48–49, 51; and BPP, 139–140; and CFAs (Community Food Assessments), 148–150, 153–54; and CSU, 11, 13–14, 17, 61, 65, 69, 72, 81, 86, 95, 98, 101, 103, 123, 156, 158–59, 182; and Nishida, Florence, 186; and RIC, 101, 103, 112, 115, 117–120, 123; and Ron Finley Project, 186, 188; and working principles, 26

colonialism, 110; and decolonizing your diet, 71, 228n16

Columbus Dispatch, 178

Comerchero, Doron, 107–9, 112, 116, 124

common cause, 11, 28, 67, 88, 105, 112, 167, 205

communication ecology perspective, 8–9, 10, 18, 27–31, 201, 208, 212–14, 221n39; and BPP, 131; and CSU, 67, 82, 84, 100, 103, 131, 146, 164, 181; goal-oriented, 29–30, 214; and RIC, 103; and Teaching Gardens Program (AHA), 168, 179

communication power, 166–68, 179

communities of color, 3–8, 17, 34–35, 159, 196–98; and alternative food movements, 48, 52–53; and BPP, 132–38; and CFAs (Community Food

Assessments), 129–131, 148–153; and CSU, 66, 71, 96–97, 126, 146, 159–160, 162, 235n61; and food deserts, 45–46; and food justice movement, 53–57, 203; and NPVM, 142–44; and RIC, 105, 107–10, 117–18, 126, 128; and Teaching Gardens Program (AHA), 171, 176; and youth food justice movement, 105, 107–10, 117–18, 126, 128. *See also* ethnic minority communities

community-based organizing, 3–4, 6–15, 17–19, 27, 31, 35, 166–68, 191–92, 195–202, 211–15; and alternative food movements, 50, 53; and BPP, 124, 130–141, 145, 233n28; and CFAs (Community Food Assessments), 129–131, 148–153; and CSU, 11–12, 25, 32, 61–62, 65–100, 103, 124–27, 130, 142, 146, 148–49, 154–160, 162–64, 180–83, 200–201; and food justice movement, 51–58, 115, 130–31; and LA Green Grounds, 186–87; and neoliberalism, 22–25; and NPVM, 144–45; recommendations for, 4, 202–9; and RIC, 12, 25–26, 102–6, 108–12, 115–122, 124, 126–28, 201; romanticizing of, 7, 52, 57, 102; and Ron Finley Project, 12, 26, 185, 187, 190–91; and Teaching Gardens Program (AHA), 12, 26, 165–66, 168, 170, 173–74, 177, 191; working principles for, 26–27, 30–31, 131

Community Build (South Los Angeles), 74–75

Community Food Security Coalition, 149, 151, 225n57

Community Food Systems, 54

Community Food Village Project (CSU), 67

community gardens, 5, 7, 17, 52, 58, 154, 196, 206

community service: and BPP, 66, 135, 140, 143, 201; and CSU, 77–78, 201; and NPVM, 143

Community Services Unlimited. *See* CSU

ConAgra, 41

Congress, US: and Farm Bill, 33, 51, 120, 197

consciousness-raising, 54, 204

consensus, 114–15

conservation programs, 197

conservatives, 22–23; and alternative food movements, 50; and "nanny state," 50

Constitution, US, 120

consumer choices, 5–6; and alternative food movements, 47, 49–50, 52, 225n53; and food justice movement, 53, 55; and Green Revolution, 39; and "nanny state," 50; and processed foods, 44–45; and risks of industrial food system, 43–45; and Teaching Gardens Program (AHA), 180

contemporary network theory, 214

co-op retail markets, 48–49; and Detroit Black Community Food Security Network (Mich.), 54, 56

co-optation, 8–9, 57, 206; and BPP, 138; and CSU, 157, 160–61, 163; and Ron Finley Project, 169, 189, 191

Cora, Cat, 170

corner markets, *32*, 44, 64, 94–95, 98, 121; Mama's Chicken, 95

corporations, 8, 195, 202–3; and alternative food movements, 47–51; and BPP, 137; chemical corporations, 38, 42; and CSU, *32*, 80, 103, 142, 156–57; failure of, 16; and food justice movement, 120; as monopolies, 41, 137; multinational corporations, 21, 41–42; and neoliberalism, 21, 23; and RIC, 123; and risks of industrial food system, 40–44; and Ron Finley Project, 189–191; and social responsibility, 51, 178–180; structural power of, 51; and Teaching Gardens Program (AHA), 168, 172, 176–180, 191; transnational corporations, 36; and La Via Campesina (The Peasant Way), 47–48. *See also* agribusiness; *names of corporations*

Costanza-Chock, Sasha, 24–25, 109

criminal justice system, 16, 46, 136, 140–41; and juvenile recidivism, 189

critical analyses, 4, 13, 215

critical consciousness, 60–61, 69, 79, 102, 117, 191

critical thinking skills, 71, 73, 75, 128

CSU (Community Services Unlimited), 10–11, 13–14, 17, 25, 31, *32*, 34, 60–62, 65–100, 168, 200–202, 209, 227n2; and alternative food movements, 61, 96–97; apprenticeship program of, 67, 70, 75, 79, 82, 84; and backyard fruit, 78–79; and "beyond organic," 77, 79, 93, 95–96, 101; board members of, 85, 110, 138, 155, 157–58, 181; and BPP, *32*, 130–31, 135, 138, 140–41, 146, 153, 155–56, 160–62, 164, 166, 200–202; and CED (community economic development), *32*, 91–92, 144, 146; and CFA (Community Food Assessment), *32*, 129–131, 148–154, 235n55; and commercial kitchens, 93–94; and Community Build, 74–75; and Community Food Village Project, 67; and community workshops, 14, 79–85, 99, 156, 182; conceptual diagram of, 31, *32;* and conflict-oriented discourse, 159–160; and documentary film, *32*, 182–83; and Earth Day South LA, *32*, 85–91, *89*, *90;* egocentric network of, 214; and electoral politics, 142; and engaged scholarship, 13–14; and farmers' markets, *68*, 78, 91, 95–96; and Food Forward, 78; and food justice movement, 11, 13–14, 17, 25–26, *32*, 53–54, 58–62, 65–100, 103, 153–164, 180–83, 191–92, 200–201; and Food Party fundraisers, 200; and Foods that Cleanse, 82; and Garden Gateway workshops, *32*, 79–85, *81;* and grant funding, 20, 34, 81, 148, 151, 153–56, 158, 161, 163–64, 201–2, 235n61; and From the Ground Up, *32*, 70–73; and Growing Healthy, *32*, 67, 69; and Healthy Food Map of South LA, 95; history of, 12, 181, 200–202; internship program of, 65, 67, 70–73, 75, 77, 79, 84, *89*, 95, 97–98, 101, 110–11, 129–130, 138, 181; and media coverage, 85–87, 89, 99, 154, 167, 169, 180–83, 192; and Mercado La Paloma, 92–93; and mini urban farms, *32*, *68*, 69, 74–75, *76*, 77–79, 83–84, 91–92, 94, 99, 182; and

CSU *(continued)*
    NPVM, *32,* 143–44, 151; online
    resources of, *32,* 86, 93–94, 181, 192; and
    origin stories, 129–131, 138; outreach
    work of, 14, *32,* 78, 81, 85–88, 90, 182;
    and Paul Robeson Community Center,
    94; and produce-bag sales program, 78,
    92, 94; and produce stands, 60, 70, *76,*
    92–93, 97, 181; revenue-generating
    aspects of, 91–93; and RIC, *32,* 54,
    101–4, 106, 110–12, *113, 114,* 116–17, 123,
    126–27; and Ron Finley Project, *32,*
    190–91; and school gardens, *32,* 67,
    69–70, 75, 151, 153–54, 174; and Soul
    Full Catering, 94; and systems-based
    approach, 67, 69, 74, 200–201; and
    Teaching Gardens Program (AHA),
    32, 173–74, 191; and 360 approach, 67,
    99; and Tree of Life, *32,* 78; and urban
    farms, 13–14, 67, *68,* 181; and videos,
    165–66, 192; and VMP (Village Market
    Place), *32,* 34, 67, *68,* 92–98, 100, 154,
    161, 181; and volunteers, 13–14, 34, 60,
    75, *76,* 77, 79, 87–88, 95, 99, 101, *113,*
    129, 138, 143, 155, 181; website of, *32,* 181;
    and youth development work, 11, 62,
    67, 69–74, 200
cultural histories, 71–74, 77, 201, 204
cultural investigation of "why," 27–30, 212
cultural knowledge, 61, 74, 80, 82–85, 97,
    99. *See also* knowledge practices
cultural pluralism, 204
Curry, Peggy, 171
Curtis, Jamie Lee, 2

Daly, Carson, 187
Day of Action (RIC), 106, *114,* 122–23, 167
Dean, Jodi, 185
Deasy, John, 2
decentralized social policy, 19–21, 35,
    219n11
decision-making capacities, 21, 41; and
    alternative food movements, 51; and
    CFAs (Community Food
    Assessments), 151; and CSU, 66, 151,
    160; and RIC, 108; and Teaching
    Gardens Program (AHA), 238n22
Declaration of Independence, US, 120

decolonizing your diet, 71, 228n16
decommodification, 55–57, 161
DeFilippis, James, 25, 91
DeFreitas, Lawrence, 13, 62, 70–72, 97,
    102, 117, 143, 147
Democratic Party, 20–21
Department of Treasury, US, 33–34
deprivation amplification, 46
Detroit (Mich.), 103; Detroit Black
    Community Food Security Network,
    17, *32,* 54–56; Food Policy Council,
    56
developing world, 5, 195; and agricultural
    history, 37, 39–40, 222n17; and food
    security, 34, 44; and processed foods,
    45; and risks of industrial food system,
    44–46, 57
Devito, Danny, 178
diabetes, 44, 65
dialectical materialism, 133
Diani, Mario, 28, 212
digital media, 11–12, 14, 16–18, 28, 31,
    165–68, 191–93, 213–14; and alternative
    food movements, 47; and CFAs
    (Community Food Assessments), 150;
    and CSU, 148–49, 163, 169, 192, 202;
    recommendations for, 205–7; and
    RIC, 12, 121, 183–84, 202; and Ron
    Finley Project, 168–69, 184–85, 190–
    91; and "spreadability," 185; and
    Teaching Gardens Program (AHA),
    169, 192; and La Via Campesina (The
    Peasant Way), 47. *See also* social media
direct action, 102, 118, 123, 205
discrimination/anti-discrimination, 5–6,
    25, 196; and CSU, 17, 53, 96, 99; and
    ethnic minority farmers, 96; and
    NPVM, 144; and RIC, 109; and Ron
    Finley Project, 190; in South Los
    Angeles, 64, 129. *See also* racial justice
disease, diet-related, 4–5, 195; and
    alternative food movements, 48–49;
    chronic disease, 5, 41, 44–46, 48–49,
    65; and CSU, 62; and LAUSD, 2; and
    risks of industrial food system, 41,
    44–46; in South Los Angeles, 65
disinvestment, 17, 64, 129
Disney, 188

obesity, 33–34, 203; and alternative food movements, 48–49, 225n55; childhood obesity, 1–2, 33–34, 49, 169, 177–79; and *Jamie Oliver's Food Revolution,* 1–3, 49, 225n55; and Let's Move, 33, 49, 225n55; and risks of industrial food system, 44; in South Los Angeles, 65; and Teaching Gardens Program (AHA), 169, 177–79, 238n22

Occidental College, 147

Occupy movement, 16, 219n3

O'Gorman, Michael, 170–71

Oliver, Jamie, 1–3, *32,* 49, 122, 188–89, 225n55, 238n25. See also *Jamie Oliver's Food Revolution*

Olympia (Wash.), 106

The Omnivore's Dilemma (Pollan), 49

open-ended interviews, 3–4, 214–15

organic farming practices, 43, 48, 77, 225n53; beyond organic, 77, 79, 93, 95–96, 101, 181; and CSU, 77, 79, 95–96, 101, 181–82; and Teaching Gardens Program (AHA), 169, 172

organizational communication ecology, 30

Our Lady of the Lake Regional Medical Center (Baton Rouge, La.), 173

outsider status, 8–9, 200, 206; and Teaching Gardens Program (AHA), 167–68, 173, 176

Palestine, 110

PANTHER (London, Eng.), 142–43, 146

Parenting magazine, 178

Participant Media, 169

participant observation, 4, 10, 13, 215

Participatory Appraisal model, 151

Partnership for Los Angeles Schools, 237n16

partnerships, 8, 167, 198, 203, 205; and BPP, 137; and CFAs (Community Food Assessments), 150–53; and CSU, 17, *32,* 53, 61, 67, *68,* 69, 74–75, 78–82, 84–85, 90–91, 94–96, 99–100, 102, 131, 138, 154–160, 162–63, 201; and Eliasoph's "Empowerment Projects," 24; and food justice movement, 51, 56; institutional partners, 203; intergenerational, 101, 110–13, 120, 126;

and neoliberalism, 25; networked partnerships, 17, 26, 61, 79, 85, 99–100, 131, 137, 190, 198, 205; and NPVM, 143, 145; public-private partnerships, 33, 49, 96, 145; recommendations for, 207–8; and RIC, 102, 112–13, 123; and Ron Finley Project, 189–190; and Teaching Gardens Program (AHA), 170–74, 180; and working principles, 26

Pascall, Dyane, 66–67, 77, 80–81, 91, 95–97, 124, 150, 162, 192

Patel, Raj, 40

Paul Robeson Community Center (South LA), 94

Peace and Freedom Party, 133, 142

peasant farmers, 47–48, 205. *See also* La Via Campesina (The Peasant Way)

Pedagogy of the Oppressed (Freire), 9

Peña, Devon G., 55–56

Peoples College of Law, 142

perseverance, 65, 206–7

Philadelphia (Pa.), 101, 106, 120–21

philanthropy, 56, 166, 168, 203, 206, 238n25; and alternative food movements, 51; and BPP, 137–38; and CSU, 156, 159; and media coverage, 169; and philanthrocapitalism, 180, 203; and pro bono assistance, 51; and risks of industrial food system, 42; and Ron Finley Project, 185, 189–190; and Teaching Gardens Program (AHA), 166, 168–69, 176, 178–79, 191

Philippines, 42

Planting Justice (Oakland, Calif.), 108

Point Dume Marine Science School (Malibu, Calif.), 169–170; Parent Teacher Association, 169

police, 77–78; and BPP, 132, 134–35, 139–141; and "broken windows theory," 165; in London (Eng.), 142; in New York City, 165; police raids, 140; police repression/brutality, 64, 132, 134, 139–140, 142; "policing the police," 132, 139; and "stop-and-frisk," 165

policy advocacy, 6–8, 14, 167, 197–98; and BPP, 124; and CFAs (Community Food Assessments), 149, 152–53; and CSU, 14, 88, 124–25; and Healthy

Wallis, Quvenzhane, 178
Wal-Mart, 41, 157
Washington, Booker T., 144
Waters, Alice, 49, 188–89
Watts riots (1965), 63–64, 139
wealth concentrations, 6, 8, 78, 195, 207;
and BPP, 56, 133, 137; and CED
(community economic development),
91–92, 144–45; and environmentalism,
118; and Great Recession, 4; and Green
Revolution, 39; and *Jamie Oliver's Food
Revolution,* 2–3; in Malibu (Calif.),
170; and NPVM, 144–45
WellPoint Health Networks, 237n14
West Adams Preparatory High School, 1
West Oakland Farmers Market, 55–56
Westwood (Los Angeles), 2–3
White Panther Party, 133
whites, 6–7, 23, 166, 168; and alternative
food movements, 52, 54–55; anti-white,
134–35; author as, 13, 200; and BPP, 56,
133, 134–35, 137, 139–140; and CSU, 71,
86, 159; and environmentalism, 118;
and RIC, 118–19; in South Los
Angeles, 63; and Teaching Gardens
Program (AHA), 166, 176; white
communities, 197; and "white flight,"
63; white supremacy, 54, 119
Wildwood Elementary (Baton Rouge,
La.), 173
Williams, Raymond, 22, 104

Will Rogers Elementary School (Santa
Monica, Calif.), 170
Wilson, Rita, 170
W. K. Kellogg Foundation, *32,* 51, 56, 156,
205; Food and Community Gathering,
54, 205
Wolch, Jennifer, 22, 24
Women's Cancer Research Fund, 170
workers, 5–6; abuse of, 195; agricultural
labor, 36–37, 41, 43, 48, 55, 97–98,
118; and farm labor groups, 123;
migrant workers, 41, 43, 55, 118; and
risks of industrial food system, 41,
43; slave labor, 37; and workers'
rights, 97
World Bank, 195

Yahoo Employee Foundation, 172
Yakini, Malik, 54–55
YFBR (Youth Food Bill of Rights, RIC),
120–24
youth development work, 8, 24, 34, 198,
204; and CSU, 11, *32,* 62, 67, 69–74,
95, 98, 160–61, 200; and *Jamie Oliver's
Food Revolution,* 3; and LAUSD, 3;
youth cooking competitions, 2
youth food justice movement, 10–12, 48,
101–28, 230n8. *See also* RIC
YouTube, 121–22, 177, 181

zoning laws, 152, 187